Indian and Jesuit

Indian
and
Jesuit
a seventeenth-
century
encounter

James T. Moore

A Campion Book
Loyola University Press

Copyright © 1982, James T. Moore
ISBN 8294-0395-7

Printed in the United States of America

For Linda

Contents

Acknowledgements

I wish to express special gratitude and appreciation to my wife Linda Lytz Moore and to Professor Herbert H. Lang of Texas A&M University for their many hours of patient advice and assistance in the preparation of this work; to Jeanette Ertel of Loyola University Press and Professors Henry C. Dethloff, Claude H. Hall, and Zoltan J. Kosztolnyik of Texas A&M University for the many hours spent in reading the manuscript and the invaluable suggestions which followed; to Mary Lenn Dixon, Associate Director of A&M University Press, for her kind assistance in translations from the French; and to Bessie and Mendom Moore for their on-going support and encouragement.

Introduction

The following chapters illustrate the extent to which the Jesuit missionaries to the Indian tribes in seventeenth-century French North America were willing to accept the principle of accommodation, a principle they applied more to themselves than to the Indians. This openness to change was based upon the Jesuits' concepts of natural revelation and natural law. For the Jesuits, *good* already existed in the native cultures and provided the foundation upon which native Christianity could be built. In addition, they shared with the Indian a belief in an imminently present spiritual world; they sought only to change the vantage point from which the Indians viewed and participated in this world. The Jesuit missionary effort, therefore, was based on the premise that native tribal culture was to be left largely intact and become the context for a new expression of Christianity.

The Jesuit missionaries carried out their work in North America amidst colonial rivalry and ferocious Indian warfare, some of which was a by-product of the machinations of the colonial powers. By 1632, when the permanent missions began, the Jesuits were starting their missionary endeavor in North America for the third time, having fallen victim twice before to English and French colonial strife. As the century unfolded, the Jesuits pressed farther and farther into the French domain, until by the end of the century, they were manning outposts all the way from the mouth of the St. Lawrence to Wisconsin and Louisiana. When, in 1649, their Huron missions were destroyed by the Iroquois, they responded by sending missionaries to the Iroquois themselves.

All of these efforts were carried out with a respect for the peoples they sought to convert—peoples among whom they were convinced good already existed, providing the ready context for their message.

I

French Jesuits among the Amerind

The first Jesuit missionaries to arrive in French North America were Pierre Biard[1] and Ennemond Massé,[2] whose ship arrived at Port Royal in Acadia on Sunday, May 22, 1611. Their ship, beset by icebergs and winter storms, was forced to detour by way of the Azores, and its Atlantic crossing required four months. But these natural difficulties were no more serious than the political ones that might have barred Biard and Massé from beginning their work in the New World.

King Henry IV, in response to Samuel de Champlain's reports on his voyage of 1603, had appointed Pierre du Gast, Sieur de Monts, as lieutenant-general to Acadia; de Monts in turn had ceded title to Port Royal to Jean de Biencourt de Poutrincourt. Poutrincourt was a nominal Catholic, although one with Huguenot leanings; de Monts himself, however, was a Huguenot. At this time, the French government allowed Huguenots to emigrate to New France, but efforts to convert the Indians were still reserved to Catholic Frenchmen. While the Huguenots had little trouble adjusting to this stricture, they still had an aversion to the prospect of Jesuits coming to North America, for they perceived them to be special agents of the Counter-Reformation and the papacy. Some Catholics, indeed, shared this aversion.

On May 14, 1610, Henry IV was assassinated, and the bulk of power fell for the time being to the queen regent, Marie de Médicis. Marc Lescarbot, a Paris lawyer and traveller, acting on behalf of de Monts and Poutrincourt, published an essay on the good progress of missionary work under the direction of secular priests among the Indians of Acadia. While he had little good to say about Huguenots, his praise of the work of Catholics in Acadia was designed to discourage the queen from allowing Jesuits to enter this domain from which both Huguenots and a few Catholic allies wanted them excluded. Lescarbot argued that there was no need in having "learned Doctors" among the Indians for they were really of more use in opposing heresies and vices at home. He also implied that Jesuits possessed an untrustworthy nature in that they tended to censure whatever did not agree with their maxims, and that they wanted to rule whatever they touched. Even the greatest rulers had not escaped their pervading influence, he said. If one wished to convert the savages, then he should join himself to a colony of farmers and move in mass to Acadia to cultivate the soil. Colonies of Frenchmen could better convey Christianity to the native than learned Doctors, for to live ". . . as the Savages do seems to me out of all reason."[3] A glowing report, sent by a Huguenot layman, giving an account of the baptism of a native "sagamore," or chief, together with twenty others, in June, 1610, at Port Royal, was cited as on-the-scene evidence that Jesuits were not needed in Acadia.

Biard and Massé had originally planned to embark from Dieppe on October 27, 1610, but their presence in the city had been discovered by Huguenot merchants who set out on a circuitous route to prevent their departure. Having obtained a contract with Poutrincourt to load and provision his ship, on which the Jesuits planned to leave, they then refused to complete the work unless the Jesuits stayed home. Prominent Catholics protested that it was the queen's wish that the Jesuits should go to Acadia, and prevailed upon her to state her wishes by letter to the Calvinist-dominated town consistory. But the queen wished to calm the situation and wrote Biard and Massé, urging them to postpone their mission.

However, local Catholics told the Huguenots to resume loading the ship, and that if the Jesuits did go, they were ready to purchase all of the Huguenot investment in the ship and its cargo. The Huguenots then proceeded to over-provision the ship so that the Jesuits' passage could less likely be bought in that way. At this point, however, Antoinette de Pons, Marchioness de Guercheville, first lady of honor to the queen, having raised a sizeable sum from the court circles, persuaded the Huguenot merchants to sell her their interest in the ship. She then purchased the proprietorship of Acadia, except Port Royal, from de Monts.[4] Thus all barriers to the venture were successfully removed.

When Biard and Massé arrived in Acadia that Sunday in May, 1611, they became the first of their order to set foot in French North America; yet, other of their Jesuit brethren were anything but strangers to the New World. Long active in Spanish territory, Jesuit missionaries were already established on the west coast of Mexico in Sinaloa, and in six more years some would be at work among the Yaquis on the banks of the river by the same name.[5] In fact, there were Jesuits who had carried on short-lived missionary work among the Indians on the peninsula between the James and York Rivers in Virginia in the 1570s, a fact which seems to have been known to the English colonists who arrived there in 1607 and seems to have added fuel to their already smouldering suspicions about the objectives of the Jesuits.[6]

Biard's evaluation of what he and Massé found did not at all agree with the glowing reports current in some Parisian circles. While he had only good to say of Poutrincourt, praising his generosity and kindness, he reported that the state of the Catholic church and its missionary effort among the natives was at a low ebb. The secular priest who had been there for a year had, indeed, baptized about one hundred Indians, but since he had not learned their language, the Indians' knowledge of the religion they had embraced through baptism was nil. Biard was incensed to find that polygamy continued even among the baptized.[7] The erstwhile missionary priest, upon the arrival of the Jesuits at Port Royal, promptly made plans to return to France, and gladly handed over his charge to the fathers. The Jesuits immediately set about learning to communicate with the Indians, using whatever means were at hand. Pictures were distributed, crosses were erected, and Latin hymns were sung before the doors of Indian huts. Formal instruction of those baptized began as soon as Biard and Massé could make themselves understood in the native language. When they asked the Indians' what their Christian names were, almost all answered with a word meaning patriarch, the same word they used for their former priest. Most were unable to recollect their new names; and, since the "patriarch" had given them the new name, they simply called themselves patriarchs. A solemn thanksgiving was held with an image of Christ carried about under a canopy with great ceremony to signify that Christianity was now laying claim to the new land.[8]

Through caring for the sick the two missionaries were able to save some lives as well as further instill the teachings they had come to spread. The son of Membertou, the local Micmac chief, a nominal Christian, fell dangerously ill and was given up for dead. According to custom, the whole tribe feasted whenever death approached their people. The Jesuits, however, persuaded Membertou to allow them to take his son to their residence, where, after much care, he was restored to health. The effect of this was salubrious for the growth of Christianity. Not only did the youth become a convert, but his father was also reestablished in the faith and numerous others of their tribe were attracted to the priests' teachings.[9]

On May 15, 1613, Father Jacques Quentin[10] and Brother Gilbert du Thet[11] arrived with a royal commission to establish a new settlement and mission; the site chosen was on Mt. Desert Island, on the coast of present-day Maine. The Marchioness de Guercheville, the principal sponsor of this move, sent fifty colonists to establish the new settlement. Biard and Massé joined them in what was to be a short-lived enterprise.[12] Hardly had a settlement been established when an English ship bound for Virginia blew off course and came upon the infant French settlement. Upon learning that a French ship was docked there, the English prepared for battle and proceeded to capture the ship. Most of the French crew were on shore at the time, engaged in building houses for the settlement. The English proceeded to capture the entire village. Brother du Thet was wounded and died the following day; the other Jesuits were taken prisoner. The English commander, Samuel Argall, secretly removed the royal commission from the French papers; thereupon he accused them all of being a band of pirates, since, when he demanded their royal warrant, they could not produce it. This was merely an excuse for letting his men plunder the spoils and for threatening to hang the "pirates." English paranoid attitudes toward Catholics, especially Jesuits, and their current fears generated by alleged plots to undermine the English government, placed the missionaries in special jeopardy. The fathers pled for the lives of their compatriots, assuring Argall that the French king had initiated the expedition. The Englishman obviously knew this. Although he continued his charade, he adopted a milder manner and even offered to return the settlers to France.[13]

The colonists were placed on two small ships. One, bearing Father Massé, returned to France directly; but the other, with Fathers Quentin and Biard, went first to Jamestown where Governor Thomas Dale—reflecting the prevalent fears of supposed Jesuit plots and English Catholic treason—raged against the Jesuits as symbolizing the very worst in religion and urged that they should be killed.[14] Argall protected them and even produced the purloined royal decree chartering their now stymied effort. Although the Jesuits' lives were spared and safe conduct to France followed, the royal commission was additional fuel in English eyes for an effort to drive the French out of their American enclave. Argall retraced his path and destroyed French forts along the Canadian coast and captured ships anchored at Port Royal. Although the vessel carrying Quentin and Biard attempted to follow Argall, violent winds blew it off course, and after many days of turbulence they landed at the Azores where the crew secured new provisions. Since he had taken the Jesuits by force, the English captain, Turnell, feared trouble in the islands; but the priests made no charges against him and even concealed their presence when the ship was searched. Ironically, when the ship reached England, the captain was accused of piracy—he was in a captured French ship and possessed no documents to verify his story. The two captive priests came to his rescue, however, by confirming his account. For their effort the fathers were treated as honored guests by the mayor of Pembroke, an unaccustomed experience for Jesuits in England at that time.[15] On such an unlikely note, the first Jesuit missionary effort in French North America came to an end.

This relatively short-lived venture nevertheless captured the interest of much of the French reading public. Biard's report of Jesuit work in 1612 had been published before his return, and a further report was published four years later.[16] During the next few years the Jesuit position in France was not always secure. Even when the king's confessor was a Jesuit, Cardinal Richelieu—the dominant political figure in France—had no use for the order, and would tolerate it only when the priests were subservient to him and supported his designs. Although Pope Gregory XV, in his instructions to the papal nuncio to France in April 1621, expressed praise for the French Jesuits because he regarded them as enemies of ecclesiastical corruption and as a bulwark against Calvinism,[17] this meant little to Richelieu, of course, except further to convince him of the ultramontane tendencies of the followers of St. Ignatius Loyola. As the 1620s progressed, Richelieu missed no opportunity to check any Jesuit efforts that he considered prejudicial to his own exercise of power. When in 1625 he raged against a Jesuit publication issued at Rome, alleging that it extended papal authority over the church at the expense of civil government, he first cajoled Jesuit authorities at Paris to renounce much of the work, and finally forced the Jesuit superior in Rome to withdraw the work for revision. Having gained his point, he rewarded the Jesuits by ostentatiously attending their Paris church.[18] He was sure of his power, and French Jesuits respected it. Fortunately for the French Jesuits, the second episode of their work in North America had begun a few months prior to the outbreak of this struggle. Otherwise it might never have begun at all.

In 1615, a branch of the Franciscans, the Recollect Fathers, at Champlain's invitation began a mission among the Indians at Quebec. In 1619 they commenced work also in Acadia. These ventures, especially the one in Acadia, met with little success. The Acadia mission closed in 1624, and the Recollects invited assistance from the Jesuits whose missionary success in South America, Asia, and Africa had won them a reputation for perseverance and success.

Three Jesuits arrived in April 1625: Ennemond Massé, Charles Lalemant,[19] and Jean de Brébeuf.[20] Father Brébeuf spent his first winter, that of 1625–26, with the Montagnais Indians near Quebec. These Indians were nomadic and roamed a wide region from the St. Lawrence to the watershed of Hudson Bay. Their language was of the Algonquian language group.[21]

After his return to Quebec in 1626, Brébeuf prepared to set out to establish a Jesuit residence among the Huron Indians. The Hurons lived around what is now Lake Simcoe and south and east of Georgian Bay, located in present-day Ontario. They were generally sedentary, subsisting by raising corn, beans, and squash, and hunting only during the late winter and early spring. They spoke a dialect of the Iroquoian language group.[22] Brébeuf took Father Anne de Noüé[23] with him to the Hurons.[24] Although Noüé returned to Quebec the following spring, Brébeuf remained among the Hurons, adopted their lifestyle, and did not return to Quebec until 1629, just as it capitulated to the English. Lalemant had remained in Quebec until November, 1627, when he journeyed to France to seek supplies for his mission. On his return voyage in May, 1628, his ship was captured by the English and it was forced to return to France by way of England. The following year, in June, Lalemant and several of his brethren were shipwrecked during another attempt to return to Quebec and went back to France on a Basque fishing boat. By this time news had reached France of the English capture of Quebec and Acadia. These events effectively put an end to the Jesuit mission in Canada for the time being.[25]

However, since an armistice had officially been declared between France and Great Britain prior to the fall of the two territories, they were retroceded to the French who again took possession in 1632. Once more the Jesuits returned to what was again French North America. Paul Le Jeune,[26] a former Huguenot, left his duties as superior of the Jesuit house at Dieppe to head the work at Quebec and returned with the French Commander, Emery de Caën, who took possession from the English. Le Jeune, Nouë, and a lay brother set out from Honfleur in April. The crossing was rough and cold. Le Jeune recorded:

> It is one thing to reflect upon death in one's cell, before the image of the Crucifix, but it is quite another to think of it in the midst of a tempest and in the presence of death itself.[27]

Le Jeune saw Indians for the first time at Tadoussac at the juncture of the Saguenay River with the St. Lawrence where the ship remained nineteen days. This was a strange, hard world to those Jesuits who first came over from France, most of whom, including Le Jeune, had been trained for professorial ranks in compliance with Loyola's dictum, "that labor of studies . . . [is] a work of great merit in the sight of God."[28] To Le Jeune, a former professor of rhetoric, these creatures he had come to convert reminded him of the "maskers" who cavorted in France at Mardi Gras. He marvelled at their brightly painted colors, but what struck him most was a firsthand view of their shocking cruelty to captives. He concluded, however, "Before the faith was received in Germany, Spain, and England, those nations were not civilized."[29]

The priests reached Quebec on July 5, 1632. After three years of English occupation, the village, at the foot of the fort, including those buildings Lalemant had had constructed during the second missionary effort in the mid 1620s, lay in ashes. Le Jeune was able to move into the small house more than a mile from the fort that Lalemant had once used. It was here he established a residence for his brethren.[30]

Some Jesuits were sent from France to Acadia and to Cape Breton Island to begin work there. Others were sent to join those already at Quebec—among these were Jean de Brébeuf who arrived once more in Quebec in 1633, and Charles Lalemant who returned there the following year. Lalemant served mainly in Quebec and as spiritual director and confidant to Champlain until that great leader's death in 1635. Lalemant returned to France in 1639. Brébeuf returned to the place for which he had longed—the Huron country.[31]

Le Jeune and the others had immediately set about learning the native languages. Brébeuf, Antoine Daniel,[32] and Ambrose Davost[33] began preparations to inaugurate once again work among the Hurons. Daniel and Davost had arrived in 1633, and that same year Ennemond Massé had returned to Canada. In 1634 a stockade had been erected by Champlain's lieutenant, La Violette, at Three Rivers, and various missionaries journeyed to carry on work with the nomadic tribes that periodically rendezvoused there.

A relatively well-ordered, European life-style developed at the Jesuit residence in Quebec, which differed greatly from that of later far-flung missionary outposts. In 1634 a group of skilled French carpenters and masons arrived at Quebec and set about under Noüe's direction to rebuild the Jesuit buildings destroyed during the English attack on Quebec in 1629, and in ruins since. A small house was also erected for those Jesuits in charge of Champlain's chapel. The workmen were not an un-mixed blessing to the Jesuits; they were young, single, and totally unaccustomed to the severe winters and fron-tier conditions of the region. In addition they had to live in one room. They fought, argued, and generally ignored their priestly employers, except to show some arrogance which, according to Le Jeune, originated in the fact that he could not take a stick to them as a lay employer would. Nevertheless, he concluded, ". . . I am aston-ished that the hardships they . . . undergo . . . do not cause them to make a greater outcry than they do."[34] But in spite of obstreperous employees, other aspects of Quebec life were pleasing to the Jesuits. Le Jeune could write to the Jesuit provincial in France, Barthélemy Jac-quinot, that life at Champlain's fort was like that of "a well-ordered Academy."[35] At Champlain's table morning and evening, men read selections from historians or works on the lives of the saints. Champlain also ordered the fort bell to sound the angelus at the appointed hours.

Beginning with Le Jeune's annual report from the mission field in 1632 and continuing for the next forty years, the reports, or "relations," of the Jesuit fathers would be published in Paris and read by much of the literate French public. Reporting on all mission news from everyday events to accounts of the martyrdom of men whom many immediately viewed as saints, the *Rela-tions* kept before the French public the trials and tri-umphs of the missionaries and their neophytes. Within a year after the event, Parisians could read of the departure of Brébeuf and his companions for the Huron country and of the conditions under which they lived.

On July 1, 1634, Brébeuf and Daniel with some lay assistants set out in a bark for Three Rivers to wait there for the Hurons. Davost followed three days later with the admiral of the fleet, the Sieur du Plessis Bochart, who wished to meet the Indians at Three Rivers where they often came to trade. The Hurons did arrive, but not in their usual great number because of a battle with the Iroquois who had been reported moving toward the Huron region in a large body, said to number about five hundred. The Hurons had surprised them with a superior force and had taken about two hundred prisoners. A smaller group than usual had had time to go down to Three Rivers that July, only seven canoes in all.

The Jesuits were soon faced with the privations of Indian life: long hours of rowing, little food, long portages, indifferent or hostile treatment. Brébeuf reported that little caches of food had been hidden along the shore on their trip down—to supply their needs, albeit in meager fashion, on the return trip. These were the only "hotels" they had, he wrote. Each morning and each evening a little cornmeal was mixed with water to equal about a bowlful. These two daily repasts comprised their entire diet on the journey.

In early August, 1634, the fathers arrived at what had been the Huron village of Toanche—where Brébeuf had dwelt in the 1620s—only to find it long since deserted by the Indians who now lived in the village of Ihonatiria, a short distance away. Brébeuf was well-received; Indians who remembered him greeted him with the cry, "Echon," the Indian name he had taken during his last stay with them. The fathers, who had been separated on their long, river journey, soon were together in Ihonatiria. There had been some difficulty at first in getting from the river to the village, since the fathers had simply been cast ashore rather summarily and left to solve the problems presented by baggage and the distance they had to travel to the new village. But the welcome given Echon made up for this. Soon the fathers had a house built in Huron style with a few adaptations done to the interior. Huron houses, reported Brébeuf, seemed substantial and presumably were used longer than those of the nomadic Montagnais near Quebec. But the fathers still compared them to brush arbors, which—except for the addition of bark strips—they literally were.

By 1635, the French had, in addition to the Acadian settlements, three enclaves on the St. Lawrence: at Quebec; another upriver on St. Croix Island, where Champlain had built Fort Richelieu; and still farther upriver at Three Rivers. The Jesuits by this same time had six residences: St. Anne at Cape Breton; St. Charles at Miscou at the southern side of the mouth of the St. Lawrence; Notre-Dame-de-Recouvrance at Champlain's chapel in Quebec; Notre-Dame-des-Anges, a short walking distance from Quebec; the Residence of the Conception at Three Rivers; and the newly established Residence of St. Joseph at Ihonatiria among the Hurons. French food supplies went no farther upriver than Three Rivers, but the missionaries in Huronia were able to get a little wine for mass and some religious ornaments, as well as a few raisins and prunes for the sick, brought in by canoe. Wine was so scarce that only a few drops could be used at each mass, but later it would be made from wild grapes in the wilderness missions. Wheat for the host, the bread of the mass, had to be grown locally in a small borrowed plot which the fathers and their lay assistants cultivated for the Huron missions. A small hand mill was used to process this grain, but they found that corn for their daily meals was best processed if pounded and crushed in Indian fashion.[36]

There were lay assistants in the early Jesuit mis-

sions who served out of a special sense of religious voca-
tion. In 1638 the Jesuit provincial in France, Étienne
Binet, gave permission to accept such individuals, called
donnés, or those who had *given* themselves for the service
of the order, and a form of contract for the work in
Canada was approved. Word of this permission was
brought to Le Jeune by Jérôme Lalemant,[37] brother of
Charles, who arrived at Quebec in June, 1638, on his way
to the Huron country. Upon his arrival there, the fathers
enthusiastically received the idea and suggested a plan
by which these laymen would bind themselves for life,
but with vows similar to those of a Jesuit novice, not
those more stringent and encompassing ones made by
the life-professed. The donné promised his service to the
missions for life; in return for which, the order promised
to feed, clothe, and care for him in sickness for the rest of
his life.[38]

Smallpox, the white-imported scourge of Indian
life, again and again afflicted the Indians of the St.
Lawrence region during the 1620s, 30s, and 40s. Although some of the missionaries themselves almost died
from it, many of the Hurons blamed this disease on the
fathers, not because of their race or origin, but for what
they believed was sorcery against them practiced in the
chapels. Repeated outbreaks of other diseases and
plagues of fever caused the Indians to threaten the
fathers with death in the Huron villages, but each time a
sufficient number of friendly voices saved their lives. In
the fall of 1636, a general epidemic of smallpox and perhaps some other contagion struck both Indians and
French. In June, 1636, Pierre Chastelain,[39] Charles Garnier,[40] Isaac Jogues,[41] and several others of their order
arrived at Quebec with the same fleet that escorted
Champlain's successor as governor, Charles Huault de
Montmagny. Chastelain, Garnier, and Jogues left for the

Huron country in July. In September Chastelain and Garnier contracted smallpox, but both recovered. Jogues came down with what was described as a fever, but of a very serious variety, if not smallpox itself. Because scores of Indians and many of the French fell ill, the Jesuit residence was turned into a hospital. Those Jesuits who were well enough visited the sick in the cabins twice daily to give out raisins, sugared water, a little soup, and meat when they had it. The priests also baptized the dying when they could.[42]

Plagues notwithstanding, in May, 1638, the village council of Ossossané agreed to build a cabin for the Jesuits in their village. On May 21, Pierre Pijart,[43] who had arrived among the Hurons in 1637, set out with two laymen to begin this work. On June 5, he celebrated mass in the still uncompleted house, dedicating it as "La Conception de Notre Dame."[44]

During this same period, faced with the problem of evangelizing the nomadic tribes of the Quebec region, Le Jeune launched an attempt to bring sedentary life to these tribes. With funds given by a French diplomat and courtier-turned-priest, Nöel Brulard, chevalier de Sillery, the Jesuits established a village[45] a few miles from Quebec, not only for converts but for any Indian willing to listen to their teachings. The village was fittingly named "Sillery." Most of those Indians who either settled or visited Sillery in the years to come were either Montagnais or Algonquin. The Algonquin were from a number of tribes speaking a dialect of the Algonquian linguistic group who lived along the St. Lawrence and in the regions to the west of the river. They were nomadic and closely related to the Montagnais.[46]

Le Jeune of course had already seen to the instruction of those Indian children he and the others could gather around them. In the winter of 1636–37, the fathers had spent more time with the young than with their elders, for they felt that their teachings would have quicker results with them than with those set in their ways. After only one invitation, both boys and girls so overwhelmed the missionaries in numbers and frequency of visits that the fathers had to tell them to wait until they were called to their classes. On each occasion as they entered the chapel—with boys on one side and girls on the other—each child received a little present. The French children came too and were useful in helping the native children to learn corporal acts and postures of Catholic worship: to sign the cross, kneel, and genuflect. It was much easier, they found, to instruct the little Indian girls, who wished in every way to imitate the French girls. At a signal, all knelt, signed the cross, and invoked the Trinity, first in Latin and then in Montagnais. The missionary in charge prayed in the native tongue for the success of the day's lesson; then led them slowly, in their own language, in the recitation of the Lord's Prayer and the Apostle's Creed. Afterwards they sang each of these; the Jesuits had set them to verse in the native language. The usual catechetical form of instruction followed and then a "feast" concluded the session. [47]

By 1637 a number of Huron youth arrived in Quebec for instruction and for the next few years formed the corpus of a separate Huron seminary. By 1639 Le Jeune concluded that educational efforts in Quebec were going well; he had no doubt that the enterprise had proven that the Indians and European intellects were equal. The Huron, Montagnais, and Algonquin youths responded well to the injunctions of Catholic piety. At the seminary for the nomadic Montagnais and Algonquins at Sillery, he recorded that the students were faithful in their prayers, and that those baptized attended mass daily and took turns carrying on the lay function of acolyte. They did this with ". . . as much grace and modesty as if they had been brought up in a well-regulated academy . . ."[48] The way to govern them, Le Jeune added, was through love, not fear, for neither they nor their elders responded well to threats or coercion. Their performance at catechism astounded him, especially some of their questions to him and the other Jesuits. He recorded one, asked by an Indian boy:

> You teach us that God existed before the creation of heaven and earth; if he did, where did he live, since there was neither heaven nor earth? You say also that the Angels were created in the beginning of the world, and that those who disobeyed were cast into Hell; elsewhere, you put Hell in the depths of the earth; these statements cannot agree very well, for, if the Angels sinned before the creation of the earth, they could not be thrown into Hell, or Hell is not where you place it.[49]

The father's answers to these inquiries are not recorded.

In 1639 Marie Vignerot, the Duchess d'Aiguillon, a niece of Richelieu and a devout Catholic—who from 1622 had devoted her life and fortune to charitable works—endowed and erected a hospital at Quebec to be staffed by the hospital nuns of Dieppe. Simultaneously, Magdelaine de Chauvigny, or as she was later known, Madame de la Pelterie, came with three Ursuline nuns to set up a school for Indian girls. Additional Jesuits also arrived that year for service both in the educational work at Quebec and tasks in the distant missions. The Indian settlement at Sillery by this time had led to the founding of a seminary for boys, another for girls, and a hospital. Also the French proprietors of New France, "The Gentlemen of the Company of New France," had granted the same concessions at their stores in Quebec to Christian sedentary Indians as to French colonists. In addition, young Indian girls were granted land if they married Frenchmen, and private gifts were sometimes made to encourage Frenchmen to marry Indians.[50]

Because the small hospital opened by the nuns was soon overwhelmed with Indian patients, cabins, after the Indian manner, were erected in the garden to provide at least some shelter for the sick. Blankets and sheets had to be cut up to go around, and nuns worked so hard that the Jesuits feared losing both them and the hospital. The sick seemed to come from all directions, and there was no letup in their number. The heat of late summer, 1639, was so intense that the stench from the infirm became so great as to drive the well away, except the sisters who continued their work despite the scarcity of fresh food and lack of time for sleep. But the Mother Superior is quoted as having only praise for her patients:

> The patience of our sick astonish me. I have seen many whose bodies are entirely covered with small-pox, and in a burning fever, complaining no more than if they were not sick, strictly obeying the physician, and showing gratitude for the slightest service rendered them.[51]

On Maundy Thursday, 1640, after mass, the governor and leading men of the city ceremonially washed the male patients' feet while certain prominent French women, the Mother Superior, and other nuns washed the female patients' feet.[52]

The Ursuline sisters leased a dwelling for themselves and their school for Indian girls upon their arrival in 1639. On November 21, 1642, they moved into a new, spacious house, described as well constructed. The new building, to enhance its security, was placed near the fort; a year later, even this building had to be enlarged. In addition to the large number of Indian girls, there were some French girls who lived there either permanently or temporarily. Besides the girls, Indian men and women were welcomed to come for instruction in religion, held almost daily in the nuns' parlor which served as the school's classroom. The nuns made it a regular part of their routine to feed the adult day students along with the boarding students and themselves. Madame de la Pelterie, who financed this work, finally became an Ursuline novice herself and died at the Quebec convent in 1671.[53]

By 1643, there were thirty-five or forty Christian Indian families at Sillery except during the hunting season; others lived there too when they wished, even though they were neither Christian nor sedentary. Almost all of them were either Montagnais or Algonquins. The Montagnais lived in the mountains near Quebec, the other tribe occupied land further inland and upriver in the direction of the Hurons. For a time the Jesuits tried to supply these villagers with French-style houses that had weatherproof lofts in which to store supplies for the winter. A few of these small houses were built for the Indians at Sillery, but the Indians seemed to develop no great attraction for them; so the project was abandoned. Most of Sillery's residents continued to construct and dwell in huts made of poles and bark strips.

In the winter of 1642-43, thirteen canoes of Atikemegues, a Montagnais tribe, came to winter with the Indians at Sillery, providing the missionaries with the opportunity to teach yet another tribe from whom they in turn were able to learn a new dialect. Jacques Buteux[54] and Jean de Quen[55], who gave instruction to this tribe, lived with them to learn their language and their ways.

Hymns in the various dialects had become commonplace and with any new encounter another version was sure to follow.[56]

In 1642 the French established the colony of Montreal, upriver from Three Rivers. Even with this outpost, however, travel on the river at times over the next years was almost at a standstill for both Frenchmen and their Indian allies. In that same year, the Iroquois tribes to the south closed access of the river to the Hurons and the Jesuit missionaries at Montreal and captured the supplies that the Jesuits at Quebec tried to send to them.

Living primarily in what is now central New York and northeastern Ohio, the Iroquois confederation consisted of five nations: Mohawks, Oneidas, Onondagas, Cayugas, and Senecas. The "Iroquoian Family" consisted of many tribes, including Hurons and Cherokees. The term "family" denotes a kinship of language; a common sedentary trait, with the chase supplying only a small part of a tribe's subsistence; and a comparatively well-developed social and political structure, in which, however, there were varying degrees of development from tribe to tribe.[57] The Iroquois confederation was beginning a push to the north and to a lesser extent to the east and west in the 1640s. In this period they reached their highest numbers and greatest prosperity, their fighting prowess greatly enhanced by a liberal supply of guns received from the Dutch at Orangeburg, present-day Albany. Their total population at this time has been estimated at about twenty-five thousand.[58] At the apex of their power, the area around and including their village on Lake Onondaga was the seat of a dominion extending from Lake Michigan and the Falls of the Ohio on the west to the Hudson River on the east and from the Ohio and Potomac Rivers at the south to the Ottawa River and Lake Simcoe on the north.[59]

One twentieth-century observer has blamed the Jesuits for the Hurons' weakness before the Iroquois onslaught, for not securing more guns for the Hurons, and for dividing them religiously.[60] Yet the records show that Christian and non-Christian Indians went to battle together, with the convert showing as much or more valor than his compatriots. The missionaries constantly begged Quebec and Paris for French aid and intervention which Paris was too slow in granting. Indeed, without Jesuit aid, even the Huron remnant might not have survived after the depredations of 1649. A more measured view of the results of the Iroquois onslaught against the Hurons brings to light certain flaws inherent in Huron society that left them a weakened prey to the Iroquois. Huron villages were moved frequently, causing a weakening in political organization; their farming methods and social structure made it both desirable and possible to frequently move their villages, and they had not reached a point where any readjustment in these factors could readily have been seen or accepted. Their social values and farming methods had deleterious effects on the environment and frequent village relocation was expedient. In addition, while they had a flexible trading system and could generally feed themselves, their political structure, far less sophisticated than that of the Iroquois, proved too inert to meet the threat presented by the power and discursive goals of the Iroquois. Even though the French and occasionally some of the Iroquois tried to bring a peaceful solution to the conflict, jealousies, feuds, and the ineffective Huron political structure, stymied these efforts.[61]

In the Huron country, in spite of disease and threats from the Iroquois, work continued to progress during the closing years of the 1630s. In the autumn of 1639, the Jesuits established a central residence among the Hurons located on the Wye River, just before it flows into Matchedash Bay of Lake Huron. Since the Hurons tended to move their villages every few years, the missionaries hoped that a central residence would give more stability to their efforts. The new residence was called Ste. Marie. From here, for the next decade, priests set out to work and live in the various Huron missions and those that they would attempt to establish among neighboring tribes. Ste. Marie also served as a center for religious retreats not only for the missionaries but for many converts as well. In the winter of 1639–40, work was carried on among the Wenrohronons who had settled near the new mission of the Conception at Ossossané. Things went so well that the decision was made not to wait for the customary times for baptism, Easter and Pentecost, but to open the door of this new church as soon as the Indians were instructed. The tribal elders, along with persons with stable marriages, and prominent heads of families, were instructed and baptized first, so that the new church's foundations would not begin to crumble and find its grave in its cradle. Public baptism was forthwith administered on St. Martin of Tours Day, November 11; and again on December 8, the solemnity of the Immaculate Conception of the Blessed Virgin. Baptisms continued through the winter and into the spring of 1640, so that by April, about sixty at Ossossané—many of whom were Wenrohronons—were actively trying to practice their Christianity. Each Sunday these sixty or so gathered at the chapel at Ossossané for Mass, the Wenrohronons having to come some distance through the snow, each clothed only in a skin thrown across his back as a "mantel," and with a skin about his feet and legs on the coldest days.[62] Of these occasions Lalemant wrote:

> In winter, we are careful to have fireplaces full of burning coals in several parts of the Chapel, to pro-

vide against the discomforts that might arise from
the cold and their nakedness. This so pleases them
that some often remain, of their own free will, whole
hours after the service, to converse about our mysteries, and to become better and better instructed.[63]

That same winter of 1639–40 a new mission
under Charles Garnier and Isaac Jogues was established
among the Khionontateronons or "Tobacco Nation," so-
called, because tobacco grew profusely along the south
coast of present-day Georgian Bay where the members of
that tribe lived. The priests were not enthusiastically received, since it was rumored that their "sorcery" conjured up disease.

Also in 1639, Pierre-Joseph-Marie Chaumonot[64]
and Jean de Brébeuf made a trip south to the "Attiwandaronk" or "Neutral Nation" who lived just north of the
Iroquois. Brébeuf was chosen to go because of his facility
with languages. They took along two lay assistants to
give the appearance of being on a trading expedition.
After getting into the country and making some acquain-
tances, they led their assistants back out and returned
without the facade of being traders. They were then met
with the charge of sorcery. Much hardship surrounded
their entire visit, and numerous times reports were received at the mission village of Ste. Marie in the Huron
country that they were dead. Each time they began their
daily devotions from the breviary they were accused of
invoking spells. Their inkstands, books, and so forth,
were looked upon as evil talismans. On their return
journey, when they were about halfway to Ste. Marie
and still in the country of the Neutral Nation, the winter
weather forced them to seek refuge in an Indian village.
A woman took them in, faced down the opposition and
its charges against the priests, helped them with the

dialect, which they adapted to their Huron dictionary, and even went out of her way to prepare special food for their Lenten fasts. All this, despite the fact that she was not a convert.[65]

The Nipissiriniens roamed a large area west of Quebec and north of the Huron country as far up as James Bay where many went to trade. However, they were nomadic on a seasonal basis, gathering at Lake Nipissing, then wintering farther south. They dried fish, which they exchanged for corn and were known thereby to have become a prosperous people. They seldom traded with Quebec, so the fathers there had no plans to attract them to Sillery, and the Jesuits in Huronia saw little chance of drawing them permanently among the nearby Algonquins or their own basically sedentary Hurons. Lalemant wrote in 1641:

> Consequently we spoke to them, not of abandoning their country and coming to place themselves near the other Algonquins already settled, but rather of receiving a few of our Fathers among them, that they might be instructed; they declared that this would be very acceptable to them. This is why Fathers Claude Pijart, and Charles Raymbault, setting out from below to come and help us, had directions to offer themselves, on the way, to them.[66]

However, at least for that winter of 1640–41, the Nipissiriniens were close to Ste. Marie, and the fathers were able to carry on work among them, not far from their now well-established missions.

After some indication in 1641 that the Ojibway tribe would be willing for missionaries to come among them, Charles Raymbault[67] went with Isaac Jogues and several Christian Hurons to the present Sault Ste. Marie region of northern Michigan. They set out late in September, 1641, and after a seventeen-day journey reached their destination and reported finding about two-thousand Indians from whom they received news of nations to the west and south who had had no contacts with Europeans. As soon as they returned to the residence at Ste. Marie, Raymbault set out by canoe to seek the Nipissiriniens, but ice formed and forced his return. He fell ill on the trip, grew weaker, and was taken to Quebec, where he died in 1642.

Claude Pijart, in the winter of 1641-42, made several trips to the lands of the nomadic Algonquins where he instructed them, confessed converts, said Mass and led them in hymns composed in their native tongue. He then left in April, 1642, with René Ménard[68] to go back to the Nipissiriniens, whose opposition to the faith seemed to be less and less.[69]

At this same time, far to the north and east, work progressed among the Indians on both sides of the St. Lawrence above Quebec. The missionary activity at Tadoussac, north of Quebec, influenced Indians on the coast and worked to the good of the St. Charles's Mission as far away as Miscou. The mission at Miscou in turn in 1642 sponsored work near present-day Bathurst, New Brunswick, at the Indian village of Nepegigwit.[70]

Nearer Quebec, that same year, Le Jeune, who was no longer superior, was sent to live at Three Rivers to work among the local Algonquins. Near the close of November, when the Indians decided to go to Montreal to hunt there during the coming winter, Le Jeune packed up and went with them. However, when they heard that some of their tribesmen were going to winter at Fort Richelieu, farther upriver, their fleet of canoes then headed in that direction. Father de Noué, there to minister to the French, was pleased to have another Jesuit with him, and a joint effort was launched to teach the Indians. Mass, public prayers, instructions, both public and individual, and hymn-singing literally filled the daily schedule from early morning to dusk until the end of the winter of 1643, when the Indians left in the direction of either Three Rivers or Montreal.[71]

When the Iroquois closed the upper St. Lawrence to the traffic of other tribes, the Indians, the Jesuits, and the French entered a new and bloody epoch in which the Hurons almost became extinct, and several Jesuits died. In June, 1642, Isaac Jogues went down to Quebec with the Huron fleet and, on the return trip, was taken prisoner—along with a number of others—by the Iroquois. Two donnés, William Couture and René Goupil, were put to death, adding to the sufferings of Jogues. Both the French and the Hurons suffered miserably through various torments: some were burned with coals, others had the nails on both hands torn out by their captors' teeth, had thumbs cut off, fingers bitten, sawed, or twisted off, and were beaten with clubs. As Jogues recounted:

> . . . as if by compulsion she cut off my left thumb where it joins the hand. Then taking in my other hand the amputated thumb, I offered it to thee, my true and living God. At last warned by one of my comrades to desist, since they might otherwise force it into my mouth and compel me to eat it as it was, I flung it from me on the scaffold and left it I know not where.[72]

In the case of Eustace, a Huron, some days before his burning and beheading, ". . . they had cut off both his thumbs, and through the stump of the left one they . . . drove a pointed stake up to his very elbow."[73] Jogues eventually was freed by the Dutch and sent to France. By 1644, he was back in America, stationed at Montreal. He made two trips into the Iroquois country to work out a peace between them, the Hurons, and the French. On the second trip, he was treacherously slain by a hatchet blow to the head on October 18, 1646, shortly after his arrival at a Mohawk village. A French aide, Jean de Lalande, was killed the next day in the same village.[74]

In 1644 Frances Joseph Bressani[75] had almost been another to meet his death at the hands of the Iroquois. After his arrival in French North America in the summer of 1642, he served as a missionary to the Algonquins at Three Rivers until 1644, when he was sent to the Huron country. On the third day of his journey he was captured by the Iroquois, taken south to their home country, and put through the usual cruelties: all but one of his fingers were either torn off or slowly burned off on a succession of evenings until a Dutch ransom effort secured his freedom and a voyage to France. Yet, he was back among the Hurons by the fall of the next year.[76]

Throughout the 1640s the Iroquois push against the Hurons continued despite Jesuit efforts to get the French to provide military means to stop it. These efforts proved insufficient to stop this onslaught before the Hurons had been virtually destroyed. Word from France charged that the Dutch were encouraging the Iroquois in order to drive the French from North America, but the Jesuit authorities in Quebec found this hard to believe.[77]

In the early morning of July 4, 1648, at the Huron village of Teanaustaiyé, just as Father Antoine Daniel finished saying Mass for the Christian villagers, the Iroquois struck. Within moments, they had scaled the palisades of the village and put to the flames the cabins and the church. Some of the women and children tried to flee through an opening in the wall into a ravine at the back of the village while the chiefs and warriors attempted to hold back the enemy. Joining this latter group, Daniel— still dressed in alb and stole—stood ready to aid the dying warriors through baptism or absolution. At one point he ran through the cabins to minister similarly to the sick and aged. As Huron resistance to the attack began to weaken, Daniel was shot by musket fire. After he fell he was shot with numerous arrows and finally thrown upon his burning church.[78]

The next year, in March, Jean de Brébeuf and Gabriel Lalemant also joined the ranks of the Jesuit martyrs when the Iroquois destroyed the Huron mission villages of Saint Louis and Saint-Ignace. About 1,200 Iroquois came early on the morning of March 16, 1649. Brébeuf and Lalemant were in St. Louis where the enemy attacked first. The village was torched and the fathers seized. They and other prisoners were beaten with clubs about the shoulders, face, abdomen, groin, and legs. Huron survivors who escaped later told other missionaries that, as long as he had had the strength, Brébeuf continually urged Christianity upon his captors and perseverance upon his fellow Christians that they might die well and be assured of an entrance into Paradise. While he was doing this, a Huron, once captured by the Iroquois but now fighting with them, who had been instructed and baptized by Brébeuf, became agitated and had boiling water poured over the priest's head three times in mockery of baptism. Hatchets were then heated red-hot, tied together into a kind of collar and placed around Brébeuf's neck. Among the Indians this was thought to be a particularly cruel kind of torment, for the victim, bound to a post, could take no posture that alleviated the pain: if he leaned forward, the pain increased on his back, and vice versa; and the same was true of his movements to either side. Then they put on Brébeuf a belt of bark full of resin and pitch which, having been ignited, seemed to cook his entire body; but, according to an eye witness, he continued to preach the faith to his executioners, a fact which caused their rage to run even hotter against him. To stop his speaking they cut out both his lips and his tongue. Flesh was then cut from his arms, thighs, and legs, which they roasted and ate before his very eyes, for he was still alive and conscious at this point. When it was evident that he could not remain conscious much longer, he was made to sit on the ground where he was scalped. Then one of them cut into his chest and removed his heart which was roasted and eaten. Others began to drink his blood, since Brébeuf had suffered courageously, and the blood of a courageous victim was thought to convey like courage to those who partook of it. Brébeuf died about four in the afternoon of March 16, the day of his capture. Lalemant lived until the next day, not having been put to the test as early as Brébeuf. Similar torments were endured by him. When he, too, would not cease preaching, his tongue was also cut out; in addition his eyes were gouged and live coals were put in their place. He died about nine o'clock on the morning of March 17. The bodies of Brébeuf and Lalemant were found later by the Jesuits, one not far from the other. With great reverence the martyrs' remains were taken to the Huron residence at Ste. Marie. There the bodies were buried, but when Ste. Marie was evacuated, the bones were sent to Quebec where they received the veneration due to the relics of saints.[79]

The plight of the Hurons was now desperate. As Paul Ragueneau[80] wrote:

Many, no longer expecting humanity from man, flung themselves into the deepest recesses of the forest, where, though it were with wild beasts, they might find peace. Others took refuge upon some frightful rocks that lay in the midst of a great lake nearly four hundred leagues in circumference—choosing rather to find death in the water, or from the cliffs, than by the fires of the Iroquois. A goodly number cast in their lot with the Neutral Nation, and with those living in the Mountain heights, whom we call the Tobacco Nation . . .[81]

There was mission work by this time among the Tobacco Nation, but this region was not to be immune from the Iroquois onslaught. Both Fathers Charles Garnier and Noël Chabanel soon joined their martyred brethren. At three o'clock in the afternoon on December 7, 1649, this mission and the village of Etarita were destroyed by a band of Iroquois. The usual slaughter resulted. As a group tried to flee they begged Garnier to go with them, but he remained, believing it his duty to do so. He hastened to give absolution and baptize where he could—in the burning cabins or in the midst of the panicked crowd. To his fleeing congregation he shouted, "Pray to God, and flee by whatever way you may be able to escape. Bear about with you your faith through what of life remains; and may death find you with God in mind."[82] As he sought to pursue his duty in the village, he was struck in the chest and stomach by a volley of musket fire. He was stripped, but continued to live. Seeing a man dying nearby, he struggled to his feet to go nearer to help the man die well; but, after much effort, he himself died before reaching the other.[83]

Noël Chabanel, Garnier's missionary companion, away at the time, was killed along the trail in the forest by the same band of Iroquois the next morning.[84]

After 1649, missionary work among the Hurons and adjacent nations, in the form in which it had existed from the 1630s, practically ceased. The missionaries under great duress, however, seemed to have even greater resolution.[85] By June 1, 1649, the Jesuit residence at Ste. Marie had been removed to the Isle of St. Joseph where many of the Hurons had fled.[86] Lack of adequate food and the spread of disease would take a great toll among the Hurons. Many survivors were taken by the Jesuits to safer ground, away from the Iroquois, to the Island of Orleans near Quebec;[87] others sought refuge with tribes farther to the west. A great change had taken place in the St. Lawrence and lower Great Lakes regions. Paul Ragueneau wrote in 1650:

> When I ascended the great River, only thirteen years ago, I had seen it bordered with large numbers of people of the Algonquin tongue, who knew no God. These, in the midst of their unbelief, looked upon themselves as the Gods of the earth, for the reason that nothing was lacking to them in the richness of their fisheries, their hunting-grounds, and the traffic which they carried on with allied nations; add to which they were the terror of their enemies. Since they have embraced the faith, and adored the Cross of Jesus Christ, he has given them, as their lot, a portion of that Cross—verily, a heavy one, having made them a prey to miseries, torments, and cruel deaths; in a word, they are a people wiped off from the face of the earth. Our sole consolation is that, having died Christians, they have entered on the heritage of true children of God. *Flagellat deus omnem filium quem recipit.*[88]

In the midst of the Iroquois push, the French made some inquiries for aid from the English of New England. A Jesuit, Gabriel Druillettes,[89] made two abor-

31

tive attempts at reaching an understanding with the leaders of the Massachusetts Bay Colony, who themselves were not to be immune to the Iroquoian threat.[90]

Druillettes began work with the Abenakis along the Kennebec in present-day Maine in August, 1646. After returning to Quebec, he went back to Abenaki territory and from there went on to Boston as an emissary of the Quebec government. The colonial officials at Boston had been hoping to work out a trade agreement with the French and now the latter wanted aid against the Iroquois. But why a Jesuit emissary? Jesuits were liable to being hanged in Boston, except, the law stated, those who came as emissaries. Perhaps the French authorities wished to dispel some of the suspicion in which the Puritans held the civil, military, and religious officialdom of New France. It was commonly held in the English colonies that all French forts had a Jesuit assigned to stir up the Indians against the English,[91] so perhaps a personable Jesuit, working with Indians in an area to which even France realized England had a legitimate claim, was seen as just the man for this ambassadorship. Druillettes was well received and obviously was a great success personally among the Puritans. To be sure, he was treated well by the governor and the leaders of the church, especially well by his fellow missionary, John Eliot; but not even a second visit succeeded in bringing about a treaty or alleviating the fears and suspicions surrounding the French and what Druillettes himself represented— fears that far outlasted the seventeenth century.[92] While the Indians of New England were suffering at the hands of the Iroquois in 1650, the English themselves were not. Besides, they saw the Iroquois as a buffer against the French.[93]

In 1653, however, the Iroquois were willing to make peace with the French, partly because of recurring

difficulties with the Dutch and the Eries. This time a
Jesuit emissary went directly to them, deep in their own
territory.[94] Father Simon Le Moyne[95] arrived at the Iroquois fishing village on Lake Ontario, August 1, 1654,
and was received well, finding many Huron Christians
among them—mostly women now in servitude. On August 5, after having been feted at villages along the way,
he arrived at Onondaga. With great skill he began an
oration in which he called out slowly, in the fashion of a
chief, the names of the various clans and chiefs, stating
his purpose of solidifying the peace between them, the
French, and their Indian allies, all of which he read from
a carefully prepared list. Presents were exchanged according to the native custom which both symbolically
and actually served to bind an agreement. Arrangements
were made for a proposed French settlement among
them, and of course this was to include the presence of
Jesuit missionaries. By September 11, Le Moyne was
safely back in Quebec.[96]

By the end of the next year a mission under
Claude Dablon[97] and Pierre Chaumonot was operating at
Onondaga, these two fathers having arrived among the
Iroquois in November, 1655.[98] After much hardship and
little response, except among the Huron expatriates, the
Jesuits were forced to leave in 1658 when hostilities again
broke out. But far from retreating from their missionary
effort, the Jesuits now looked in another direction—to
the west.

In the early 1660s, Father René Ménard pushed
past the Iroquois to Lake Huron and to the Lake Michigan region where he preached the faith and looked for
new missionary sites. He died on this journey, but his
reports reached Quebec and helped open the way for the
"apostle" of the western tribes, Father Claude Allouez.[99]
Allouez set out for the west in August, 1665,[100] and he

spent the next twenty-five years, until his death in 1689, in missionary work among the Indians of the west, possibly giving instruction to as many as one hundred thousand, and baptizing about ten thousand.[101] It was through his efforts that the Ottawas, Potawatomies, Miamis, Illinois, and various other tribes, including some Hurons who had fled to the west away from the Iroquois, were reached. In 1670 Father Jacques Marquette established Saint-Ignace, a mission on Mackinac Island in Lake Michigan. From here, mission work radiated to such mission stations as Sault Ste. Marie, St. Joseph on Lake Michigan, Immaculate Conception on the Illinois River, St. Francis Xavier on Green Bay, and Le Pointe du Saint-Esprit on Chequamegon Bay, to name only a few. The Immaculate Conception mission work actually included several smaller missions among the tribes along the Mississippi River.[102]

Father Marquette had arrived from France in 1666, and was soon sent into the regions so newly opened by Father Allouez. After having worked at Sault Ste. Marie, then at another station on Chequamegon Bay on Lake Superior, he retreated with his flock of Ottawas and Hurons, under threat from the Sioux, to a bark chapel on the Mackinac straits. This became Saint-Ignace, the central point of western missionary labors.

In May, 1673, Marquette set out with Louis Joliet, an explorer sent out by the governor at Quebec, Louis de Buade, Count Frontenac, to explore and, in effect, discover the Mississippi, going as far south as the juncture with the Arkansas. They returned north and wintered at the Jesuit mission at what is now De Pere, Wisconsin. Joliet returned to Quebec in the spring. Marquette, having become ill, remained at the mission until October, 1674, when he made his way to the Illinois country for further missionary activity. But after a difficult winter on the banks of the Chicago River, illness forced him to set out for Saint-Ignace at the Mackinac straits. He died enroute on May 18, 1675, at what is now Ludington, Michigan, and his remains were buried the following year under the altar of the Saint-Ignace mission.[103]

In 1667, the Iroquois were sufficiently weakened by the French that Jesuits could once more enter their regions to begin missionary work. For the next twenty years they continued to do so. The hostility towards the Jesuits resumed and eventually led the priests to establish a village for Christian Iroquois across the St. Lawrence from Montreal; but from fear of too much contact with the French settlers, the village was soon moved some distance away.[104]

Work continued with the Huron colony near Quebec, and in an earlier move to protect the Indians from being corrupted by European influences, the Jesuits in 1673 had set up the village of New Lorette, a few miles from Quebec. This town became a great center of devotion and pilgrimage for all Christian Indians in the late seventeenth century.[105] In 1673, the fathers began work once more among the Indians of Acadia, with their main headquarters at Port Royal. Without slackening their efforts in the west and along the St. Lawrence, they so efficiently did their work in Acadia that by 1700 it was said that all the Acadian Indians were Christians. After the departure of Druillettes in 1657, Jesuit work among the Abenakis went into a decline until the 1680s when work was started once again.[106] This region by the 1680s had become the site of the work of Sébastian Rasle.[107] He was killed and scalped in August, 1724, at his Norridgewock, Maine, Abenaki mission by New England troops who later auctioned the scalp in Boston.[108]

Not all the opposition to the Jesuits' work came from hostile Iroquois or Puritan New Englanders. Some highly placed French officials also opposed the kind of missionary work these priests carried on in the last half of the seventeenth century. While the Jesuits in the early 1600s had never really pushed the "Europeanization" of the Indians, after the 1640s the missionaries expressed virtually total opposition to the spread of French *civilization* among their Indian converts. This order of priests from the beginning of its missionary activity had sought to build on the good it believed was already present in a culture. They came to believe that contact with most of the French was destructive to the Indians.

For the wandering tribes they sought no change in native life-style except what affected Christian moral standards and general church discipline, and with the sedentary tribes they sought to form villages apart from the French where Christianity and the native life-style could blend. After the ascendancy of Colbert in France, this practice was directly contrary to Louis XIV's stated policy. When the Count de Frontenac was sent to New France as governor in 1672, he was told by Colbert that the Jesuits in New France had too much influence; therefore, Frontenac was ready to write what he knew Colbert wanted to hear about Jesuits. Among the charges he leveled against them in his correspondence with the court was that they were opposed to Colbert's frenchification policy toward the Indians; and, indeed, they were. Yet the Jesuits still had enough influence with the king, whose confessor was a Jesuit, to get a grant in 1680 of additional land, which was some distance from Montreal, on which to move their Iroquois converts who would then be father away from French influence. This was done over Frontenac's opposition.[109] At the same time, in France, Blaise Pascal attacked the order's approach to its work. Although not all Jesuits were alike, and the methods of the Spaniard Pablo de Arriaga in Peru differed vastly from those of Le Jeune or Allouez, it is, nonetheless, hard to reconcile Pascal's acrimony with the historical record, especially that of his fellow countrymen.[110]

During the seventeenth century and on into the eighteenth, the Jesuit missionary enterprise spread worldwide. Missionary explorers such as Marquette and Allouez had their counterparts elsewhere: Eusebio Kino in northern New Spain, Wenceslaus Linck in Baja California and the lower Colorado River area, and Ignacio Nápoli among the Cora Indians of Baja California. They did not always use identical methods, but an intrepid nature and single-minded devotion seems to have been common to each of them. They were men who refused to remain aloof from the various peoples and differing cultural environments which they encountered.[111] Their efforts literally circled the globe: they were in China, in Russia, and hoped in this period to open an overland route from Europe to China for the work of their order.[112] It was controversy over the Chinese work that indirectly put an end to the publication of the annual reports from the French North American missions in 1673.[113]

The missionary efforts of the Puritan New Englanders pale by comparison to the work done by the Jesuits a few hundred miles away. The justly acclaimed John Eliot, who respected Druillettes, if not his religion, had no real successor in missionary activity. There was in Eliot's approach a strong desire to civilize the Indian in the European, or English manner, and Puritan missionary work in the early eighteenth century was deemed an Anglicizing influence. Various excuses were offered then and later for the Englishman's lack of missionary zeal toward the Indian; particularly, however, after King Philip's war in the late seventeenth century, a conflict in which a league of tribes from Maine to Connecticut led by "King Philip" killed hundreds of colonists. Indians were seen as threats, as enemies, as a kind of savage nuisance to be removed, not Christianized.[114]

Jonathan Edwards in the eighteenth century worked for a time among the Indians because he simply had no other position open to him, having just been removed from his previous pulpit. When missionaries were sent among the Iroquois about 1700, it was an open question whether it was for the spread of Christianity or the winning of their allegiance that provided the prime motivation for those who sent them.[115] As the century drew to a close, the Jesuit work in the far-flung French territories in North America was continuing and in a measure was expanding to the south in Louisiana and along the Gulf Coast; however, while Jesuits were still exploring new territory, the emphasis of their effort shifted from the west to the St. Lawrence valley in the early years of the eighteenth century. This did not prevent much of their frontier missionary network from surviving until 1763—the end of the French period in North America. Then came their own suppression by the Church itself. With the lifting of the ban in the early nineteenth century, however, the Jesuits returned to what had been French North America and even sought out some of the same nomadic tribes known to Allouez and Marquette. For example, they ministered to the Potawatomies in 1838, who by that time had been pushed to what is now Linn County, Kansas.[116]

What they accomplished is astonishing, and what they might have accomplished, but for the Iroquois onslaught against the Hurons, as the historian Francis Parkman concluded, could well have changed the direction of North American history.[117]

The succeeding chapters will examine the Jesuits' perception and evaluation of the Amerind as he existed within the context of his native culture, and how in turn the missionaries sought to adapt both themselves and their message in order to enter into the native cultural environment. This adaptation on the part of the Jesuit missionaries affected not only the missionaries' life-style but their didactic methods; it even affected the Catholic cultus itself—that amalgam of ritual and devotion at the heart of the Church's life.

II

"Maker of the Earth"

Jérôme Lalemant wrote of the Hurons that ". . . never in France have I seen illiterate people more susceptible to the mysteries of our Faith. . . . And. . . no heart continues to be barbarous when Faith has taken possession of it . . . ,"[1] but how did the missionaries view this barbarism? Some missionaries—both Catholic and Protestant—tended to find no good in cultures untouched by either the message they sought to impart or the kind of civilization they themselves represented.[2] The Jesuit fathers in French North America tended, however, to note the good as well as what they considered the bad in the Amerindian cultures. For them the good had its origin in God who made man in his own image; an image that had been blurred by the fall of man, but not entirely obliterated. They believed that through nature and reason man could find hints of the existence of the true God, and form a concept of what is good.[3] Here, of course, the followers of Loyola were being faithful to Catholic doctrine as expressed in St. Gregory the Great and expounded and refined by St. Thomas Aquinas. According to this doctrine, 'natural revelation' or 'natural theology' is that knowledge of God which man can achieve by the use of human reason as distinct from the more complete knowledge expressed in the Christian revelation. 'Natural law' is the concept of morality believed to be inherent in nature and which any rational human being can perceive through the use of reason. Such knowledge of the good in nature that might be found by man is not sufficient by itself to lead him to a state of salvation; this comes only through the Christian revelation and the grace supplied through the sacraments, prayer, and good works. The Jesuits, however, retained a keen awareness of what the Church in earlier ages had acutely sensed: the Christian revelation is the fulfillment of all strivings for good in man, so that wherever good survives or appears, the foundations of Christianity are there present. Needless to say, one can find in the four centuries of Jesuit history some exceptions to this rule,[4] but in their work with the American Indians, the Jesuits tended to remain in the lineage of those, beginning with St. Paul, who sought to respect and incorporate into Christianity whatever in a given culture was not alien to it and what was believed to confirm it.

If the divine image in man was not entirely obliterated by the fall, then the Jesuits in French America were eager to find and to report the vestiges of this image in the aborigines whose souls lured the missionaries to the New World. The Jesuits were not the only Europeans who rejected the view that the American aborigines were simply brutish beasts, fit only for slavery or annihilation: Marc Lescarbot had visited New France in the early 1600s and praised the charity and wisdom of the Indian.[5] In 1670, the German explorer John Lederer, in the service of the Governor of Virginia, wrote:

> Though they want those means of improving Humane Reason, which the use of letters affords us, let us not therefore conclude them wholly destitute of Learning and Sciences; for by these little helps

which they have found, many of them advance their natural understanding to great knowledge in Physick, Rhetorick, and Policie of government . . .[6]

He reported having heard tribal elders, in consultations and debates, give evidence of as much "Judgement and Eloquence" as did Europeans of great education and literary talent.

As a vast collection of testimony, however, in which the intelligence and laudable attributes of the Amerind are cited over and over, seventeenth-century Jesuit literature is without parallel. Writing from the mission in the Huron town of Ossossané in 1639, the Jesuit François du Peron went so far as to declare that nearly all the Hurons—in oratory, in business affairs, in "tricks and subtleties," and in the daily matters of life—showed more intelligence than the most sagacious "citizens and merchants" of France.[7] Although this may have been an overstatement, the fathers were eager to voice what their experience had taught them and to dispel the view that simply because the Indian lacked European civilization he was, therefore, dull, slow-witted, and brutish. The Indian lacked only education, not intelligence, they reported, and association with him for a relatively brief period should convince the European of this. Le Jeune wrote in his report for the *Relation* of 1634, published in France, the following rather frank conclusion:

> I naturally compare our Savages with certain villagers, because both are usually without education, though our Peasants are superior in this regard: and yet I have not seen any one thus far, of those who have come to this country, who does not confess and frankly admit that the Savages are more intelligent than our ordinary peasants.[8]

43

The fathers obviously were eager for the French court and reading public to have as high an opinion as possible of the Indians in order to insure the future of the Jesuit missionary work in French America; yet, in view of their observations recounted in this chapter and in later chapters, it is logical to conclude that more was at play in their thinking than a desire to convey a favorable impression. Intelligence in the Indian was seen as a sign of an otherwise blemished divine image still to be found in each of them, and this was the basis upon which the missionaries hoped to build native churches to outshine the faith and practice of old Europe.

In Le Jeune's *Relation* of 1635, he stated that although their vision had long been "obscured," some individuals, nevertheless, had a kind of knowledge of God. Although it was a knowledge clouded by what he called "superstitions," these were superstitions that the Jesuits hoped ". . . to change into true Religion, and, like spoils carried off from the enemy, to consecrate them to the honor of our Lord . . ."[9] In a few Indians this natural revelation of God was relatively free from "superstition." Such an Indian is quoted in the *Relation* of 1638:

> It seems to me . . . that I have had from my youth some little knowledge of the things you teach; I was wont to think thus when I was alone, 'There is one who has made all, upon whom we depend, who gave us our life, and causes us to find something with which to sustain it; and that one hates evil doers! I had a desire to know him, hence I was greatly rejoiced when I heard you speak of him.[10]

Other evidence of natural revelation was cited in the same *Relation:* a woman reported that in her past, during an illness, it had occurred to her that there was a higher power who could cure her; she invoked this power and quickly recovered. Later, when she went to Quebec, she heard the missionaries speak of God. She decided that this was the one to whom she prayed, and that the missionaries could reveal more of him to her, and provide her with his name. Another, a young man who was reported to have had no prior contact with Christianity or the French, stated to the missionaries his long-standing conviction that there was a powerful, beneficent spirit who created all things. He now identified this spirit as the God whom the Jesuits proclaimed.[11]

Again, in 1639, Le Jeune cited several individuals attracted to Christianity as if it were for them the fulfillment of some long-cherished belief or inclination. For example, an Algonquin, arriving at Three Rivers with about eight hundred tribesmen, responded to the fathers' didactic entreaties with the statement that he had long wished to hear such things. Since childhood he had believed in a benevolent spirit who healed men in their sickness—a spirit to whom men might have recourse when in need.

Another example was an old woman, who in 1640—immediately after her baptism at Sillery—was quoted as saying:

> It seems to me that our Ancestors believed something of what the fathers teach; for I remember that when I was quite young, my father who was very old, related to us that he who had made all, and who provides our food, was displeased when any one did wrong, and that he hated the wicked and punished them after their death.[12]

The most notable convert in the Huron missions in 1642 was one Ahatsistcari, thought by many to be the

Huron's chief warrior. Shortly before his conversion he was reputed either to have captured or put to flight an entire band of three hundred Iroquois with only fifty men of his own. The Jesuits maintained that by his reason—reason emanating from the divine image in man—he had apprehended the existence of a spirit that is all good. To this spirit he himself is said to have attributed his prowess in battle and his preservation. They quote him to the effect that he had this inclination long before having heard any preaching of Christianity.[13]

Paul Ragueneau in the *Relation* of 1647-48 called this knowledge "a secret idea of the Divinity and of a first Principle, the author of all things, whom they invoked without knowing him." This "secret idea" they invoked in the forest during the hunt, and when in danger either in battle or on the water. Although the various tribes had different names for this concept of the "first Principle" and although they might give it various names according to the role it was seen in at the moment—whether as a protector, as a witness of their courage or honor, or as the supplier of game for the hunt—it was still the same concept of divinity they were seeking to invoke. This only confirmed early Christian thought, Ragueneau concluded,

> So true is what Tertullian said of the most infidel Nations, that nature in the midst of perils makes them speak with a Christian voice, —*Exclamant vocem naturaliter Christianam*, —and have recourse to a God whom they invoke almost without knowing him, —*Ignoto Deo*.[14]

According to the missionaries, then, some Indians, in spite of inescapable involvement in their native tribal religion, maintained a clouded notion of the existence of the true God.

Writing in 1653, after having returned to his native Italian soil, Father Bressani stated that even though the pagan North American Indian was totally uncultivated and possessed of a corrupt nature, he was better off than the "libertines" of Europe, for even in his paganism he maintained a belief that the soul was immortal and that it would be appropriately rewarded in a life to come. Furthermore, he was not an atheist, for he believed in the existence of good and evil spirits and had a vague notion of a deity. Although his beliefs were couched in "a thousand fables," he was no worse off in that regard than the Greek had been with his Elysian fields.[15]

The fathers believed they detected this "secret idea" of God in certain individual Indians, not only among the sedentary Hurons but also among the Algonquins, the Montagnais, and the other nomadic tribes beyond them to the west. Father Allouez, working in the upper Great Lakes region and in the Mississippi valley in the 1660s, reported that among the Potawatomis and Illinois Indians he encountered this same "secret idea" on a rather large scale. One aged Potawatomi told him that he had always fasted for long periods; that he had visions of the "Maker of the Earth"; and that he made sacrifices to God by throwing tobacco frequently upon the fire while he uttered exclamations of praise. It is noteworthy that Allouez assumed that this man had been seeking the true God before his baptism, and that although Allouez recorded in his journal how he told the neophyte that it was not necessary to honor God through sacrifices of tobacco, he does not record that he forbade this practice.[16]

According to Allouez, the Illinois honored many spirits, but they held one to be preeminent among all others and gave a special worship to this one who they said was the "Maker of all things":

> Such a passionate desire have they to see HIM that
> they keep long fasts to that end, hoping that by this
> means God will be induced to appear to them in
> their sleep; and if they chance to see him, they deem
> themselves happy, and assured of a long life.[17]

Allouez implied not only that the "secret idea" of God
had survived among these tribes but that at least on
occasion what might be termed an inchoate spiritual relationship had developed between the Indian and the true
God. The presence of an idea of God in individual Indians or within an Indian community did not, as will be
shown in a later chapter, prevent the missionaries from
generally attributing the native cultus,[18] as this was expressed with various tribal variations, to 'demonic' forces. The native cultus as exercised through the medicine
man, or *shaman*, had, however, become basically tainted
with evil. On the other hand, natural revelation and the
survival of good in the 'fallen' Indian probably lay behind
the fact that a faint idea of God was preserved through a
few individuals in each generation.

　　　This rudimentary idea of the Deity was not the
only evidence to the missionaries of the existence of good
within the native cultures. There was also the Indian's
belief in the soul's immortality. Long before the flowering
of the Jesuit missionary enterprise, the French traveller
Lescarbot had pointed to the Indian's belief in life after
death as evidence of a wisdom exceeding Pliny and certain other classical philosophers.[19] In evaluating this almost universally held belief among the Indians, the missionaries found evidence again of the survival of natural
revelation comprehended through reason. Once, in one
of the cabins at Sillery, when Father Buteux was speaking
about the immortality of the soul and was using some of
the Indian's own imagery—such as their idea of the

village to the west where, they believed, the soul continued to hunt and to do many other things after death that the person had enjoyed in this life[20]—he was challenged by a newcomer. The Indian asked why he made the effort to convince them of this belief since they needed no convincing to know that the human soul was far different from that of a dog. A dog's soul, he said, perceived only through its senses, but a man's soul knew many things not perceived through the senses; therefore, it could exist without the body and was not material, but immortal. Father Vimont, who reported the incident, saw this as conclusive evidence that:

> . . . the savages whom we instruct are not satyrs roaming through the woods, and that the saying of the Prophet is true that God has impressed upon the most barbarous souls a quality of reason, which is a ray emanating from the light of his countenance.[21]

Father Jérôme Lalemant went so far as to say that "emanation" from the divine countenance was even to be discovered in the languages of the various tribes, or at least in those of the Algonquian language group encompassing most of the tribes with which the missionaries worked along the lower St. Lawrence.

> Their compounds are admirable; and I may say that, though there should be no other argument to show that there is a God than the economy of the Savage languages, that would suffice to convince us. For there is no human wisdom nor skill which can unite so many men, so as to make them observe the order which they maintain in their languages, wholly different from those of Europe; it is God alone who holds the guidance thereof.[22]

The Jesuits, however, did not confine their search for vestigial truths among the Indians to their theistic concepts and ideas of immortality. If the light of reason were still operative in the Amerind, then, at least to some measure, they no doubt apprehended the natural law as well. Though there were many times when the fathers doubted, their attitudes generally affirmed that in some respects the Indian reflected a morality in conformity with the Catholic church's concept of natural law, and sometimes to a degree that put many Europeans to shame. Certain prominent aspects of native morality horrified the missionaries, but the Jesuit writings do not present a people devoid of what the fathers understood to be all *'moral* consciousness.' The significance of this evaluation is that the Jesuits saw cultures that in their view ought to be changed, not destroyed.[23]

Pierre Biard, who with Ennemond Massé was a member of the first group of Jesuits to arrive in French North America, wrote as early as 1616 that according to his experience in Acadia, or what the English called Nova Scotia, and to the south along the Maine coast, the natives were not given to thievery; and that, on the contrary, these Indians thought of the European as a thief. Yet, he wrote, that, as a group, the tribes he had known were stunted in their moral development; but not so stunted that some praiseworthy moral attributes had not survived. Biard praised the convert, Membertou—an Indian from the area of Port Royal in Acadia—because in all his years as a pagan, wrote Biard, he had always kept himself to one wife, knowing from the use of his reason that polygamy produced a "troublesome" life. Among these tribes wife beating and fornication were rampant; yet, in the midst of such disorders, few *divorces* occurred and relatively little adultery, Biard believed. The girls and women seemed quite modest, and the men at least not overtly immodest. Some Frenchmen caused the Indians great offense when they tried to take liberties with the Indian women. They were not a quarrelsome race of people, Biard wrote; in fact, not as quarrelsome as the French. It seemed to Biard that the tribal leaders were generally able to work out any differences that arose between members of their own tribe. Serious offenses were avenged by the injured party; or, in case of murder or manslaughter, by his family; vengeance upon the guilty party settled the matter without blood-feud. Once vengeance was taken, the families and descendants of both the injured and the guilty lived in peace with each other. And, like Lescarbot who reported of the same tribes, Biard cited their generous and sharing nature.[24]

According to Biard, natives did not hurry as the French did, and this was to their credit, for hurrying accompanied worry, an ever-present shortcoming of the French ". . . who can never do anything without hurry and worry; worry, I say, because our desire tyrannizes over us and banishes peace from our actions."[25] The Indian life-style helped relieve the Indian of malice and worked toward producing a pleasant, happy, and generous disposition.[26]

Although Paul Le Jeune, in the 1630s, pointed to good in native morality, he was less apt to find good there than some of his brethren. He, nevertheless, pointed out in his report for the years 1632 and 1633 that Europe too had passed through an uncivilized era—the demise of which, he wrote, was due to the acceptance of Christianity. Before the triumph of the faith in Spain, Germany, or England, the inhabitants were no more civilized than the Indian, he said. He went on to recite a long list of the Indian's faults; although, as offenses go, he stated that they were not many in number.[27]

Among the Montagnais tribe around Quebec,

thievery was rarely found, but among the Hurons the matter was different. According to reports Le Jeune had received, the Hurons were quite artful in purloining others' possessions and were held in great esteem by their tribesmen if they attained notable ability in this "art." In fact, if caught and punished for their efforts, they patiently endured their sufferings, since they considered themselves deserving of it for being so foolish as to be caught.[28] They stole from each other, he wrote, and when they came down to trade in Quebec they stole from the French as well. He believed that no people were more given to stealing than the Hurons. While in their presence, he said, one had to watch them at all times, and even this vigilance little retarded their abilities. He had had a carpenter's tool disappear almost from before his eyes, even as he was trying to watch everyone in the room, fearing that this very item would attract their attention. "It is necessary to have your eye both on their feet and on their hands, when they enter a place. It is said that they steal with their feet as well as with their hands."[29]

By 1634, Le Jeune had decided that the Montagnais, though not given to thievery, were self-centered and were not inclined to reverence their tribal leaders. To them their birthright was the "liberty of Wild ass colts."[30] They obeyed their chiefs, he said, only if it pleased them.

That same year he wrote of the Montagnais that they were incredibly slanderous even about their nearest relatives, but that they generally ignored the slander and behaved toward the backbiter as if nothing had been said. About this propensity to slander and inclination to ignore it, Le Jeune explained:

> . . . it seems to me, that their slanders and derisions
> do not come from malicious hearts or from infected

mouths, but from a mind which says what it thinks in order to give itself free scope, and which seeks gratification from everything, even from slander and mockery.[31]

Furthermore, he said that lying to strangers was as natural to them as speaking, and that he did not trust them except under circumstances that brought punishment, should they fail to keep their word. They were unbelievably gluttonous, eating as long as the food held out. He recounted being told once that if he wished to pray everytime his Indian companions wanted to eat, then he should prepare to recite his *benedicite* more than twenty more times during the course of the night. Le Jeune found the Montagnais to be foul-mouthed at all ages—they used as exclamations the words for the private parts of the body. Also he decried their drunkenness, but knew the cause to be his own people. After pointing out that if the liberty to do so existed in Christian societies, some Christians would far exceed the debauchery of the Indians, for "dissoluteness strides more openly there than here."[32]

For all the faults Le Jeune cited, his praise was ample for the good he found; and, like Biard before him, he lauded the Montagnais for their patience with each other. Le Jeune recorded that in November, 1632—on a day when the weather had turned wintery—he spent much time in one of the large Montagnais houses in the company of many families who had numerous children. He could only think of how in France, if there were several families gathered together under one roof, there would be brawls, disputes, and quarrels. But such was not the case here. Cursing of one another was practically unheard of among these Indians.[33] He believed they surpassed the supposedly Christian Europeans in the exercise of the virtue of patience, much to the Old World's shame. In their toils and hardships their patience held sway, particularly in sickness. One could jump, dance, and yell in a sick man's presence with his never complaining; and in the midst of privation in the forests it was the Indians who encouraged him:

. . . they said to me, "We shall be sometimes two days, sometimes three, without eating, for lack of food; take courage, *Chihine*, let thy soul be strong to endure suffering and hardship; keep thyself from being sad, otherwise thou wilt be sick; see how we do not cease to laugh, although we have little to eat."[34]

If anger or punishment should be commensurate to the offense, then the Montagnais was the most forgiving of creatures. Once, in the midst of the forest in winter, Le Jeune recorded, in a situation much like that just described, a young Indian stole for his own use the day's provisions, the only food the band had in the midst of a famine. The young man who was from another area had been given a generous amount of food along with the others before supplies were exhausted, a factor which compounded his treachery. Yet no curses nor epithets were hurled at the thief; the worst were only sneers aimed in his direction. Later, when he returned to the group, he was received by them; Le Jeune wanted to upbraid him, but was silenced by his host who said that the theft was no doubt attributable to ravenous dogs, and the thief, with his family, was allowed to move into the household. Le Jeune wrote that this occurrence should "confound many Christians." To behave in such a fashion, the Indians still reflected the light from the "divine countenance," and, he wrote, "possessed souls which were naturally good."[35]

At times, even in the midst of praise, it is obvious that he questioned both the depth of the Indians' virtue,[36] and the motivations that lay behind it;[37] yet, in 1636, in the midst of the immorality, the disorder, the hostility of Indian society, Le Jeune thought of France:

> The din of Palaces, the great uproar of Lawyers, Litigants, and Solicitors is heard here only at a thousand leagues' distance. Exactions, deceits, thefts, rapes, assassinations, treachery, enmity, black malice, are seen here only once a year, in the letters and Gazettes which people bring from Old France. Not that we have not our maladies, but they are easier to cure . . .[38]

There is little doubt in Jean de Brébeuf's reports from the Huron missions that moral virtue was present among these Indians. Brébeuf, who has been called a "second St. Paul," believed that to convert the Huron, he had to "become a Huron with the Hurons . . ."[39] He readily pointed out the admirable aspects of Huron life: there were some loving and secure marriages among them in spite of their permissiveness toward polygamy and adultery; they were generous to each other, remarkably unselfish, with the door always open to strangers. Indeed, their charity and hospitality were implanted in them by God himself, wrote Brébeuf. Besides, they could cope with the prospect of death better than many Christian "gentlemen and ladies to whom one would not dare to mention it." Surely, Brébeuf wrote, it was on the basis of virtue found within them ". . . that we hope, with the grace of God, to build the edifice of the Christian Religion among these people . . ."[40]

There was lasciviousness among them but in some respects less so than among Christians "who will blush . . . in their presence" at the day of judgment; and while there were liars, thieves, and the slothful among

55

them, they were not alone among the earth's peoples in these failings. Some of their failings, too, were directly attributable to sickness, so prevalent among them: ". . . we know very well how sickness alters the disposition and the inclinations even of the most sociable."[41]

Even Jérôme Lalemant, who, as one commentator said ". . . did not understand Indians, nor even like them very much . . .,"[42] and who in 1638 found the "stench" and "wretchedness" of Huron customs incredible,[43] in 1645 praised the Indians:

> . . . I can say in truth that, as regards Intelligence, they are in no wise inferior to Europeans and to those who dwell in France. I would never have believed that, without instruction, nature could have supplied a most ready and vigorous eloquence, which I have admired in many Hurons; or more clear-sightedness in affairs, or a more discreet management in things to which they are accustomed . . . in those practices which among them are regarded as evil acts and are condemned by the public, we find without comparison much less disorder than there is in France, though here the mere shame of having committed the crime is the offender's punishment.[44]

Lalemant had only landed in the New World a few months before writing of his chagrin at what surrounded him in the Huron country in 1638. Whether he liked Indians "very much" or not, he devoted years of his life to them, and one can detect a lessening of judgment against them as the initial cultural shock wore off. In 1648, of the Atikemegues, he went so far as to say:

> It seems as if innocence, banished from the majority of the Empires and Kingdoms of the World, had

withdrawn into these great forests where these
people dwell. Their nature has something, I know
not what, of the goodness of the Terrestrial Paradise
before sin had entered it. Their practices manifest
none of the luxury, the ambition, the avarice, or the
pleasures that corrupt our cities.[45]

While the Indians in their natural state, untouched by Christianity, were deemed to be savages
without the hope of heaven, they were not, in the Jesuits'
view, devoid of intelligence and reason. The 'image of
God' in which man had been created, though blurred by
the 'fall', was still to be found in the Indian. His intelligence and reason were signs of this blurred image, and
through these the Indian might perceive to a degree both
natural revelation and natural law. Indications that to
varying degrees the Indians had done so were to be
found in their vestigial theism and corrupted ideas of the
immortality of the soul. Additionally, though this presented some difficulty at times, the Jesuit writings reflect
a belief in the survival of a vestigial perception of the
natural moral law.

In the reasoning of the missionaries, if natural
revelation and natural law could be perceived through
man's innate reason regardless of any attributes of civilization, then Christianity, which is the highest fulfillment
of natural revelation and natural law, obviously could
also exist in conditions considered by the standards of
European civilization to be primitive or savage. Only to
the extent that Christian moral principles might lessen
the brutality of Indian life can it be said that the Jesuits
hoped to be a "civilizing" influence upon the Indians; yet
even this moral understanding was to be based upon the
natural law.

These conclusions provided the basis for the

missionaries' approach to the Indian tribes: good existed already in the tribal cultures, and all good had its origin in God. The good the missionaries found provided a foundation for what they came to build, a foundation that a native Christianity might not only rest upon but with which it could also coalesce and thereby renew the blurred image of God in the Indian. Such a concept could only lead to a policy of preservation and adaptation, not destruction. It seemed obvious to the missionaries that the survival of good in the native cultures had had nothing to do with the amenities—food, dress, or shelter common to contemporaneous western civilization. They concluded that Christianity ought to be planted in native soil, be fed and watered with what was indigenous to the native culture, and be presented to the Indians in a manner that was not foreign or artificial to them. The amenities of European civilization were irrelevant to the missionaries' purpose.

III

"Holding out One's Hands"

If the Jesuit sought to build on native foundations, without interjecting a "civilizing" imperative, then it was the missionary, not the Indian, who had to change the methods by which he survived in the human environment and to adapt himself to living conditions foreign to his experience. In this context, it was the European who was being *Americanized* rather than the converse.

On August 1, 1626, Charles Lalemant, then superior of the inchoate Jesuit work in New France, wrote to his brother and fellow Jesuit, Jérôme, who was still in France. Charles raised the question of exactly how a Jesuit was to relate to the Indians with whom he worked. Charles described to Jérôme what it was like, for example, to journey to the villages of the sedentary Hurons, far up the St. Lawrence. To reach his destination, the missionary had to paddle constantly by day; and frequently he had to carry canoe and gear over lengthy portages. After the arduous trip, he would find himself among Indians who, though not nomadic, often suffered great privation during winter, because they had neglected to store supplies for the bitterly cold months. But what is more to the point, they were, Lalemant wrote, more "savage" in some respects than the nomads of the Quebec region, for they were given to many acts of immorality. Could "Religious eyes" bear to look upon so much nakedness and immorality? Although there is no record of his brother's answer to this question, the collective answer of the Jesuit order is clearly written "large" in the history of seventeenth-century French North America.[1] Jérôme himself came to North America and would write in the *Relation* of 1642 that when necessary one must become a "barbarian" with the "barbarians" in order to lead them to Jesus Christ.

Another missionary had made a similar comment. In a report that Father Le Jeune sent to France in 1632, he, too, had expressed the Jesuit intent to live at the native's level and "to become a Savage with the Savages."[2] He wrote that a missionary must be willing to give up life as he had previously known it and to accept village life with its reprehensible morality as well as its privations. It was true that at times one might go for days without food and be required to sleep exposed to the cold. But the only way to know the Indians and to learn their language was to live with them. To avoid offending them, he advised that when one was offered a morsel of what might appear to be unsavory food served on a piece of bark, together with water served from a bark dipper, that one should not only graciously take it but also show no repulsion when his hosts wiped their greasy hands on their hair or on the mongrels that gathered about the fire.[3]

After large-scale work was resumed in the Huron country in 1634, more and more of the Jesuits learned what it was like to travel with Indians. They learned to paddle for hours and to carry baggage or a canoe during long portages. Paddling was hard on any priest recently arrived from France, and although he might take along a sheet to serve as a sail on the wide St. Lawrence, he usually ended up paddling against the current.[4]

Based on reports sent to him from the Huron country, Le Jeune wrote an entire chapter in the *Relation* of 1636 for those who felt called to America as missionaries. He wrote that the trip to the Hurons took at least four weeks. During the day one had to face the hardships of river travel. The sun burned by day and mosquitoes tormented by night. Numerous times travelers incurred the risk of being drowned or thrown upon the rocks. The only food was a little crushed, dried corn that was boiled in a small amount of water. Since those just arriving from Europe did not know the native language and the best place to learn it was at their destination, the trip would pass basically in silence. If one should become ill or injured along the way, one could expect no help from one's companions, since there was virtually nothing they could do and no way for them to obtain additional aid. In fact, the Indian might abandon any companion who could not fend for himself.

Le Jeune went on to say that when the aspiring missionary arrived in the Huron country, the fathers there would surely greet him with love and charity, but they would have only a humble native hut of arbor-type construction for him to dwell in, and they would be able to offer no more than a mat or skin for him to sleep on. In addition to the mosquitoes and sandflies, fleas were a plague of the villages and helped keep one awake all night.

Beyond the physical hazards, there was also the matter of pride: whereas in France the Jesuit was considered a respected scholar, among the Indians the opposite was true—every man, woman, and child considered the priest strange and a dolt. Furthermore, the missionary must be willing, without rancor, to accept their laughter and derision.

The Huron language will be your Saint Thomas and your Aristotle; and clever man as you are, and speaking glibly among learned and capable persons, you must make up your mind to be for a long time mute among the Barbarians. You will have accomplished much, if, at the end of a considerable time, you begin to stammer a little.[5]

In the villages as well as among the nomads, the cold was a formidable problem, especially for those Jesuits who were accustomed to carpeted rooms and tight-fitting doors and windows. New missionaries were advised by veterans that the cold was best endured if, like the Indians, they did not struggle hard against it, but rather accepted it and allowed an adjustment to occur. This was what Le Jeune termed "holding out one's hands" to the cold instead of waging war against it.[6]

Ultimately, however, it was the Indian himself to whom one had to hold out one's hands, and this meant more than the acceptance of ice, wind, and snow. An entire life-style had to be embraced. Hands had to be held out to good and to bad, to the Indians' joys and sorrows, to times of plenty and the frequent times of winter famine.

Adjustment to a strange diet posed understandable difficulties, but among the nomadic tribes both the missionaries and the Indians might go for days at a time with no food at all. Even among the sedentary tribes this could occur if crops failed or if adequate preparations for the winter had not been made. If careful planning had been done, having enough food was much less a problem in the villages of sedentary tribes than among the nomads. The missionaries learned to barter for food and to store it for the winter. They could generally count on enough corn, squash, and dried fish to ward off hunger. Among the nomadic tribes of the north and west, however, all depended on the hunt; what little corn these tribes were able to cultivate had to be raised during a short growing season.

Among the Hurons in the 1630s the Jesuits adjusted to a village life-style which was to typify their existence in sedentary villages of the Great Lakes region, regardless of tribe. Morning and evening they ate a kind of porridge made of water and cornmeal. Like the Indians, their porridge or "sagamité" was sometimes seasoned with cinders to enhance the flavor. Sagamité was sometimes considered to be both a food and a drink, since it was served in the form of a liquid. For that reason, the Indians often drank nothing with their sagamité meal, water being their only beverage. On occasion, when the supply of dried corn was more than ample, an unleavened cornmeal mixture was baked in the embers into a kind of bread which might contain either beans or wild berries. Raspberries, blackberries, strawberries, and grapes were abundantly available in season, at least along the Great Lakes and St. Lawrence. Fresh meat and fresh fish were likewise available in season—meat, in winter; and fish, in the warm months. Another Indian favorite was a fish full of waterflies, which the priests compared to the "gnats of Provence." The Jesuits decided that at least for the Indians ". . . the more tainted the fish . . . the better."[7]

The ordinary street dress of a Jesuit priest or lay brother in Europe was a casssock, more ample in cut than the usual Latin or Roman cassock of later times; and this was how the fathers dressed in the New World. They even slept in their cassocks. François du Peron[8] wrote from Ossossané in 1639 that he had worn his one cassock since leaving France some months before, except for the times when he changed his linen underclothing. In this the fathers imitated the Indians who also slept in their clothing.

If some weighty cause arose, however, the fathers did not hesitate to dress in something that might not so easily exacerbate a delicate situation as would their black habit. When in 1646 Father Isaac Jogues planned to go into the Iroquois country, he was warned by Algonquin friends that he would create a friendlier atmosphere along the way if he removed his habit, since it "preaches as well as your lips . . ." Jogues followed his friends' advice and Jérôme Lalemant concluded that it was wise "to treat the sick as sick . . . [and] that one must become all things to all men, in order to gain all to Jesus Christ."[9]

Generally, when on the trail away from a village or with the Indians on a hunt, in addition to whatever habit he might have on, the Jesuit wore a hat, carried a bag for his breviary and writing material, and a blanket which served as ". . . robe and cloak, as mattress and cushion, for a bed, and for every other convenience—even for a dwelling-place, when in the open country, and when they have, for the time, no other shelter."[10]

During the 1640s the missionaries to the Hurons had occasional respites within the crude masonry and timber walls of Ste. Marie. But for these, however, when the missionaries did have "other shelter"—whether in the villages of the Huron, the Montagnais, the Iroquois, or later in those of the Ottawa, Illinois, and Miami far to the west—at best they could expect a cabin constructed like an arbor, with bark, sticks, and branches of trees and bushes spread over a pole framework. These obviously were extremely flammable almost from the time they were first erected. Although some were no bigger than 10′ square, among the tribes of the upper St. Lawrence and Great Lakes such structures were as large as 90′ × 20′ and 20′ high at the very center. Among these tribes, cabins had no windows or chimneys—only a hole in the roof to allow some of the smoke to escape.[11]

Among the tribes along the St. Lawrence, the fathers reported that the procedure of construction was almost always the same: women went with axes to cut poles while the men drew the plan of the structure on the ground. In winter, they noted, this was done by cutting out a three or four foot hole in the snow, the sides of which formed the lower walls of the cabin. Poles were set up either in the ground or snow and tied together at the tops from side to side. Bark, sticks, and branches were then laid upon this framework. Branches were used to line the floor, and a skin was hung over the doorway in winter. The fathers reported that in the northern regions the winter wind hardly noticed the bark and branch walls; and that in summer there were infestations of lice, gnats, and mosquitoes.

The missionaries at times made some adaptations in their own cabins so that they could be better arranged for their purposes. For example, the cabin built for the Jesuits in the 1630s at Ihonatiria was of the usual Huron style, except that the missionaries divided it into three parts: an ante-chamber which served as storeroom; an inner room, which served as kitchen, shop, refectory, parlor, workroom, and bedroom; and a third room, which was divided in two by carpentry work, and was used as both chapel for daily Mass and as sacristy. In the inner room, the shelves along the walls, in Huron fashion, served for additional storage, but underneath, where the Hurons stored wood, the Jesuits made their bunks out of bark, boughs, skins, and clothing.

In order for a missionary operating in a native village to convert an interested Indian, he had to visit him in his cabin more than once a day, or so the fathers decided after five years among the Hurons. By European standards what greeted a priest upon entering a dwelling was utter and complete confusion. Several families would be gathered around the fire, whose smoke, usually not inclined to go readily out of the hole in the roof, filled the bark cabin, making it hard to see and breathe. (In their own cabin, the Jesuits, at times, could hardly see their breviaries.) People and dogs intermingled throughout, with the latter sharing the food, bark plates, and beds of their masters—and all in a cloud of dust. Before one could traverse the length of the cabin, he was invariably covered with dirt, soot, and perhaps some refuse. As a missionary walked through the cabin, usually words fell on his ears to the effect that his teachings were worthless. By 1639 he would hear that it was Jesuit sorcery that had brought contagion to the villages. The Jesuits often had to wait for hours in this milieu before the din subsided enough so that they might speak to the object of the visit, and there was always the danger of an angry response which might be accompanied by an arrow or a blow from a hatchet. Even sessions of apparently successful instruction might still be brought abruptly to a halt by a catechumen's dream or that of someone else living in the same cabin. At those times when opposition against the Jesuits made public preaching impossible, the cabin visits were still continued.

There was really no escape from this kind of life even in the Jesuits' own cabin. It was only the regimen of daily Mass and the divine office, along with the wearing of their tattered, rotting, black cassocks, that differentiated their village life-style from that of the Indians around them. Experience in the Huron villages showed that once the doors to the priests' houses were thrown open, as they were most of the daylight hours, the Indians came in crowds to see and examine everything. Only insults, complaints, and quarrels resulted from any prohibitive action. As Jérôme Lalemant wrote:

> And in all this, one must act submissively; a blow
> from the hatchet is soon given by these Barbarians,
> and the bark set on fire; as to seeking redress for the
> crime, there is none in the country, and the most
> one could expect would be a few presents.[12]

Patience and watchfulness, he concluded, must be cultivated by the missionary in what was always for them a
land of uncertainty. Nevertheless, the fathers, in the
midst of a new and alien life-style, except in times of dire
emergency or when they wintered among nomads, were
able then and throughout the rest of this period to carry
on the imperatives of the Catholic cultus, saying Mass—
usually in a bark cabin or chapel, or in the corner of a
cabin provided by a friendly Indian in a newly visited
village, or perhaps by a trail or a stream, or in a lean-to
built over a dugout in the snow. The fathers seem to
have adjusted well to these surroundings, as different as
they were from those in which they had grown up; yet,
these conditions did have their toll on the missionaries
and brought more of a "savage" appearance to them than
could be imagined by French clerics nurtured in a
scholar's environment. Father Daniel's appearance at
Three Rivers in August, 1636, after two years in the
villages of the sedentary Hurons, is described thusly:

> At the sight of Father Daniel, our hearts melted; his
> face was gay and happy, but greatly emaciated; he
> was barefooted, had a paddle in his hands, and was
> clad in a wretched cassock, his Breviary suspended
> to his neck, his shirt rotting on his back.[13]

During a sojourn of any length among the Indians, it was common for a Jesuit to adopt or allow the

Indians to give him a native name since his own was unfamiliar and often unpronounceable to them; this name might remain the same from tribe to tribe since a linguistic group inhabited a large continuous area and comprised numerous tribes. By August, 1638, the ten missionaries among the Hurons all possessed Indian names: the six at Ossossané were François le Mercier, called Chauose; Antoine Daniel, called Anwennen; Pierre Chastelain, called Arioo; Charles Garnier, called Ouracha; François du Peron, called Anonchiara; and Jérôme Lalemant, called Achiendassé. Four missionaries were at Teanaustaiyé: Jean de Brébeuf, called Echon; Isaac Jogues, called Ondessone; Paul Ragueneau, called Aondecheté; and Simon Le Moyne, called Wane.[14] For much of the Huron period it appears that these names were usual forms of address without the appellation of "father," which seems not to have come into use until later, the Hurons having some difficulty with the word since it could be construed as referring to a dead parent, and such reference to the dead was not often or lightly undertaken by them.

The fathers spent much of their time in the villages and along the trail caring for the sick. They sometimes found an Indian lying in the brush or snow, left there by a nomadic tribe according to custom, since the sick were viewed as burdens which the whole group could not afford. Sometimes the sick Indians were abandoned near the French, perhaps in the hope that they would be found and nursed to health. The fathers, of course, always tried to instruct and baptize a sick or dying patient—but the Jesuits seem not to have been hasty in baptizing anyone, except a dying infant or young child. The Jesuit reports give frequent evidence that the missionaries wanted the patient to understand and really want this sacrament. Sometimes it was after a recovery that an Indian in Jesuit care would finally express a desire for baptism; some, of course, never did. No doubt, on the part of some, the fact that a French missionary would come and nurse him to health was enough to turn him in favor of what the missionary taught in both word and deed.[15]

During epidemics the missionaries often worked around the clock. As previously mentioned, they had the first of many encounters with such a village epidemic in 1636 while among the Hurons, and the priests were themselves victims of it. They shared with the sick Indians the game the still mobile priests brought in; and the Hurons did the same for them. Priests who were able to do so visited the cabins each morning and evening to give the villagers soup and meat, "always taking occasion to exhort them to have recourse to God, and to gently influence them to Baptism."[16] The raisins, and other remedies they were accustomed to give the sick, they used sparingly during their own sickness in order to have an adequate supply left for the villagers. Each day they doled these out by strict count: prunes, raisins, and small portions of senna as a purgative. Bleeding was also part of the treatment they used, in conformity to the custom of the day. These daily visits to the sick—whether they were among the Hurons in the 1630s and 1640s, the Iroquois in the 1660s and 1670s, or the nomads to the west—were a usual part of the Jesuits' regular daily regimen.[17]

The fathers also succeeded to a large extent in entering into the social life of the various tribes. At first the Jesuits were reluctant to do this because of the immoral life of the Indians and the fact that so much of their social life centered around the native cultus, which the fathers sought to supplant. But they gradually selected and adapted various native social forms which they used as a vehicle for teaching Christianity. This practice will be discussed in a later chapter, but it should be kept in mind that, after initial hesitation, they began actively to seek ways by which Christianity and the native social life could coalesce. For example, the fathers at first disdained the use of tobacco in any form for its own sake as well as for the fact that it was often burned as a sacrifice to native dieties. But they soon learned to benefit from tolerating it. In the summer of 1637, for example, the missionaries at the Huron village of Angontenc were invited to attend a council at which, according to the Indian custom, the Jesuits, as guests, offered a tobacco cake in a dish to the assemblage. The leading chief broke it and distributed it among the prominent people present, and the council was conducted amid the smoke of their pipes. This setting proved a favorable one in which the missionaries were allowed to present their views. Even though at the time they were suspected by some of bringing disease to the villages through sorcery; nevertheless, they were invited to return for future visits.[18]

It should be noted that, after three years among the Hurons, the fathers surely understood that tobacco rituals had a religious significance to the Huron. Tobacco, both in a dry state and burned, had sacrificial overtones for the American Indians in general, and tobacco was thought to be of divine origin.[19] While the missionaries no doubt viewed their own participation in the Indian ritual as devoid of any religious significance, the same could not be said of the Indian onlooker. At the very least, he would have seen evidence on the missionaries' part of a respect for forms sacred to Indian life. The Indians were showing the Jesuits great respect by allowing them to open a council in this way; usually a ranking chief presented the bowl of tobacco at such a gathering.

Jesuits not only entered the Indian social milieu

at almost all levels, but skillfully incorporated much of what they came to teach around the framework of native life. A bold appreciation of native customs and social forms, and a willingness to adapt to them, came to be characteristic of their approach to Indian life. When a new village was entered for the first time, after greeting the village elders and finding lodging in a friendly villager's cabin, the missionary might call a council, using a particular tone of voice according to tribal custom, and announce at this gathering the purpose of his visit, a procedure often followed by the Indians of the Great Lakes region when visiting villages other than their own.[20]

From the standpoint of physical demands, the most difficult aspect of native life-style to which the missionary might have to adjust was the winter hunt, for even assuming he had managed to adjust to other aspects of nomadic or sedentary tribal experience, the rigors of winter brought new and sometimes desperate situations, unlike anything most Europeans had ever faced. There was at these times often no chance for the celebration of Mass for weeks or even months, as well as little opportunity even for the reading of the breviary, which meant disorganization and confusion for the accustomed regimen of the devotional life of a priest. In addition, the constant movement, bitter cold, varying moods of hostility on the part of the Indians, and not least of all the ever-present specter of starvation, put the missionary's continued physical existence in question and brought all the miseries which accompany the life of an ill-housed, ill-clad, starving tribe, struggling against the elements in the midst of freezing cold. However, even more than danger to his life, perhaps no greater evidence of his determination to adapt to native life can be shown on the missionary's part than his willingness to

71

live with the Indians in situations where the saying of Mass and even the recitation of the breviary might be rarely possible.

Life was uncomfortable enough for a priest among a nomadic tribe in summer. Their unsettled and less regulated existence made any regimen difficult, even when they remained for a time in one place. The 1641 report from Tadoussac reads in part, "the Sun did not regulate my rising up, or my lying down, or the hour of my repasts, but convenience alone which was hardly advantageous or favorable to my body."[21]

At least in summer, Mass could be regularly said, perhaps in a hastily erected arbor, or—as Claude Pijart and Charles Raymbaut did among the Nipissiriniens and Algonquins in the early 1640s—by simply throwing up blankets to mark out a space in one of the always crowded, noisy arbor-like cabins. Although Pijart wrote that the men of one village went about entirely nude, he concluded that most of the others were basically modest and industrious, and the missionary showed no disdain for carrying on the holiest act of his faith in such confused and disordered circumstances.[22]

Jérôme Lalemant's expressed opinion in 1642, that it was required of a Jesuit to become a "barbarian" with the Indians if he were to win their souls, was repeated by others time and again over the succeeding decades. In writing in the *Relation* for the years 1666 and 1668 of Father Allouez's work among the Ottawas and thirty other tribes to the west, François Le Mercier,[23] then superior, reiterated the necessity of leading a savage's life: of living perhaps on pounded fishbones that were used as a kind of flour; or on moss growing upon rocks; or living for a time on nothing, going for three or four consecutive days without any food.[24] As the fathers moved farther and farther west—farther from any French influence—the success of their work depended on their complete willingness to live as savages in the most dire of circumstances. On his way to the Algonquin mission near the Ottawas on Lake Superior in 1663, René Ménard recorded the desperate situation in which he and his Indian companions found themselves after their canoe was shattered and their food supply, exhausted:

> We remained in this condition six days, living on some offal which we were obliged, in order not to die of hunger, to scrape up with our fingernails around a hut which had been abandoned in this place sometime ago. We pounded up the bones which we found there, to make soup of them; we collected the blood of slain animals, with which the ground was soaked; in a word, we made food of everything.[25]

In April, 1697, François de Crepieul[26] described his life as a Montagnais missionary. He lived in an Indian cabin in winter, as did everyone else. He sat or knelt so close to the fire that he might perspire much of the day. He almost froze at night, as he slept in his clothes on the frozen ground or—if he were away on a hunt—on fire branches laid over the snow. If a cabin were small, he might scorch his clothes or the blanket on the side near the fire, as his head rested against the bark wall and the ice and snow which the flimsy barrier invariably let in. He ate from an *ouragan*, or dish, which, in the process of his and the Indians' communal eating, was rarely clean and usually got licked by dogs or wiped with greasy pieces of skin as the meal progressed. (That is, he ate from this bowl when there was anything to eat.) The meat, by French standards, was only half-done and quite tough. Besides, only one ample meal a day was the rule even if food were available. Water, drunk from the greasy ouragan was the only beverage. The only napkin was the hair of a nearby dog. In the mornings he awoke to find himself surrounded by dogs. Vermin was constantly on or about the Indians, particularly the children. The smoke, always present in an Indian house, was so strong in winter, he wrote, that it was difficult to open his eyes upon awakening in the morning. He daily tended the diseased, the stench of whom often brought nausea; he ate and drank after them as well, for it would have been insulting to them to do otherwise.[27]

Whether they were in the relatively settled villages of the Huron or Iroquois, or among the nomads of the west and north; in summer surrounded by blackflies, or half-frozen in winter dugouts hacked out of the snow, the Jesuit fathers were called upon to live their lives in a way that was altogether foreign to the average European of the seventeenth century. The kind of life they lived among the Indians in 1626 was exactly the same as that of their successors who lived among the Indians in 1697, a little over seventy years later. Native daily existence had changed little except for the introduction of Catholic religious observances and, except in a few specific settlements, this had brought no Europeanization of the Indian life-style and social structure.

This is, perhaps, the surest indication that the Jesuit fathers had sought only to modify, not to destroy, the culture they found. They sought to build on the good that they found in Indian society, not supplant it with something else, for European civilization in their view was no more endemic to Christianity than was the Judeo-Roman civilization in which it was born. A Jesuit might be a mandarin in China or a Brahmin in India or a Montagnais, a Nipissirinien, or a Huron.[28] They were sagacious enough to seek to modify only what they believed necessary to establish the religion they had come to teach. To insist on changes not necessary to this purpose, or to foster outside forces insistent upon change would in their view only bring disaster.

The desire to conserve and respect the ways of the Indians is exemplified in Brébeuf's sensitive instructions to aspiring French missionaries to the Hurons, in 1637: be always sincere with the Indians for they are your brothers, redeemed by the same Christ; do not keep them waiting when embarking; bring a tinder box or burning mirror to help them light their fires at night; eat their food the way they prepare it even though it may be dirty, for to do otherwise is to insult them; the Jesuit habit should be worn in such a manner as not to get in the way of travel, in canoes, at portages, or along the trail; do not inconvenience them and never be ceremonious with them; be strong and learn to "carry the load of a horse upon your back, as they do . . ."[29]

This willingness to respect and accommodate themselves to the cultures they found, while simultaneously seeking out things endemic to these cultures which could be used to support their teachings, produced a scene unique in the western world of the seventeenth century: the fathers were men who traveled far beyond the range of the meager French defenses into regions which had been in some instances previously unseen by European eyes. They willingly shared and endured a life-style alien to anything they had ever known before. Neither their education nor their rearing amid the amenities of European civilization prepared them for their work in the American wilderness. Because of their view of man and creation and the relativity of human cultural values, they went unaccompanied by force of arms into hostile regions where some of them died under horrible circumstances. Those who lived experienced another kind of martyrdom,[30] for once they left the confines of Quebec and the St. Lawrence Valley, they had no choice but to submit to a life amidst lice, filth, cold, and starvation. But amidst these horrors they continued to perceive good in the Indians, whom they called brothers, and to respect the cultures these Indian brothers had produced.

IV

Native Religions

No *one* American Indian religion was apparent to the Jesuit missionaries in the seventeenth century; rather they noticed that religion varied from region to region, if not from tribe to tribe. To a large extent, however, similarities in these religions far outweighed the differences.

The religion of the Indian of Acadia whom the Jesuits first encountered in 1611 had a cosmology built around spirits, both good and evil. There was a good god, personified in the sun and called by that name, with whom good spirits cooperated; and an evil god who was the chief of the evil spirits and who occasionally appeared to men in varying forms, such as a snake or horned animal. In short, these beliefs comprised a kind of polytheism—a rudimentary Manicheism[1]—common to the tribes of the northern Atlantic coast. Basically, this religion was similar to the religion of the tribes who lived along the lower St. Lawrence in the region of Quebec. Common to their sacred tales was the story of a deluge— a story that is found, of course, in many cultures throughout the world. In this version it was Messou (the Noah figure) who led in the restoration of the world. The creator was known as *Atachocam*. There were, in addition, various lesser deities or spirits, who were good or evil, depending on their moods, the seasons, and certain natural phenomena. Furthermore, each animal species had a semi-divine progenitor which looked like the ordinary animal but was much larger and co-existed in both the spiritual and physical worlds. If one of these appeared to an Indian in a dream, the Indian believed he would have success on the hunt and kill many of those animals whose progenitor had appeared to him. No great contradiction was seen in this since slain animals continued to exist in the spiritual world.[2]

Among the Huron and Iroquois there was great similarity of religion, although the deities' names might vary according to dialect.[3] Good and evil were personified in the sun and moon, and again man was viewed as being surrounded by good, evil, or indifferent spirits. As pointed out in Brébeuf's writings, these Indians had a strong belief in an afterlife, which was for them a continuation of physical experience on a higher level where men were impervious to death.[4] Also, according to Huron mythology, man had once lived in peace with himself and the animals. All in creation had been at peace and in communication with the *upper*, or spirit, world, but jealousy brought about chaos and an end to this golden age.[5]

Among the nomadic Algonquin tribes, religion seems to have been less developed and little more than a primitive animism, although there are hints of a belief in a supreme god or spirit. It is very difficult with some tribes to ascertain exactly what their religion consisted of, since the Europeans who first recorded these encounters may not have understood what they were told by the Indians or what they themselves observed.[6]

As mentioned in chapter two, Claude Allouez was convinced that, in spite of their rudimentary understanding of the divine, the tribes south of Lake Michigan and west to the Mississippi River believed in and worshipped a supreme being whom Allouez called God, implying that the Indians in their imperfect understanding were trying to adore the true God.[7]

The Jesuits believed that, in addition to the account of a deluge, they also detected in Indian beliefs some vestiges of other biblical material: an account of the 'fall of man' and an account that suggested the story of Cain and Abel. The Jesuits learned, for example, that the Hurons believed themselves to be descended from Aetaentsic, a woman who literally fell from another world into this one when, to please her husband, she cut down a special tree in order to give him the fruit which it had borne as food for the higher beings of heaven. After Aetaentsic fell to earth, she had a daughter who in turn had two sons, Iouskeha and Tawiscaron, who as adults met in mortal combat. Iouskeha used a stag's horns as a weapon and Tawiscaron used wild rose blossoms as his weapon. In this story, Iouskeha, using the stag's horns, was the victor. As shown later, Aetaentsic and Iouskeha became divine personages in Huron cosmology. Although the Jesuits were eager to draw these connections with biblical material and were ever ready to believe that the Indians had certain insights into truth perceived through natural revelation and natural law, they generally agreed with Pierre Biard who viewed the native tribal religion as a cultus that was chiefly inspired by the devil and carried out through the ministrations of the shamans.

Biard stated that the religion of the Acadian tribes was supposed to have a kind of power within it which the shamans were able to invoke and appeared to direct; but to Biard all of this was either clever trickery or the shaman's ability—as we might put it today—to *psychologically* influence his devotees through the *power of suggestion*. According to Biard, the activity of the shaman consisted in optical illusions, purported charms, and tricks. While he denied that the shaman's spells had any power, he maintained that what the shaman and his devotees were doing was a direct worship of Satan. Decades after Biard, however, in the reports of Allouez and Dablon, there is the hint, cited earlier in this chapter, that possibly something approaching the worship of God existed in what certain tribes did in carrying out the practice of their religion. There is also the tendency to withhold immediate condemnation of what might technically be termed "paganism" in order to effect an evolutionary change within it and build upon it later on.

Le Jeune, in the early 1630s, concluded that not only were the shamans tricksters, but that they also used their position to extort valuables from the credulous Indians. He cited one Montagnais who fell ill, consulted the "sorcerer," and was told that an evil Algonquin, out of revenge, had had a spell cast upon him in the form of a disease that would cause his death. The shaman had assured him that if certain presents were forthcoming, he could see that the Algonquin died instead; however, since the victim of the alleged sorcery had, by the time he related this episode to Le Jeune, given the shaman all his porcelain beads and beaver skins, he believed himself sure to die, since he had nothing more to give the "sorcerer."[8]

A change of attitude occured in the early 1630s among the missionaries. At first they had laid all manifestations of a shaman's power to trickery and optical illusion, but gradually they reached the conclusion that at times certain shamans were in direct contact with Satan. In the *Relation* of 1634, Le Jeune wrote of attending an Indian ceremony (a ceremony that still survives among some American Indian tribes) in which the spirits, manifested as sparks of fire, would enter the darkened room where the ceremony occurred.[9] He was not quite ready then to admit outright the reality of any supernatural occurrence, but at the same time he did not attempt to explain away the event. By the next year he recorded his conclusion that demonic power did reveal certain future facts to some shamans and other Indians, but usually in a garbled form and not in a manner that was reliably clear or intelligible.[10] In 1639 he wrote:

> I am inclined to think that there are, really, some among them who have communication with the Demons; but the majority of them are only imposters, practicing their enchantments to obtain presents from the poor sick, to render themselves popular, or to make themselves feared.[11]

The term *juggler* was used by the Jesuits to denote the imposters, or those Le Jeune thought in 1639 were the majority of the shamans or medicine men. These jugglers, he believed, were basically frauds who resorted to sham and trickery to extort a good living from their fellow tribesmen. Their treatment of the sick consisted in rattling a drum, howling, striking two sticks together, blowing on the drum, the fire, and the sick person, while simultaneously hissing, shaking, and contorting themselves into innumerable positions. The theory behind these dramas, Le Jeune concluded, was to frighten the disease away, and he found no real Satanic connection involving this class of shaman; indeed, he even tolerated this routine himself while he lay sick among the Indians.

> For quite a long time I was sick among them, and although I begged him to moderate a little and to give me some rest, he acted still worse, hoping to find his cure in these noises which only made me worse.[12]

And so by 1639 the chants, dances, and contortions, mistakenly thought by the Indians to frighten away diseases, were considered a nuisance rather than any-thing evil. The missionaries tried, of course, to dispel belief in the efficacy of such treatment and sought to channel the chants and dances in other directions. The *juggler* for a time was tolerated as he carried on his rather harmless charade.

The term *sorcerer* as distinct from juggler came to be applied to a second and a third type of shaman who the fathers decided could be at times in communication with Satan. The only apparent distinguishing feature in the Jesuits' evaluation of the two types was that one type (often called *magician*) rarely sought to kill by means of demonic power, whereas the other type regularly did so.

In the missionaries' mind there arose an obvious connection between the native sorcerer and the European witch or warlock. Several varieties of spiritualism, some no doubt stemming originally from the Druids of Gaul and Britain, while remaining partially distinct had co-alesced sufficiently to produce the occult of Medieval and Renaissance Europe. The Catholic church, of course, had always condemned this phenomenon as the inspiration of Satan. It is certainly understandable, then, that this same attitude should prevail in the New World as the missionaries appraised the Indian shamanistic cultus, which even when it claimed the existence of a benevolent spirit did not seem to present a clear-cut idea of this spirit's goodness.

Biard believed that he had found among the Indians of Port Royal the concept of personification of a good god in the sun. The Hurons, to an extent, seemed to make such an identification, but they associated the sun with Iouskeha, the grandson of Aetaentsic, who was an evil god personified in the moon. As stated earlier, she had fallen from heaven where she had had a hus-band.[13] While from this the fathers could draw certain parallels with the Genesis account of the fall, they could not, to their satisfaction, draw any connection between God and the Hurons' personification of a good god in the sun, since he was said to have had an evil grandmother, Aetaentsic, and had himself killed his brother Tawiscaron. The conclusion on the part of the missionaries generally was that evil forces had gained control of native religious beliefs and were behind their cultic rites.

It also became obvious to the fathers that the Indians, be they Hurons or Montagnais, invoked many spirits to whom they accredited little intrinsic goodness or evil. How or whether the spirit responded to the suppliants' wishes seemed to affect its standing as good or evil. Since some sorcerers periodically sought to kill selected individuals by their invocations and poison concoctions, the missionaries were reinforced in their relegation of this variety of shaman to Satanic realms. As Le Jeune put it, they could be called nothing else but sorcerers since they performed some of the very same demonically inspired acts as the sorcerers of Europe.[14]

The Jesuits came to believe that the sorcerers could kill just as the Indians believed they could. The Indians looked upon the shamans as *doctors*, but the missionaries denied that the shamans could heal. These doctors were not the neighborhood jugglers whose routine the fathers might tolerate, but were "true Sorcerers, who have access to the Devil";[15] and these, the fathers concluded, had at times brought about the death of selected individuals, usually of another village or tribe. According to the missionaries, most Indians as they lay dying seriously entertained the notion that a sorcerer had cursed them.

In February, 1634, Le Jeune, wintering with the Montagnais near Quebec, lived in a cabin where his host and a sorcerer performed a rite designed to bring death to another sorcerer miles away in the region of Cape Gaspé at the mouth of the St. Lawrence. The Jesuit wanted very much to see this ceremony and refused several invitations to leave. All women and children were dismissed except one woman who seems to have had an assigned role in the ritual. Le Jeune described the scene: after all were seated, a young Indian brought in two sharply pointed sticks. His host then made a charm by wrapping in a piece of leather various articles, such as pieces of broken knives, small bits of iron shaped like fishhooks, pieces of wood shaped at each end like a snake's tongue, and some iron arrow points. All present began to chant and cry out as the sorcerer started beating a drum. After this had gone on for awhile, the lone woman who had remained arose and passed once behind the backs of those in the circle and then took her place again. The shaman then took the two sharpened sticks and drove them into the ground as he shouted, "Here is his head." A kind of ditch was then dug, a sword brought in and used to strike one of the sticks; the sorcerer then took the sword and descended into the ditch; there, he went into a violent frenzy, striking with the sword as if a heated struggle were in progress. After a time he ceased long enough to get the leather bag, which he took into the pit with him; then he proceeded once more to go into a violent struggle. At last he stopped and pulled the sword, now bloody, from the ditch. The ditch was covered and the announcement made that the victim was wounded and would soon die; some said they had heard faint outcries, as if coming from a great distance.[16]

When this was witnessed in 1634, the fathers at Quebec gave the event little credence, believing the blood to be that of a moose which the sorcerer had hidden somehow in the pit. Even at this time, however, they had begun to wonder about the possibility of demonic power being manifested through the shamanistic rites. By 1637 Le Jeune decided that certain native rites, once written off as subterfuge and fakery, were in fact to be taken at face value. One such rite was the previously mentioned rite of communication with spirits who were believed to manifest themselves as sparks of light. This was at first written off as pure fakery, but in the *Relation* for 1637 Le Jeune indicated that he had decided otherwise. According to the fathers: when the spirits were to be consulted, a tent of robes or blankets was constructed and the sorcerer entered it; then chanting began and, when the spirits were invoked, the tent would begin to shake violently. At first the missionaries had thought that the sorcerer shook the tent, but later they began to wonder. Le Jeune wrote in 1637 that he had witnessed a confrontation between a sorcerer and the spirits inside such a tent, called an *apitouagan*. At the time, he suspected the shaman had moved the tent. Upon subsequent reflection, however, of how the tent was erected, its weight and the duration of its quakings, coupled with the testimony of those whom he trusted, he was inclined toward the position that the movements were caused by non-human forces.

While in the Huron country, Father Pierre Pijart witnessed a sorcerer going into a frenzied state, during which he clasped a red-hot rock between his teeth, with no ill effects. Pijart had brought the partially calcified rock to Le Jeune in Quebec. Le Jeune attested to the presence of teeth marks in the rock and sent the rock on with the annual report to the Jesuit provincial in France.[17]

Pijart reported to Le Jeune that, in May of 1637, he had attended an *aoutaeroki* feast at Ossassané among the Hurons—a ritual held to bring health to those for whom it was done. Dancing and shouting were carried

on for much of the night; but, in the midst of this, a
shaman took into his mouth a rather large red-hot coal
which he proceeded to convey to the sick, one by one,
each of whom was some distance away from him. Beside
each patient he made growl-like noises, all the while
distorting his face as he blew upon them. Soon the coal
broke in his mouth, and the shaman declared the feast a
failure and that another must be done the next night.
After the first feast, a French lay assistant to the Jesuits
went forward to inspect the shaman's mouth. The coal
had broken, and it had apparently filled his mouth, but
the lay assistant reported finding the shaman's mouth
free of burns.[18]

On the ensuing night, stones were again heated
in a fire which Pijart declared "was hot enough to burn
down the cabin," and that he almost withdrew except
that he was determined to see if all he had heard about
such events were true. As the stones were being heated
in the fire, about two dozen singers chanted in a fashion
that the missionary described as extremely "lugubrious"
and "frightful." To Pijart's amazement, as the red-hot
stones were removed from the fire, several sorcerers
came forward, took them between their teeth and went
to the patients to repeat the growling and blowing Pijart
had seen the previous night. One of these stones, with
the teeth marks, was the one sent on to Le Jeune in
Quebec.

> You will be astonished that a man can have so wide
> a mouth; the stone is about the size of a goose egg.
> Yet I saw a savage put it in his mouth so that there
> was more of it inside than out; he carried it some
> distance and, after that, it was still so hot, that
> when he threw it to the ground sparks of fire
> issued from it.[19]

This apparent immunity to fire on the part of certain shamans and their devotees is recounted a number of times by the missionaries and shown to have manifested itself in several ways. Jaques Buteux, while working among the various tribes who moved in and out of Three Rivers in 1640-41, wrote that during one three-day feast, particularly grand in scope, the women and girls began to dance while certain men took the shaman and caused him to walk over red-hot embers; he was not burned, reported the missionary.[20]

The fathers, who often pointed to the failure of a shaman's predictions to come true, were sometimes astonished when they did. One new magician in the region of Ossossané in 1640 made certain predictions in several villages. One entire village publicly scoffed at these, whereupon the shaman announced that those who had believed him would soon do well in bringing in a catch of fish, but that fishermen from the unbelieving village would die. The fathers reported that that was exactly what happened. The doubters died in a storm while out from shore. The conclusion was that the power of Satan was behind this tragedy.[21] Although the missionaries have left no evidence that there was ever any doubt among them as to the sufficiency of divine power to thwart whatever evil influences certain shamans might be able to conjure up, some of them did believe that such influences, though never permanently debilitating, were aimed at the priests. Lalemant recounts that in late 1639 or early 1640, while among the Hurons, Pierre Pijart was having a heated dispute with a village sorcerer when the latter finally threatened all of the Jesuits with death and stated that Jean de Brébeuf was even then prostrate with sickness. Pijart responded with laughter for he had just seen Brébeuf in perfect health, not three hours previous to this encounter. With an ominous warning, the sorcerer ceased all talking, whereupon Pijart returned to the Jesuit residence of St. Joseph at Teanaustaiyé where he found Brébeuf heavily feverish, with head and abdominal pains. Pijart and Lalemant ascertained that no Indian could possibly have known of this sudden illness at the moment the magician spoke in the other village some distance away. Lalemant did go on to record his view that spirits under divine command were more powerful than the evil ones, since Brébeuf was well by the ensuing day.[22]

The sorcerer who reputedly could cause death or sickness was held in great awe, of course, yet could be brought down very quickly if he or she practiced this "art" indiscriminately. In April, 1637, a woman at Ossossané was summarily executed as a sorceress because she had conjured evil in her own village and against the *wrong* person. She named her executioner and was dragged from the cabin, burned on the face and body with lighted pieces of bark, then brained with a tomahawk. Her body was reduced to ashes the next day in the center of the village. It seemed to Le Mercier and the others who witnessed this event that all that had distinguished her from the other sorcerers who were highly revered in the local villages was that she had used her "powers" to cause death and destruction within her own village unit.[23]

Among some of the shamans, a phenomenon described as a "throbbing of the breast" was considered indicative of certain imminent events. A Montagnais at Three Rivers in the 1630s told a group of French hoping to meet the annual Huron fleet not to return to Quebec because a seer of some local repute had experienced the breast-throbbing phenomenon, which was taken to mean that the Hurons would arrive the next day. They did.[24] Le Jeune witnessed a similar incident at Quebec. But incidents such as these often proved false, said Le Jeune, who laid the whole matter not to coincidence but to Satan, who occasionally gave the Indians correct prophecies, but more often tricked them.

There were many of the Hurons in the 1630s and 1640s who were much inclined toward Christianity, but who had great difficulty in forsaking their native religion in its entirety, especially that aspect of it dealing with their *aswandic* or, as the fathers put it, their "familiar demons." They believed this spirit was the source of "their preservation and that of their families, and the source of all their good fortune."[25] The aswandic in the Jesuit writings is often shown to have been associated with a charm carried in a special leather pouch, usually brought out only when it was addressed in a petition. The Hurons told the fathers that everyone had them, that they could be bought, sold, or inherited, for they resided wherever the charm was and with whomsoever had it. Christians, of course, were exhorted to give theirs up, and many of them did. One very faithful convert, however, after throwing his charm away by the trail, always felt hesitant about going past the spot, lest the charm should somehow get back into his pouch. The fathers believed some converts who told them they had wished they still had their charms and that after such a wish the charms mysteriously reappeared.[26] Charms contained in a kind of leather bag are still in use by some Indians even today.[27]

Sometimes the missionaries believed they witnessed a struggle by the familiar demon to hold on to its devotee right before their eyes. Du Peron wrote from Montreal in 1643 that an Indian had presented himself there for baptism, declaring that he was willing to give up his demon, a demon whose power, he said, had always gotten him whatever he had asked for, ever since the demon first came to him at the end of a seven-day fast. Du Peron reported that when he asked the Indian to publicly renounce his demon, he began rolling his eyes and taking on a frightening countenance. He continued to answer lucidly the questions put to him, but he refused to denounce his spirit or demon, saying that it was within him and that he feared it. The next day, however, he was able to renounce his demon and was forthwith baptized. The missionaries believed the spirit had not returned to the convert after baptism. Du Peron was convinced Satan or some demon had been fighting for this Indian and had lost the battle.

The fathers believed their conflict with Satan to be real and vivid, especially as they came to accept the reality of demonic power which they believed they saw expressed through the sorcerers or shamans. They also came to feel that sudden frenzies, such as that just related, or fits of anger against them, were still further signs of demonic power and possibly of demonic possession.[28]

The aboriginal belief and reverence for dreams posed a problem to missionary work throughout the Jesuit period. The Indian believed that messages from the spirit-world were conveyed through dreams, and that it was through this medium that a young Indian had his personal, familiar spirit revealed to him. Orders coming in a dream were to be obeyed. Charles Lalemant, writing from Quebec in 1626 to his brother Jérôme, commented on the extensive power that dreams could have on Indian life:

> If during the night they dream they must kill a Frenchman, woe to the first one whom they meet alone. They attach great faith to their dreams. Some of them will tell you two days before the coming of a ship the hour of its arrival, and will give no other

explanation except that they have seen it while asleep.[29]

In May, 1633, a Montagnais near Quebec reported he had had a dream in which he learned that some Frenchmen would be killed; and, said Le Jeune, on June 2 the Iroquois ambushed and killed three Frenchmen who, with their party, were trying to go up the St. Lawrence. The father concluded that, while it may have been been a coincidence, it might also have been the influence of Satan which had allowed the Indian to see the future in his dream.[30]

Writing in 1639, after a few months in the Huron country, du Peron said that he was convinced that the unchristian Indian had all his actions dictated to him directly by the Devil who might appear in dreams as a bird, a ghost, a flame of fire or any one of a variety of forms. He related how the Indians often fasted before receiving these dreams, from which they sought guidance for hunting, warfare, fishing, trading, dancing, and holding feasts.[31] Le Mercier, who had been living with the Hurons, also concluded that the Indians' dreams were the the messengers of Satan and that Satan made it very difficult for Huron converts who refused to act on their dreams. He stated that Satan through some "diabolical trick" had recently caused those who had the "best" dreams to be successful hunters, while a Christian convert who had forsaken his dreams returned home from the hunt with no game. Dreams seemed to work, or at least were being used by Satan to bring scorn on those who refused to act upon their dreams.[32]

Ironically, the convert cited by Le Mercier as having lost out in the hunt because he had foresaken his dreams was Joseph Chihwatenhwa, one of the most faithful and influential Huron converts the fathers ever made. Although the missionaries frowned severely when a convert gave heed to his dreams, they knew, of course, that the Indians could not be prevented from having dreams. The Jesuits rationalized that Satan was served only if the Indians heeded their dreams. After some years this same Joseph Chihwatenhwa had a dream which he felt necessarily should be related to a fellow convert, René Tsondhiwane. In his dream he was attacked by three or four Iroquois who threw him to the ground, scalped him, and then split his skull. The missionaries recorded that in fact all of this soon happened to him. The dream had recurred, and he had revealed to René that he had been told in the dreams that if a sacrifice and feast of dogs were held, all would be averted. The fathers accepted his dream as a demonically inspired foretelling of the future, sent as an attempt to subvert the faith of Chihwatenhwa. The Devil was holding out his life as the prize, a prize he had rejected by refusing to make the prescribed sacrifice.[33]

Father Étienne de Carheil, in his work among the Iroquois in the 1670s, found the dream phenomenon no less an obstacle to his work than did those laboring among the Hurons and Montagnais years earlier. He believed it to be the central point of the Iroquois' religion and that which, more than anything else, strongly bound the Indians to that religion. It was the chief means of receiving direction from the spirit-world, and there seems also to have been the prevalent idea that during at least some dreams the soul left the body and participated in the activities dreamed of.[34] Although de Carheil discounted this possibility, not all the fathers were so sure. This phenomenon of *astral projection*, or the "out-of-body" experience, is accepted still among some American Indians.[35]

While a dream might just happen, they were

often sought through fasting, as at adolescence when a boy sought out his *familiar spirit*. Sometimes the fathers were not sure whether it was simply a familiar spirit the youths sought in these dreams or what might better be termed a deity. De Carheil inclined to the view that the familiar spirit was conceived of among the Iroquois as a kind of god. Vincent Bigot[36] and Dablon expressed the same view in the *Relation* of 1679.[37] In the west among the Outagami, or the Fox tribe, in 1673, Allouez had to exert special effort in order to prevent his young male converts from blackening their faces and fasting in the chapel in order that God might appear and speak to them in their dreams.[38]

When the Indian sought out his familiar spirit or demon, he did so usually as an adolescent. He believed that if he fasted for a time, the spirit would appear to him in a dream or in a waking vision. In time the fathers came to accept the reality of these apparitions. From the reports of Daniel and Chaumonot among the Arendaenhronon group of Hurons in the winter of 1641-42, Lalemant related the experience of an Indian who, years before, at the age of fifteen or sixteen, had gone into the forest to fast and to seek his special vision. After fasting sixteen days, he stated that suddenly a voice from the sky called on him to end his fast, after which an aged but handsome man appeared to him announcing that he was now the Indian's master and would protect him from other spirits. The Indian was assured that he would live to a great age. He would have children, the spirit said— two males, a female, then another male. His wife would be as a sister to him following the birth of the fourth child. Then the spirit held out to the youth a piece of raw human flesh. When the youth was unwilling to eat it or even taste it, he was then offered a portion of bear fat, which he consumed. Then the spirit ascended into the sky. The spirit had appeared to him intermittently since, the Indian reported, with promises of assistance in times of difficulty. The Jesuit added, "nearly all that he predicted to him has happened." He had four children in the predicted order, and following the birth of the last, an illness left him impotent. Except for that, his health was and had been excellent, although he was then nearing old age. His great prowess had always been in the chase, where he often received signs that aided his success. The Indian credited this to his eating the proffered bear's fat; and his lacklustre performance in battle, to his refusal to eat the human flesh.[39] Lalemant wrote, "Such things are so common in this Country that it is no wonder that these poor Barbarians are so attached to the service of the Devil . . ."[40] The reality of this and many similar apparitions was not doubted by the missionaries.

The *Ondoulaehte*, or the war-god, came often to the Indians, Daniel and Chaumonot reported. Sometimes the apparition took the form of a woman with a furious countenance, or of a man raging with anger. The fathers reported that a raging apparition, "a Megaera" waving firebrands and flames, entered the cabin of a thirty-year-old man and so aroused him with anger that he frenetically threw himself into the cabin fire. But he showed no sign of feeling pain. Subsequently, for a number of days, the man sang and gave war cries with no weakening of voice. When some of his fellows tried to lay hold of him, the demon within him cried out, presumably by means of the Indian's voice, and demanded a suit of native armor, a standard showing a wolf's muzzle, and various weapons. When they were unable to supply these items, the apparition became visible to the man a second time, the fathers reported, and predicted doom in the coming summer's warfare as punishment for their failure to produce all of the things demanded. The demon went on to say that it would now make its offer to the Iroquois, and thereupon disappeared from his sight.[41]

As fanciful as the Indians' visions had seemed at first, the missionaries reached the conclusion that these preternatural events, which they ascribed to the Devil, were central motivating factors in the native religions. They likewise concluded it was Satanic power, not some flaw in the Indians' reason or intellect, that had corrupted their approach to the Divine. The Indians' world, the missionaries came to believe, was so full of "demonic" manifestations that their religion had become simply a response to these phenomena. It wasn't until the missionaries came to believe in the reality of these phenomena undergirding Indian life that they understood the existence of religious observance among the Amerind. The failure to recognize initially the signs of any deep-seated religious observance caused the missionaries to believe at first that tribal conversion would be swift to follow. Such, of course, was not the case. One finds in Lalemant's words the realization that there was something formidable at the heart of Indian life with which the Jesuits were struggling:

> It is not only an erroneous opinion that has obtained footing in their minds, through their having received it as a tradition from their Ancestors; but frequently these Demons show themselves only too visibly, and make their appearance in such a manner that these people cannot doubt their existence.[42]

To appease these spirits, sacrifices were necessary. Captives were sometimes viewed as potential victims, and Jogues, during his captivity among the Iroquois, witnessed the burning of an Indian woman captive as a sacrifice to Aireskoi, the Iroquois personification of the sun. The woman was tortured to death by fire, then her body was cut into pieces and sent to various villages to be devoured.[43] Except in time of warfare, however, bears, stags, dogs, grease, and tobacco were those things ordinarily offered in sacrifice. Tobacco was by far the most commonly offered item. The fathers were present on numerous occasions when it was ceremonially offered and they seemed to have patiently tolerated the tobacco sacrifices since these were so much a part of Indian social life.[44]

Although they viewed the Indian's religious practices that centered around the shaman as demonically oriented, they came to believe in the reality of the phenomena upon which the Indian cultus was built. They came to conclude that the shamanistic practices they so detested, were, indeed, an understandable, if erroneous, response to certain phenomena which they believed permeated Indian existence. It was not a blighted intellect or a warped sense of reason that had produced the native spiritualism, but real, definite, describable phenomena, resulting from an evil intervention in the Indian's experience of existence.

It is possible to fault both the seventeenth-century Jesuit missionaries for their credulity or their superstition, and the seventeenth-century concept of "the powers of darkness" as exemplified, for example, by the Salem witch trials. In justice to the Jesuits, however, it should be noted that when the missionaries first came among the Indians they did express skepticism about the power of the shamanistic rituals. It was only after living with the Indians for a period of time that they reached the conclusion a supernatural power, albeit demonic, lay behind at least part of what the shamans practiced.

Furthermore, it is interesting that the May, 1973, issue of the *Smithsonian* carried an article written by a non-Indian, an author and photographer, a man of our own century, who had spent much time observing a Sioux medicine man at work. This twentieth-century observer reached a conclusion similar to that of the Jesuits three centuries before. He described the ceremony in which the spirits are supposedly contacted, a ceremony not unlike that which the fathers saw at another time among other tribes:

> I have heard the voices . . . and I have seen the lights. . . The Sparks were moving all around me and high on the ceiling where no man could reach them. And once an eagle came into the room. Nobody could see it, but . . . I could hear its high-pitched cries and feel the touch of its wings. And during a sun dance, in full daylight, I saw a medicine man make a circular motion over his head with a large feather, asking an eagle to come and circle the sacred pole. And within minutes a black dot appeared in the west, out of the clouds, and became a huge dark brown eagle. It circled slowly and silently four times above us, then sailed away without moving its wings. I and all the Indians saw this thing . . . I have no explanation.[45]

V

Angels, Demons, and Visions

The nineteenth-century American historian, Francis Parkman, stated in the *Jesuits in North America*, one of his
volumes on French colonial America, that the Christianity
brought by the Jesuits to the Indians in the seventeenth
century was the only version of that religion which the
Indians could have accepted.[1] By such a statement, however, Parkman was disparaging the Jesuit effort rather
than praising it. Parkman believed that the religious concepts of the Jesuits were only a little less primitive than
those of the "savages" whom they came to convert. Although Parkman records his great respect for what he
believed to be the intellect, brilliance, and devotion found
in many members of the Jesuit order,[2] his own rationalistic
world view (and, perhaps, the Puritian roots from which
he sprang) militated against his viewing the religious and
metaphysical concepts of the Jesuit fathers as being anything other than primitive or "medieval" at best.

   Parkman was correct to suggest that the Indian
and Jesuit had in common some religious or metaphysical
criteria, but his understanding of them as something
primitive shows little or no insight into exactly why an
Indian might have been attracted to the new religion of
the Jesuits instead of, for instance, that of the Puritans of
New England. It was not simply that the Jesuits were

Catholics, which made their approach to Christianity different from that of the Puritans, but that the Jesuits as an order had grown out of, and were the chief spokesmen for, the Counter-Reformation, that movement which sought to preserve, purify, and strengthen the traditional spiritual values of Western Catholicism.

The Jesuit missionaries preached to the Indians a religion based on the concept of the immediate reality of an invisible world, a spiritual order which was often, though not always, imperceptible to the senses. This chiefly invisible domain surrounds and encompasses man and the material world in which he lives. This concept theoretically permeates all of Christianity to a degree. The Nicene Creed, accepted not only by Catholics but by most Protestants also, proclaims the Creator to be maker of "all things visible and invisible."

Before we can understand the metaphysical interaction which took place between Jesuit and Indian, we must understand who the Jesuit was in the seventeenth century, and how the traditional pre-Reformation understanding of man, man's place in creation, and the nature of this creation was reflected by the Jesuit and by his order. This can best be comprehended within the context of the Reformation itself and the divergence of thought regarding man and his place in the universe that took place at that time. To understand the Jesuit work in French North America, we must once more look at the religious upheaval of the sixteenth century, not quite a hundred years before the first arrival of the Jesuits among the Hurons.

With the Reformation, a cleavage developed as to exactly how the invisible world might be perceived; whether, indeed, it could be perceived at all by those still housed in the flesh. Until the Reformation, the Catholic church had assumed that the unseen world from time to time impinged upon the physical order by making itself manifest to certain individuals; hence, pre-Reformation Christianity is rife with accounts of visions, dreams, and miracles. It does not follow that the Church sanctioned all of these accounts: some were strongly doubted, others were encouraged, and still others were treated with indifference. But philosophically the medieval Church had no problem handling these phenomena, for in both Platonic and Aristotelian thought the relationship between the physical and invisible world is a close one. If the eternal, spiritual realm, as Plato said, is to some extent reflected in the physical world, then the two can never really be separated. The parallel between the 'incarnational' principle lying at the heart of Christianity and the Platonic idea that the eternal order reflects or reveals itself in the physical world is plain enough. But, in addition to this, the Catholic church had centered its whole cultic and spiritual life around sacraments that are based upon, and, it is believed, in themselves carry out, this same principle—that of the eternal and invisible order making itself present and known through and in matter. In the case of the sacraments, the physical elements are bread, wine, water, and oil.

In the late Middle Ages, William of Occam[3] largely denied the reality of this manifestation of the spiritual or eternal order in the realm of the physical; and later, Luther, in portions of his theology, expressed some of the same 'nominalist'[4] views. Calvin did likewise, even to a much greater extent. Luther expressed this view mainly in his writing against visions and other such phenomena, whereas Calvin went on to apply it to the sacraments as well. In the general classical Protestant view, then, the spiritual world is apprehended in this life by faith alone and experienced only after the physical life ends. This is not to say that in Luther's and Calvin's

101

theologies the spiritual world cannot in various ways manifest itself in the visible world; but, philosophically speaking, such phenomena would be highly suspect. Luther in his own writings seems to imply that while visions, for instance, may occur they are more likely than not the phenomena of Satan.[5] This line of thought is indicative of what is later expressed in the seventeenth century by many Puritan writers: what might be called supernatural phenomena are by no means denied, but rather are affirmed as the work of Satan.

It is interesting to note that in the seventeenth century the only kind of Protestant Christianity the Indians of the upper St. Lawrence (such as the Iroquois or Huron), or those of Acadia (such as the Abenaki), were likely to encounter was New England Puritanism. This particular version of Calvinism found it especially difficult to allow for supernatural phenomena except that which found its origin in Satan. Here the Puritan records abound with accounts of visions, voices, and so forth. It is ironic—although perhaps not the idea that the sixteenth-century Reformers intended to convey—that in reading certain writings of the Puritans one is left with the notion that while Christianity seems divorced from any manifestations of spiritual phenomena, evil often manifests itself in witches, visions, and various other supernatural forms.

When Increase Mather wrote of metaphysical events, the devil was usually the source; and Mather relegated visions of the Virgin and the saints, that Catholics sometimes had reported, to the same source, saying that while such phenomena may be truly classed as 'visions,' they are inspired by evil sources.[6]

Cotton Mather, Increase's son, at times exhibited in his writings an obsession with witchcraft and its phenomena, but when he recounts his own daughter's illness, from which she subsequently recovered, he relates that as he prayed for her when death seemed imminent his Bible "accidentally" fell open to the account of the raising of the young girl in the eighth chapter of St. Luke.[7] Evil might have its definite signs and portents, but good rarely would. Mather hesitates to say that God directly caused the book to open as it did, but uses the word "accidentally" to describe the occurrence. This is significant when contrasted to his frequent and ready ascription of a metaphysical understanding to witchcraft phenomena. While, of course, the Mathers must not be viewed as the only spokesmen for seventeenth-century Calvinism, they are spokesmen for what the English in New England spiritually and philosophically offered with little success to the American Indians as a replacement for their native religions. By relegating almost all supernatural phenomena to Satan, they did exactly what the Jesuits did not do, which was to effectively close the door to an acceptance of the Indians' understanding both of man and the universe, and how man and the world around him relate and interact. It is helpful to understand the Puritans, therefore, in order to understand the Jesuits, who, ironically, worked geographically, if not philosophically, in such close proximity to them.

The Counter-Reformation, officially expressed in the decretals of the Council of Trent, which closed in 1563, was the Roman Catholic response to the work of the Reformers. While the Council of Trent sought to purify the Church from both moral and doctrinal corruption, at the same time it placed renewed emphasis on a theological heritage that is based on tradition and classical philosophy. 'Nominalism' was completely rejected.

The Society of Jesus was instrumental in countering the theological influence of the Reformation while seeking to bring about reforms at the same time. Jesuit theology, their view of man and the world of matter, as well as their view of the invisible or spiritual world, were what classical philosophy and the medieval Church had declared these to be. This is what the Counter-Reformation reaffirmed.

Whatever modern man may think of how or why the Indian experienced what he thought he experienced, there can be little doubt that the Indians believed they perceived and often experienced a transcendent side to existence which not infrequently manifested itself in their lives. There was for the Indian very little distinction between the physical world and the realm of spirits and supernatural phenomena. The Jesuits, too, believed in the impingement of the invisible world upon the physical order, and what really differentiated them from much of Protestantism, particularly Calvinism or Puritanism, was that they believed the divine was as likely to manifest itself in a supernatural manner as was evil; in fact, even more so, since the sacraments were an ever-present means of participating in the divine order by means of the physical. The Jesuit missionaries, in short, were able to come to terms with the Indians' world. They were able to accept the reality of supernatural phenomena in the native cultus, because of their conviction of the reality of the supernatural within their own cultus. When exhorting the Indian to accept Christianity, instead of attempting to deny him his perception of an unseen world which was an important part of his existence, the Jesuits provided the Indian with a way to retain it—albeit from a different vantage point.

This is not to say there were no problems in this for the fathers, but what problems arose were not insurmountable, because of the existing commonality of metaphysical perception between the two ostensibly disparate groups—the pagan Indians and the Christian Jesuits. To put it simply: the Indians had visions; the Jesuits had visions. The Indians experienced signs and portents; the Jesuits, also, though perhaps not as often. The Indians believed supernatural properties might dwell in matter; the Jesuits said spiritual power resided in certain material elements divinely ordained for that purpose. Paradoxically, while there was, on the one hand, no comparison between what the fathers taught and what the unconverted Indians believed, yet, on the other hand, there were certain preconceived factors regarding the existence of an imminent spiritual order that made an understanding between the two possible.

The Jesuits came to accept some of the phenomena surrounding native shamanistic rites as evidence of the direct intervention of Satanic forces in the native cultus. They, of course, did not need such displays to convince them of Satanic powers in the lives of people; but such manifestations confirmed all the more what they believed to be the reality of the evil power which opposed them. This was a spiritual power, and the Jesuits believed that they too were in contact with power emanating from the unseen world, but a power that was always working for the good of man. It was to the same plane of existence, as it were, that both Jesuit and shaman looked for help, but the Jesuit saw this aid as coming from two diametrically opposed sources: good and evil—God and Satan. Needless to say, the Jesuits believed the power of God to be greater. They knew they often faced death among the tribes, but they believed that death could never overtake them unless God allowed it to happen; and such allowance would only occur in order to accomplish the divine will. Therefore, while it was likely that at sometime an Indian or a group of Indians at the instigation of demonic powers would kill some or most of the missionaries, there was really nothing to fear since their demise would not happen until God willed it.

For the missionaries, their struggle with the forces that opposed them and the possibility of martyrdom were all part of an unseen conflict which, though involved with this world, was basically concerned with an unseen realm where good and evil continued their age-old struggle. Just as the shaman called on the aid of forces from the spiritual world, the missionaries did likewise; confronting openly and directly, they believed, the demons themselves; rebuking them and exorcizing them. As the shaman called on spiritual beings for assistance, the Jesuits and their converts called upon God, the angels, and the souls of the dead for strength and protection. And more particularly, as the shaman used charms that were the bearers of spiritual aid, so the missionaries directed the Indians to the sacraments and used the relics of the saints, and sacramentals such as holy water, medals, statues of the saints, and rosaries. To the missionaries, these material objects had been brought into such close relationship to the spiritual world that they had become special channels through which spiritual power passed into the physical order.

Much of what the Indians invoked in the spiritual world, they abjectly feared; therefore, if the missionaries were successfully to oppose these forces, they had to show no fear in the process. Le Jeune cried out in the presence of a terrified medicine man, ". . . come, demon; murder me if thou hast the power, I defy thee . . . thou hast no power over those who believe and love God . . ."[8]

While few of those who communicated with evil forces were viewed as possessed, some shamans exhibited at times a high degree of what the Jesuits considered derangement. These were viewed by the missionaries as demoniacs. It seemed to the Jesuits that their madness only created a greater reverence for these shamans among their fellow tribesmen. The missionaries concluded that

Satan, through long contact, had possessed their minds and was using the manifestation of possession as a further means of controlling the Indians. Jérôme Lalemant cited one of these in the *Relation* of 1647 as having attacked Isaac Jogues during his first sojourn among the Iroquois.[9] As further indication of demonic possession among the Indians, the missionaries noted that, as they approached some Indians to mention Christianity, the Indians refused to listen and made distracting, incoherent sounds. Daniel and Le Moyne, working among the Huron clan known as Arendaronons in 1640, reported that as the priests approached, certain of the Indians began to howl like wolves; their conclusion, that demon-possession was the source of this activity, led them to "outwardly exorcise them *per Dominum nostrum Jesum Christum*," whereupon, wrote the missionaries, the Indians became silent.[10]

This visible and outward opposition to what the fathers believed was the source of native shamanism was carried out among the converts as well. At the Huron mission of St. Joseph in 1642, a captain, desiring baptism, was summonded before a council of village Christians to declare his faith; instead, he began to act like a madman. He went to several villages wrecking canoes, crashing down cabin doors, crying out all the while that a demon had entered and taken hold of him, that he now belonged to this demon and must try to kill all the French. The fathers recorded that he took on unusual strength and resilience, running through the thickets seeming not to notice as thorns ripped his flesh. He began a general harassment of Christian Indians: throwing water on one woman in imitation of baptism and threatening to burn another. When the missionaries approached him, they were met with violent blows from his fists. At this point the priests "saw very plainly that the issue of this affair must be referred to God alone."[11] They prayed for him to

God and the "possession" left him in a few days, the missionaries reported. Later, the man returned to the priests, asking their forgiveness for what he could only vaguely remember and for what others told him. He stated that at first he recalled being affected by a "force" or invisible power, or as Lalemant put it, "an occult force." The missionaries restored him to the fold, holding that he could hardly be guilty of any crime since a demon had directly governed his actions.[12]

Whenever an Indian, convert or not, was troubled with visions or apparitions which brought fear or foreboding, the Jesuits were equipped to deal with the situation in terms he could understand. At the Jesuit mission at Three Rivers in 1640, an Indian of high position visited Father Buteux. The Indian related that a demon had appeared to him in his cabin. He begged the priests to "offer the prayers appointed to drive him away." Buteux went home with him and said the prayers he had requested. The Indian was no longer troubled and was soon instantaneously delivered from a pain in his side after praying to God. He was not baptized at the time; yet, significantly, instead of seeking a medicine man to deliver him from a frightening apparition, he had sought out Buteux who not only accepted the reality of his difficulty but was able philosophically and ritually to cope with it. Buteux regarded the Indian's deliverance from pain as a result both of the Indian's willingness to turn to a priest for help and of the priest's invocation of good which had descended upon the cabin and removed the source of the Indian's fear.[13] It is not too surprising then that, as Buteux reported, this experience caused the man to be well-disposed toward Christianity, for here was something the Indian could understand. The new religion had not only met an immediate need, but had moved within a context familiar to the Indian's experience of life.

The "evil spirits" did not go away just because an Indian became a Christian. The voices, apparitions, and dreams might well recur, but the Indian was taught how to resist them through prayer, the sacraments, the use of holy water and blessed objects, or the recitation of the rosary—all things which were believed to bring him into contact with forces in the invisible world which would aid him in his conflict with evil forces that emanated from the same metaphysical realm.

The fathers assured the Indians, who themselves had always so believed, that mankind was surrounded by spirits. But the fathers explained that the Christian faithful had, as allies, spirits called 'angels,' which protected them from evil spirits. The Indians readily understood this for they had always been taught to seek out a "personal spirit" through fastings; and, as has been shown, they learned to trust in the power of their personal spirits—or demons, as the missionaries called them. It is little wonder then that the missionaries' teaching concerning the ministrations of angels was so attractive to the Indians. Those baptized invoked the aid of their angels, and some saw visions of them just as they had once seen visions of their personal demons. The missionaries reported that those converts who saw their angels were struck by the beauty of them. An old, dying Huron asked one of the missionaries who the young man was who stood at his side. He decribed him as possessing "rare beauty . . ." and added that just to look upon his being ". . . enraptured his heart with joy." The missionary with the sick man reported seeing no vision. Ragueneau related the event:

> The Father answered him that there was no one. "No, no," he replied, "I have lost neither eyes nor judgment; I see him quite near thee. He accompa-

nies thee; and I know by his face that he comes to help me to die well; do both of you have a care for my soul." We know nothing more of this, but we are not ignorant that the Guardian Angels of these good Neophytes labor, much more than we, to guide their souls to Heaven.[14]

Charles Garnier, killed by the Iroquois in December, 1649, was himself particularly devoted to the angels. Those Indians among whom he labored in the Tobacco nation reported to the missionaries later that they had often "seen" him accompanied by a spirit which they described as a "young man of rare beauty and majestic glory," who at times of instruction had urged them to heed what Garnier was telling them.[15]

Lalemant concluded that good angels were particularly interested in the conversion of the Indians, since the Indians so frequently reported seeing them. One Huron woman who had sought baptism for more than a year fell deathly ill and was only then baptized. Shortly before her death, she told those nearby that a company of beautiful beings were at her side, the likes of whose faces she had not seen before, and that they seemed to be offering her a beautiful garment. The woman received great satisfaction and joy from the vision and expired peacefully soon afterwards. The fathers believed this was a pledge of eternal happiness conveyed to her by spiritual beings. Similar to this is the account of a young girl who desired baptism on her death-bed. Her relatives argued against it until she announced that she beheld beings who were warning her not to allow herself to go the route of a lately departed unbaptized sister. The relatives seriously received her account and ceased their protestations.[16]

There is perhaps no clearer example of the common metaphysical bond between the missionaries and the Indians than that represented by the attachment or bond that can exist between individuals and spiritual beings. The Jesuit fathers met the Indians, as it were, in the same metaphysical context, but influenced them to experience a new perception of the spiritual world. As a result, in place of having visions of detached, grotesque faces and flying heads, the convert Indians reported having visions of great beauty, from which they gained encouragement and strength. This readily found a place in the metaphysical understanding of the missionaries.

After the Indians had been exposed to Christianity a few years, those who became converts seemed to feel especially devoted to the idea of angelic beings. Le Jeune, the superior in Quebec, wrote in 1638:

> It is a very wonderful thing that the Savages, when strongly moved, are usually devoted to their good angels. In reading over again the memoirs of our Fathers, scattered in different regions, I have been astonished in seeing how the Holy Ghost gives always the same sentiments to these Neophytes. For, without having any communication with one another, they ask light from their good Angels when they come to be instructed; they feel the same astonishment at the greatness and goodness of God, although they express it differently . . .[17]

In the native understanding of the spiritual world, not only was it filled with demons and demigods but with the souls of the departed who generally dwelt in the "land of souls," far to the west. However, a kind of communication might still be possible between the living and the dead through the powers of a shaman; or it might be experienced through spontaneous apparitions;

or be brought about through prayer or mental communication. The souls of infants were thought to be especially nearby and, until the periodic feasts of the dead, common to most of the tribes with which the Jesuits worked, the souls of all those having died since the preceding feast were thought to be very close at hand.

The missionaries, basing their teachings on the Catholic doctrine of the "communion of saints," taught that the dead could be invoked since they existed in a spiritual realm not totally separate, and by no means distant, from the everyday physical world. This communication with the dead was, of course, carefully guarded and restricted by the church. Generally, this communication entails only requests for prayer on the part of the dead, now in the nearer presence of God. Even so, the Indian's world could readily comprehend such a practice; and this custom, like the presence of angels, quickly became a part of native Christian devotion, for it was not in principle a foreign concept.

As a Christian Indian lay dying, he was often exhorted to pray for those left behind when he reached the abode of God. A Christian Indian of the village of Sillery, known for his fasting and other devotions, was out hunting when he came upon a dying Christian woman. He helped care for her as best as he knew how. As the women who had been with her were enshrouding her body, he dug her grave. Then, as they buried her, he led them all in prayer, after which he invoked the deceased:

> . . . good woman, who art dead, pray for us. When thou art above, pray for those who are baptized, so that they may persevere in the faith; pray for the others, that they may believe in him who has made all.[18]

If the prayers of departed adult converts were sought by those still living, even more so were those of departed baptized infants who had an assuredly high place in the "land of souls," since they were guilty of no actual sin. In Huron and Iroquois belief, the souls of infants were usually considered to remain near their village, and the Jesuits, in their own understanding of the spiritual world, believed the souls of baptized infants had special regard for their own tribe, village, and family. The soul of a baptized Indian baby was viewed as needing no purgation and, therefore, could offer very effectual prayers for those it left behind in the physical world. The missionaries believed that it was important to baptize as many dying infants as possible, primarily for their own salvation, but secondarily for the conversion of a tribe or village, which might be hastened through the effectual prayers that these infant souls would offer in the nearer presence of God. Hence in 1642, Charles Garnier wrote from the Huron country to his brother about a departed child, "Pray to him, and so many other little Angels, that they may advance the Conversion of their country, and that they pray with you for me."[19]

This understanding, then—of the cooperation of the physical and spiritual orders of existence between men, angels, and spirits of the dead—fitted well into the aboriginal scheme of things and further illustrates that the missionaries did not wish to destroy the Indians' experience of the unseen world, but wished to change the vantage point from which they viewed it and the means by which they entered it. The Jesuits did not basically deny what the Indians believed they had experienced emanating from a spiritual realm, but the missionaries wished to quicken the Indians to a side of that same realm which, in the Jesuits' view, the Indians had not seen. The traditional Catholic openness to events of 'supernatural' origins undergirds this meshing of view-points that took place in French North America. The Jesuits' own desire to build on the good they discovered in the native cultures, plus their own experience of the "supernatural" while among the Indians, enhanced this coalescence. The missionaries not only saw evidence of what they considered manifestations of demonic power in the shamanistic rites, but believed they experienced the supernatural themselves on a number of occasions—most of such experiences were considered to be of divine origin.

The visions seen by Brébeuf and Jogues, and the vision shared by several fathers of a martyred brother, fall into the classic pattern of visions, which are, in the Catholic understanding of them, signs to incite or strengthen faith and trust.

The martyr Jean de Brébeuf had, as early as 1640, "seen a sign" of martyrdom in the form of a great cross that appeared to him one winter evening as he labored in the "Neutral" nation. The cross came from the direction of the Iroquois country. Then a number of crosses appeared to him; and on the next night, while at prayers, he heard a voice telling him to read. When it was light he picked up a copy of the *Imitation of Christ* which fell open to the chapter entitled *De regia via sanctae crucis.* He reported that this chapter brought him "great peace, and repose in occasions of suffering." Brébeuf is reported to have had frequent visions of Christ, the Blessed Virgin, angels, and various saints.[20] In 1640, he had received a vision of the blessed Virgin which he took also to signify his own earthly course:

> Our Lady appeared to him, having her heart pierced
> with three swords; and at the same time he was
> aware of an inward voice, which told him that the

most blessed Virgin had always been perfectly submissive to the will of God, although often her heart had been deep in affliction: and that he must take her in his adversity for an example of what God wished from him.[21]

Brébeuf also recounted at least two apparitions which could be classified as Satanic in origin. These visions were sent, he believed, either to frighten or cause him to sin: the one was of a skeleton threatening death; the other, of a lewd woman enticing him to immorality.[22]

During his second and final captivity among the Iroquois, Father Jogues recounted in letters to Quebec that he experienced several visions while praying before a cross in a small retreat he had erected in the woods. He reported that on one occasion he suddenly seemed to find himself in the presence of several Jesuits whom he had once known, but who had since died: Jacques Bertric,[23] Étienne Binet,[24], and Pierre Coton.[25]

I begged them . . . to commend me to the Cross . . . that it might receive me as disciple of him who had been fastened between its arms . . . While still in that same retreat, I found myself all at once in a shop of a Bookseller, stationed in the Holy Cross Cloister, in the city where I had my birth. I asked him if he had not some Book of piety . . . when it was put in my hands, I heard this voice: "This Book contains . . . the acts and deeds of men Illustrious in piety and of hearts brave in war.". . . as I was leaving that shop, I saw it all covered with Crosses . . .[26]

Writing from the Huron country in May, 1649—just prior to the defeat of the Huron by the Iroquois—Paul Ragueneau, with some reticence, recounted how on two occasions Antoine Daniel—who had been killed at Teanaustaiyé the year before—appeared to Pierre Chaumonot. Daniel appeared the first time in a radiant state and seemed to be about thirty-years-old, though he had been forty-eight when he died; the second time he appeared to Chaumonot it was during a gathering of the fathers who had met to discuss mission strategy. Although he seems to have actually been seen only by Chaumonot, Ragueneau recounts that the others felt his presence. Father Daniel had come to them, the missionaries believed, for the purpose of ". . . strengthening us with his courage, and filling us with his light, and with the spirit of God with which he was completely invested."[27]

Since the missionaries themselves believed it was possible to see visions and hear voices from the spiritual realm, the Indians, who had fully acknowledged such phenomena all their lives, likewise continued after their conversion to consider such phenomena as a possible experience. The faith preached by the missionaries obviously allowed for such phenomena. The fathers, shortly before the fall of the Huron country, recorded the experience of a fifteen-year-old Huron girl who had been taken by the Iroquois as a slave. She had been under instruction at the time of her capture, but was unbaptized. Among the Iroquois she frequently prayed that she might be baptized before she met death. As she labored in the cornfields one day she heard voices from the sky singing very beautiful music which she said was like music she had heard when the missionaries of Ste. Marie chanted the daily offices. She looked around her, saw no one, then fell to her knees in prayer. A few days later, the same thing happened. Upon hearing the voices the third time, she hastened from the field and came upon a trail unfamiliar to her; nevertheless, she set out upon it:

without victuals, without provisions, without escort, but not without the guidance of him alone who had inspired her, and gave her sufficient strength to arrive here . . . without any evil encounter.[28]

Given the missionaries' understanding of the universe and how the spiritual world related to it, they had no problem understanding such an account. They interpreted this supernatural experience as a sign of divine intervention on the girl's behalf.

Indeed, the spiritual perception of the Indian convert was often a source of amazement to the missionaries. In 1642 Lalemant wrote of René Sondihouane, a Huron convert, that he was "taught by a better Master than ourselves." He prayed long hours in an ascetical fashion, not uncommon among Indians; and, like his unconverted fellow tribesmen, communicated with an unseen spiritual world. He prayed in the chapel in the coldest weather, despite the fact that he was only lightly dressed. On one such occasion he reported a strange encounter:

. . . he felt a person kneel near him . . . [and] . . . heard an unknown voice repeating the same Prayers as himself . . . as it was dim . . . , he asked who it was. No one answered, and yet he still felt that person near him. He stretched out his hand to discover who it was, but the other suddenly disappeared.[29]

He asked the fathers for an explanation, but they could only conclude, "We knew no more than he does on that point; but we are not ignorant of the fact that God is pleased to converse with the simplest Souls."[30]

The missionaries, of course, did not base their lives on the premise that supernatural phenomena are a daily occurrence. Hunger, disease, and death were expected and accepted; yet the miraculous was always a possibility, particularly in the realm of physical healing. The power of evil was real enough to the fathers, but it was manifestly weak where healing was concerned. Miracles and wonders it might produce, but nothing that was of real or long-lasting good for man. On the other hand, the power of God could and did show itself through physical healing. The Catholic cultus, centered as it is upon the idea of the sacramental—the use of matter by the divine power—provided the missionaries with the means of seeking this healing in ways immediately understandable to the Indian, and with which he could identify.

Native religion held certain objects to be sacred. A rock or a bone of an animal was carried in the Indian's leather pouch as a means of seeking help from the spirit-world. Of similar importance to the Indian were the fire or red-hot coals, stones, and liquid concoctions used in shamanistic healing rites. Likewise, Christianity, as the missionaries taught it, could operate in a context which in the Indian's mind was not far removed from this. Based as Christianity is on the principle of the divine revealing itself in human flesh and bearing within itself the "signs" of this principle, that is to say the seven sacraments and the "sacramentals" such as holy water, sacred relics, blessed pictures, medals, and rosaries, Christianity was readily equipped to demonstrate on its own grounds the impingement of the spiritual world upon that of matter in which man dwelt.

Holy water or relics might very well help to bring about a healing, but the missionaries did not view these sacramentals as "magical," in the sense that miracles were automatic upon their use, for all ultimately depended upon the divine. Yet the possibility was always present that the divine would use these sacramentals as a means of expressing his will. If the prayers of a particular saint were requested as the sacramentals were applied, or if the relics used were that of a certain saint, then the prayer of that saint would be believed to enhance the possibility of aid in the particular circumstance.

Chaumonot wrote in 1640 that a Huron, baptized during an illness, recovered the use of all his faculties except his sight. Sometime later, one of the Jesuits washed his eyes with holy water, saying as he did so, "May the Father, the Son, and the Holy Ghost, in whom thou believest, heal thee . . . ," and by the next day he could see once more. The priest went on to recount that a Christian woman had been blinded by a demon since she had refused participation in a shamanistic rite; in this instance too, holy water restored her sight.[31]

Vimont in 1643 wrote that God sometimes healed converts because of their resignation to his will and "sometimes, also, by virtue of the holy water which is given them to drink." As an example, he wrote of a young man at Tadoussac who came down with a severe "pleurisy" and was at last brought to the Hospital Nuns at Sillery, where he became progressively worse. Yet one day he resolutely dragged himself to the hospital chapel where one of the Jesuits found him. The Jesuit recited over him the appointed gospel reading for that day and made him drink some holy water. From this point on, Vimont wrote, the Indian began to improve until he was fully restored to health.[32]

Relics used in healing rites by the Jesuits during their work among the Indians in the seventeenth century were usually those of either canonized saints or the revered North American Jesuit martyrs; or else they were fragments that were believed to be from the true cross. In

1672 after a winter of much suffering and deprivation at Tadoussac, Father de Crepieul wrote:

> The comfort afforded me by looking at the likeness of my beloved Father St. Francis Xavier, and my reliquary, in which I carry a piece of the true Cross, greatly ameliorated my little suffering.[33]

Sometimes a relic was applied to the body of the infirm while appropriate prayers were said, or a small portion might be ground into powder, mixed with water and given to the patient to drink, as was done once in Quebec with a relic of Jean de Brébeuf.[34]

At the mission in Montreal, it became the custom in the 1640s for the Indians to gather each evening for prayers in the chapel or in their cabins. On one such occasion, after they had knelt in their cabins for prayers, a young boy collapsed into deep unconsciousness and could not be stirred in any way by his parents, who shouted, threw water on him, and shook him, all to no avail. Finally at about midnight, after the boy showed no sign of life at all, the parents sent a message to the missionaries that he seemed to be dead or close to it. The priests went to the cabin and placed relics on his chest; hardly had they done so, Lalemant reported, when the boy opened his eyes and regained consciousness to the awe of all those in the cabin.[35]

In 1672, Henry Nouvel[36] wrote from the Mission of the Apostles, which was located among the Ottawas who lived around Lake Huron, that a family had despaired so much of their child's health that they had called in the jugglers, but upon their appearance the child only grew worse. Finally, the child was brought to the missionary who thought there was little hope of recovery. However, though they were not baptized, he told the parents to seek the help of Christ for healing. They were told also to ask the martyred Jean de Brébeuf for his prayers, since Christ might be moved by the prayers of one who had died in the Huron country seeking to spread the knowledge of Christ among the Indians. He then told them to bring the child to the chapel where he gave it a little water into which had been dipped a relic of Father de Brébeuf. They were told to bring the child for two more days for this purpose; however, after the second dosage of water, Nouvel reported that the child was healed. The father of the child gave a feast in Indian style, after which he himself was baptized. The next day, a young woman was cured of a malady by drinking some of the same water.[37]

As the century closed, Father Jacques Gravier,[38] on a voyage down the Mississippi to Louisiana, reported that the application of a relic had been the source of a number of healings. It ". . . is the most infallible remedy that I know of for curing all kinds of fever," he wrote.[39]

Because of their obvious association with the dead who were now believed to be living in a spiritual world, relics were accorded by the native convert a special devotional significance. Relics were brought early into the Huron country. The faithful Indian convert Joseph Chihwatenhwa brought some of these in by canoe. The relics were exposed upon the altars of the various Huron missions from time to time with great reverence. Joseph Chihwatenhwa's own reported testimony exemplifies this reverence:

> Then I addressed myself to the Saints whose relics are here, and the chief part of which gave me much trouble to bring up here from Quebec. I said to them: "Great Saints, I do not know your names; nevertheless you cannot be ignorant of the fact that

I have brought your relics to this country. Have
pity on me; pray your master and mine, Jesus,
for me."[40]

Some of these relics were on occasion given to
individual Christian Indians who carried them on their
persons, showing them great respect, just as they had
once carried about the sacred symbol of their personal
"demon." Lalemant reported in the *Relation* of 1648 that a
Christian captain at Quebec asked with great reverence
that the fathers allow him to have a relic of his own.
Since all that pertained to heaven, he said, was of far
greater value than earthly things, and since holy relics
were particles of the bones of those who had now entered heaven, if they thought him worthy he would like
nothing more than such a relic which he planned to bear
about on his person in "a small copper cross that could
open and shut." To his great satisfaction, the priests
granted his request, Lalemant reported.[41]

The parallel between carrying about on one's
person stones and other objects considered sacred, and
the carrying about on one's person sacred relics, is obvious. What was more commonly done, however, was the
carrying about of a Christian image, which was kept
securely in a leather pouch. The fathers may have delib-
erately suggested this as a substitution for the Indian's
charms. Vimont at Tadoussac in 1643 specifically pointed
out that a child was cured after a missionary called upon
all to pray for the child's health and then suspended a
crucifix over the child's head "in the place of the pouch
of magic."[42]

A religious image was carried about as a sacred
object in a leather pouch or was kept in a special place
within the Indian's cabin whenever travel was restricted.
One Montagnais, returning in the spring to Sillery, ex-

plained the darkening in color of an image that had been given to him the past year:

> . . . it is the smoke of the cabin that has blackened it. I took it out of my pouch every day, and hung it up in my cabin; and my wife, and I, and all my family, knelt down to say our prayers night and morning.[43]

When an image was removed from its pouch or from wherever it was kept from common view, it was kissed and handled with much devotion.[44]

Just as the Indians and the missionaries believed that a presumably evil force could cause a charm previously discarded to reappear in its pouch, so the divine power could effect the reappearance of a holy image that had been lost. Lalemant recounted that a shaman approached a Christian and offered to heal his sick son; the Christian refused and went on to utter regret at having lost an image that he used in his devotions—one that he had always carried about in a pouch. The shaman expressed the desire to see such an image. The convert bemoaned the fact that, while he had always carried the image about in the pouch, he had looked there and other places several times to no avail; nevertheless, he thrust his hand once more into the pouch and found it where he had formerly kept it. Lalemant pointed out that those standing around had seen that indeed the pouch had not previously contained it. The Indian placed the newly found image in a prominent place, had all kneel, and prayed to God for the healing of his son, which soon occurred—to the amazement of both Christian and non-Christian.[45]

Images also might be placed before the eyes of a sick person as a means of seeking his cure, or might also be applied directly to his body.[46] In the metaphysical understanding of the missionaries, it was not impossible that, like the mysterious swaying of the shaman's tent, spiritual power might objectively display itself through and in a holy image. One catechumen at St. Joseph's Mission in Teanaustaiyé is reported in 1640 to have sought baptism for some time, but to no avail because the fathers had found him lacking in regularity and reverence in daily prayers. But one day while praying in the chapel, he suddenly exclaimed that the picture of Christ had moved and looked displeased in his direction. The Indian, it was reported, became frightened and confused. A Jesuit, in the chapel at the time, had seen nothing extraordinary, but assured him that such things could and did happen. After much questioning of the catechumen, the missionary was convinced that it had occurred as the Indian had said. The missionaries reported that reverence and discipline became evident in the Indian's life after this event, and that eventually he was baptized. This was seen as further evidence that the reported phenomenon in the chapel had really taken place. At least the missionaries among the Hurons had little doubt that it had.[47]

The dream phenomenon was, in the Jesuit's view, the most common means of contact between the Indian and the demonic powers of the spiritual world; therefore, it was very difficult for the Jesuits, at least in the early years of contact with the Indians, to accept any Indian's dream as being of divine origin. This hesitation occurred in the face of the dream's prominent role as a spiritual medium in both scripture and church history.[48] Gradually the fathers came to believe that a Christian Indian might very well experience a dream resulting from divine inspiration; and they even came to wonder if an unbaptized person might not also receive such a dream in order to bring about his or her salvation.

Le Mercier in the *Relation* of 1638 records that Brébeuf was called to the bedside of a sick, unbaptized woman at Ossossané. The woman cried out that she had just had a dream in which a young man in a white robe went about baptizing all in the village; she recounted experiencing great delight during the dream and expressed the desire for baptism herself. Brébeuf is recorded as having explained to her the "nature" of dreams; perhaps proclaiming their meaninglessness. Yet it is possible that he might have wondered if this dream were not a sign of divine intervention for the purpose of engendering good in a woman whose culture placed so much importance on dreams. This conclusion may be inferred from the fact that he does not seem to have followed the usual procedure of protracted testing and instruction of a would-be convert, but after brief instruction straightway baptized her. The words of Le Mercier seem to confirm this interpretation, "There was nothing urgent as far as the symptoms of her disease were concerned, but the father, feeling himself strongly inspired, granted her request."[49]

About fifteen years later, the same Le Mercier also recorded a story about a former Algonquin captain, Paul Tessouehat. As Tessouehat lay dying he attempted in every way to keep all the tenets of the faith, preparing himself for a holy death and requesting a priest to come often to speak to him about Christianity. During this time, he experienced a dream to which Le Mercier and Le Moyne were willing to attribute a divine origin. He recounted that in his dream he had found himself before a high mountain, so high that the top was completely lost to view. A voice kept telling him to climb the mountain, that it was absolutely necessary for him to undertake this task. As he heard this voice, he recounted, he felt frightened and suddenly very weak. He noticed that the mountain seemed not only too high, but full of treacherous precipices as well. Then, in the depths of depression, he beheld a gigantic ladder. Beside the ladder there was a man who appeared to be a missionary, standing by to assist him in what soon became an almost effortless climb over the mountain. The dream had given him great comfort, said Le Mercier, who concluded that the mountain leading to heaven symbolized Christ; the ladder and the missionary obviously stood for the faith as taught by the missionaries, which was the means of opening the way into heaven for the Indian's soul.

Whether it was in their understanding of dream phenomena and visions or in their use of relics, images and holy water, there was in the Jesuits' approach to the Amerind a factor which both the Jesuits and the Indians held in common. For while there were many aspects of the Indians' perception of the spiritual world which the Fathers hoped to displace, there was an important sense in which the Indians' spiritual world and that of the Jesuits were already in agreement. Both already shared something very basic in how they viewed the invisible world and its relationship to the physical order of things: mainly, the spiritual world is imminent and it impinges upon the physical order; and both good and evil spiritual forces constantly seek to express themselves in the world of matter and can do so in numerous ways. The Indians traditionally had sought to deal with these forces; the Jesuits were providing them with a new context in which to view these forces, and with different means to deal with them. While one may disparage both the fathers' metaphysical understanding and their consequent missionary approach to the Indians, yet, as Parkman vaguely sensed, a basic cultural conflict was avoided because of certain spiritual criteria which both Jesuit and Indian shared. Both afirmed the reality of an ongoing interaction between the spiritual and the material worlds; and the Jesuits provided the Indians with a new framework in which this interaction might be experienced. The accounts of the starkly different approach to Indian work by the seventeenth-century New England Puritans only serve to illustrate further the value of the Jesuits' ability to enter the Indian's world instead of demanding that the Indian entirely turn his back on his traditional concept of reality.[50]

Even as the fathers accepted and adapted the metaphysical side of native culture, we shall see that they also adapted the social forms Indian society had produced; reorienting, but not destroying them, just as they had changed, but not destroyed the Indian's participation in the *unseen* world.

VI

Old Customs–New Ways

If the Jesuits' metaphysical preconceptions allowed them access into the Indian's world, their accompanying concept of cultural relativity allowed them to move with ease and little conflict within that world. As Le Jeune once wrote regarding native decoration and attire, ". . . all the nations of the world have not yet been able to agree as to what is true beauty and adornment."[1] This high sense of cultural relativity enabled Jesuits, wherever they went, to come to terms with non-European cultures in situations where other missionaries had greater difficulty.[2]

In contrast to the Jesuit approach, John Eliot, who worked among the Indians in Massachusetts, believed the Indians should be "taken off" their "wild" way of living and put into some kind of "civilized" society centered in Europeanized Indian towns.[3] Eliot founded several such towns which lasted for a time. There he taught the Indians to read their language, which he had adapted to the English alphabet. He translated the Bible for the Indian—the first Bible to be printed in New England. There were those among his fellow clergy in New England who thought he had compromised too much with native culture by not teaching the Indians to read the Bible in English: Cotton Mather implied that the truths of Christianity simply could not be put into the Indian's "penurious" tongue.[4]

As the Jesuit fathers trudged north to work among the Montagnais at Tadoussac; or moved south and west into the lands of the Huron, Iroquois, Ottawa and Illinois; or sailed southward along the Mississippi to visit the Natches and Bayagoulas, they had little thought of introducing a foreign culture or of communicating their message with the tools of such a culture. They were not concerned with teaching the Indians to read or write French or Latin, for this would only have served to complicate the main purpose of their being among the Indians. There were other ways of communicating with the Indians, Indian ways, that in the Jesuits' view would be better than ways that might be unnecessarily disruptive of native cultures. Those matters which did not deal directly with Christian doctrine and morality or with church discipline were accepted on the grounds that they were culturally relative.

The fathers, wherever they were, knew they must first accommodate their teaching and preaching of Christianity to the village life-style. In his work among the Hurons and the Iroquois, for example, a missionary usually moved into the village cautiously. He first visited the village elders and acquainted them with his purpose. He began instruction and continued to live in accordance with the regimen of village life. The Jesuits' early work among the Hurons took into account the dances, feasts, games, and councils which involved the men during much of the day. The adults, particularly the men, had to be approached always at their convenience in order not to conflict with their personal or collective participation in village life. It was, of course, viewed as especially good to convert those in authority or those held in special regard for reason of age, since this naturally tended to have a favorable impact on both the young and less important members of the village or tribe. As for the women and children, the missionaries simply moved daily through each cabin in a village, addressing any of those who would listen.[5] After several months, special classes in the missionaries' cabins might be arranged for the children, but the lessons would be kept short, since "one must learn to put one foot before the other, before he can walk."[6]

If a sizeable group of Indians converted, they organized themselves in order to make it possible for them to carry on their prayers and catechetical instruction, should no missionary be with them. This was particularly important to nomadic tribes who spent much of the year in the wilderness, away from missionaries. Sometimes they carried on their duties with much zeal; for example, when some Christian Montagnais returned to Tadoussac from a sojourn in the woods, the convert captain decreed that, in the absence of the priest, public prayers would be held twice daily under the direction of a young Indian whom he designated. The captain forthwith gave him a cord whip with which he was to punish those who failed to attend. Later the chief directed that all charms and other instruments of their former religion were to be burned in a solemn Indian-style council which, when held, ironically began with the smoking of the *calumet*, a custom associated with their former religion.[7]

Sometimes the zeal of the Christian native was too much for the fathers and had to be toned down. At Sillery, in 1641, a group of non-Christian visitors almost attacked a group of converts who had zealously reviled the native religion of the visitors. The missionaries admired such zeal, but they strongly rebuked the provocation of non-believers who, they explained, could never be attracted by such severity.[8] As Le Jeune wrote, ". . . we must not yield to all their desires; the customs of a people do not change so soon, —it is necessary to proceed with skill, gentleness, and patience."[9]

Where a sizeable number of conversions had been made and special gatherings either for Mass, public prayer, or instruction were held, opposition by non-believers was almost inevitable. Such opposition was met, however, with a bold retort from the missionary. In 1640 and 1641, a resurgence of native religion occurred at Sillery. One of the captains of the Island Nation, an Algonquin clan, whose people had helped bring on this resurgence, wished to discourage them from being baptized, implying that it was for old women and children who could not hunt. He cried out among the cabins:

> Go, good old women, go: and you, little children, who have no way of finding food, go to the black Robes and be baptized, so that you may not die from hunger; let those who resemble you, imitate you.

The next day the missionary Jean de Quen called the Indians to Mass in his usual manner, which was to follow the native custom in assembling councils. This custom was to cry out the announcement in an imperative tone of voice while walking among the cabins. It was as de Quen did this that he gave his rejoinder to the captain:

> Men and women who are not baptized; go to Teswe-hat [the captain] . . . he will give you all food; it is he who kills beavers, and knows well how to catch the moose.

The captain, although angry, no longer publicly associated baptism with weakness.[10]

The missionaries did not try to teach French or Latin to the Indians. Instead they tried to communicate with the Indians through their native written medium. The *pictography* of the Indian has long been of interest to anthropologists and ethnographers. Recent research suggests that the pictography of North American Indians was a kind of hieroglyphic system, possibly based on ancient European and Mediterranean influence.[11] The *Jesuit Relations* mention pictography numerous times and relate how the missionaries used this medium to communicate their teachings to the Indians, and how sometimes they added new symbols especially suited to the new religion.

In the early 1640s when the nomadic Atikemegues encamped near Sillery, the method of instruction employed by the fathers was similar to that used with all the nomadic tribes. It included the use of pictography in catechizing the Indians. Since there was no village chapel, instruction was given alike to men, women, and children in one of the villager's cabins. Each individual was encouraged to paint, on a piece of bark, pictographs that would enable the novice to remember the lesson. The missionary also made drawings, which he fastened high enough in the cabin for all to see. Also, as the various tenets for that lesson were presented, the missionary taught the Indians to use their fingers to number each tenet and to associate each tenet with a particular finger. When the missionary finished, those who believed they comprehended the day's lessons took the priest's pointer and began to explain again to the class the major points that had been learned, using the hieroglyphs which the priest had used in his lecture.[12]

From the land of the Iroquois, Jean Pierron[13] wrote in 1669 that the use of pictographs to communicate Christianity had brought many to class who otherwise would not have come. These drawings created so much discussion that they became "preachers to themselves" and caused the conversion of some who were otherwise untouched by the missionaries' words. The pictographs also indirectly helped the missionaries to learn the native languages, since these pictographs often engendered spirited discussion to which the missionaries intently listened.[14] In addition to the use of many figures familiar to the Indians, designs based on native symbolism were often devised, such as those used by Allouez at the St. Francis Xavier Mission located in what is now Wisconsin on the shore of Green Bay. These devised symbols represented the twelve tenets of the Apostles' Creed.[15]

Sticks, painted a certain color or notched in a particular manner, another means of native communications, were also used by the fathers as teaching devices. The sticks had particular value whenever the Indians were separated from a missionary. Jérôme Lalemant wrote in 1646 that when one of the nomadic groups of Christians left Quebec, they were given a *book* of five *chapters* which consisted of five sticks so fashioned that they could *read* the meanings the missionaries had assigned to the five sticks. The first, a black stick, was to remind them to have horror for their former demon-oriented religion; the second, a white stick, was fashioned in such a way as to remind them how they were to offer their daily prayers, devotions, and good works to God; the third, a red stick, was so shaped as to remind them of their duty on Sundays and feast days:

> . . . how they are to assemble in a great cabin, hold public prayers, sing spiritual Songs, and above all, listen to the one who shall keep these Books or these Sticks, and who will give the explanation of them to the whole assembly.[16]

The fourth was wound with little ropes to remind them that delinquents must be corrected, but with "love and charity." The fifth was carved with various native designs signifying how Christians were to behave in both famine and plenty by always giving thanks to God and hoping in him. These "books" of five chapters were given to the Christian chiefs, who based their exhortations around them as they periodically called their fellow Christians together for instruction.[17] Also, when an Indian went to confession, he sometimes used a bundle of sticks to help him remember his sins. As one penitent put it while drawing forth such a bundle, "There are all my sins, I have written them upon these pieces of wood, after our fashion, for fear of forgetting them."[18]

Pictography, or picture-writing, was universal among the Indians of North America. Most nineteenth- and twentieth-century observers have held that almost all symbols served a mnemonic purpose. The symbols did not convey ideas as such but only brought forth memories or assigned meanings, as in the case of those contrived symbols used by the Jesuits. The symbols were used to commemorate events, anniversaries, and such like, or were simply used for decorative purposes.[19] Although the origins of Indian pictography are unclear,[20] there is evidence left by the missionaries that they suspected the writing of the Indians served more than a mnemonic purpose. Father Sébastian Rasle wrote from among the Abenaki in Maine that the Indians understood each other by their picture-writing "as well as we understand each other by our letters."[21] Father Vimont wrote of the Montagnais at Quebec that they sometimes recorded what the missionaries taught them by means of "certain figures which represented for them the sense of some clause . . ."[22] The missionaries evidently saw some system underlying native pictography or else they could not have so readily adapted and used it in their instructions to the Indians. The shamanistic songs and rites were recorded by pictography, and the fathers, finding

135

much similarity in the use of picture-writing among those tribes with which they dealt, found it was easy to communicate the new religion in this same medium.[23]

The use of sticks by the Indians was also a means of conveying messages. The sticks might be set up in the ground to serve as a sign to those passing by.[24] The fathers simply adapted the use of these sticks to their own didactic purposes.

The use of the rosary was very popular among the Christians of the various tribes. As Vimont wrote:

> It is incredible how much these good people are inclined to this devotion . . . and how eager they are to have them—especially those which are rather large and handsome, to wear them suspended about their necks.[25]

But in addition to their attraction to something that was so like beaded jewelry, the rosary, too, like the sticks, was a kind of mnemonic device and fitted well into the Indian use of symbols. Primarily, of course, in Catholic devotion the rosary is a meditational device; but its mnemonic purpose is obvious. It not only provided the Indians with a means of learning certain prayers and calling to mind certain meditations, but it was adapted by the missionaries to serve as a kind of calendar device for neophytes when they were on the hunt. With it they would always know which day was Sunday and would be able then to mark that day with special devotions. One each of the five decades of the rosary was said Monday through Friday; on Saturday another devotion was said, signaling that the next day was Sunday, when the entire rosary was recited.[26]

The attachment to the rosary was no doubt partly due to the Indian custom of carrying about sacred articles and to the importance of symbols in a culture where symbolic gifts were used to supplement native picture-writing. As will be shown later, the gifts, often made of beads, served to symbolize the invoking of acts and agreements. The rosary was often worn by the neophyte as a symbol of the pledge of God's love and protection to him, as well as his own devotion to God and his love for the Virgin. The rosaries were "holy things, dedicated to God."[27]

The rosary was also used to participate in the sacrificial side of religion among a people who had been accustomed to offer frequent small sacrifices of tobacco or animal fat to the powers of the spiritual world. Le Mercier wrote in 1653 of the Huron Christians, then living on the Isle d'Orleans near Quebec[28]:

> . . . in order that the frequency with which they repeat it may be to their good Mother's honor, they put aside, each time, one of their pearls or diamonds—these are their porcelaine [*sic*] beads. Every Sunday, they bring to the Father who directs them the little pile they have amassed during the week, in order to draw from this store the material for making a Crown, or Scarf, after the fashion of the country, for the image of the blessed Virgin.[29]

Whatever, then, was at hand, either directly from Indian culture or what could conform to that culture—pictographs or hieroglyphics, adapted symbols, and carved pieces of wood—was used for the teaching of the faith. There was little or no attempt to introduce the reading of French or Latin books, not even by men of deep scholarship. The laborious effort of Eliot, who put the native language to the English alphabet and then translated the Bible into that language, does not characterize the main thrust of the Jesuit missionary endeavor. The reason for this was that their aim, an aim often at odds with that of the Paris government and of missionaries of other Catholic religious orders, was to engender a Christianity that would evolve and grow within the native cultures free from destructive alien forces. To the Jesuits, conversion to Christianity and Europeanization were *not* inexorably linked.

In 1636 Brébeuf said to the Hurons that the missionaries wanted all men to have a knowledge of God, and that peoples and nations differed throughout the world in their customs, manner of dress, architecture, and life-styles, and that knowledge of God did not presuppose conformity in these realms.[30] The missionaries were agents of the Catholic church which they considered to be one entity united under the authority of the pope; yet, this one entity was not for them a monolithic structure, particularly as it related to cultural variation. Throughout their seventeenth-century writings, they spoke of establishing new "churches" based on tribal groupings; the "Huron church" or the "Iroquois church" was to reflect an ecclesiastical expression molded by the native tribal culture. Cultural differences are assumed and expression of them are fostered within the native churches.[31]

While the fathers always gave a "Christian" name to their converts, they in turn took on Indian names themselves, and these were sometimes referred to in the official reports sent to Europe.[32] While the name of a saint was always adopted at baptism, the convert still retained his Indian name and sometimes took on another Indian name, as was native custom, if some later event or circumstance required it. They did so with no disapproval from the missionaries.[33] The very name for *Dimanche,* or "Sunday," was changed according to the native language: in the Algonquin tongues it was called "the day

which is respected;'' in the Iroquoian languages, including the Hurons, it was ''the true day.''[34] Among themselves and the French, the fathers frowned on working
on Sundays, but they realized that the Indians, who lived
from hand-to-mouth, could not always be expected to
follow this example.[35]

The liturgical life of the Jesuits while among the
French in Quebec, of course, conformed to accepted
French Catholic customs of the day. Indians in Quebec
were encouraged to participate as acolytes by carrying
the *flambeau*, or ''torches,'' in processions and serving at
the altar,[36] but within the village of Sillery the liturgy
took on a different character. Here, the missionaries were
quite willing to accommodate the ordinary proprieties of
Catholic worship to the ways and needs of their neophytes. For example, it was not unusual for the preacher
at Mass to be stopped by an Indian who had a question
or a request for clarification. Furthermore, it was not
unusual for the questioner himself, after receiving an
answer, to deliver a short discourse, usually to reiterate
the answer the priest had just given him. The *Relation* of
1640 records the following episode that occurred during a
sermon in which the sacrament of penance was being
stressed as a remedy against sin. One captain got up and
loudly proclaimed:

> My Father, they do nothing but gamble in our cab-
> ins. Listen, young men, do you understand clearly
> what the Father is telling us? You are not doing
> right; mend your ways! You gamble too much; come
> and confess, and be careful not to hide any of your
> sins.[37]

The captain sat down; the preacher finished the sermon.
Le Jeune wrote that this sort of interruption was not

unusual and was completely acceptable. While expressing his pleasure at this accommodation to native ways,
he admitted that in France the event would be most
extraordinary; among the Indians, it was altogether appropriate.[38] There were other exceptions to the ordinary
quiet reverence observed in traditional Catholic worship:
the Indians, just as they had done for centuries around
the council fire, expressed their agreement when something said by the preacher at Mass particularly touched
them. At Sillery, cries of *ho-ho* or *mi hi,* expressing approval, or *mi ke tiang,* meaning "we will do that," often were
responses to something the speaker had said. Occasionally someone might call out that the speaker should proceed slower, so that he could better be understood.[39]
This exuberance in worship took many forms and was at
times an expression of religious awe of a type unknown
to Europeans. Anthoine Sylvy[40] reported in 1677 that at
the elevation of the Host—one of the most sacred moments of the Mass—a neophyte suddenly seemed to go
into convulsions. After investigation, the missionary concluded that this behavior was engendered by ". . . the
respectful Awe that the good Christian felt at that august
mystery. . . . It would be an exceeding consolation to
have many neophytes like them."[41]

Piety caused some of the Indian converts to re-
furbish their cabins in a new style, yet with an Indian
motif. One pious woman near Quebec, out of her own
devotion and during her daughter's final illness, adorned
a portion of her cabin's interior with bark, intricately
embroidered moose robes, and beaver skins. These were
hung on the walls at one end to form a kind of shrine-
like enclosure for a crucifix that was fixed to the wall and
candles that were mounted on a floor carpeted with
leaves.[42] Such shrines also served the needs of Sunday
worship when a priest was absent from a village: here, a

villager could lead certain devotions for his fellow Christians to mark a holy day.[43]

The Jesuits translated into various dialects vernacular prayers and hymns for public worship, which they taught the Indians to say, or to sing, the words being set to a native chant. Although the Jesuits had taught the Indians prayers for private devotions, they did not always insist greatly on the prayers being used. An Indian at Quebec was asked if he prayed in his cabin, and replied that he did not, since he had not learned what to say to God, but, he went on to say, he thought always about God and was aware of his presence. The missionary who asked the question concluded that the Indian was already praying without knowing it.[44] Paul Ragueneau wrote some advice from the Huron mission in 1646, which he considered worthy of consideration by missionaries in other fields. They had taught the Huron neophytes an act of contrition—the prayer to be said whenever one was aware of sin and repented of it. But one of the Indians responded that lying was such an easy thing for him and his people, that a certain prayer to be said automatically might be simply another lie. He advised:

> . . . rather, without giving us any form of prayer, tell us that we must detest our sins with all our hearts and with all our strength; and that God does not look upon our lips, but that he penetrates into the depth of our souls, insomuch that none can deceive him.[45]

Without doubt, the missionaries did not cease teaching their converts the act of contrition; but, significantly, Ragueneau wished to share with his brethren not only that he had converts of profound wisdom but that the truth of what this particular neophyte had said was worthy of consideration by learned French churchmen, and that a different approach might be needed in the respective cultures of the Indian tribes.

Cultural needs demanded accommodation. What would not be tolerated in France might be acceptable among the Illinois, the Iroquois, and the Ottawas. An aged chief at the mission at Sault Ste. Marie referred to Christ as "Jesus, The God of war." There was no disapproval expressed by Father Druillettes, because the village was under constant threat from the fierce Nadouessi tribe[46] and warfare was a reality of life the Indians had come to accept. Fridays and other days of abstinence, as well as the Lenten fast itself, could not be observed among the Indians. The fathers concluded that, like the Sabbath, these days were set apart for man, not man made for them.

The Lenten fast, which in the seventeenth century involved a rigorous abstinence from flesh-meat, was made entirely optional for the native converts; for, after all, Father du Peron had concluded, "the Lent of the Savages is continual."[47] What made it even more difficult was that Lent occurred at the very time of year when the hunters traditionally returned from the hunt, and therefore meat was more plentiful than at any other time. The fathers made it plain that those who abstained, as some insisted on doing, did so of their own accord. The normal Indian diet was more meager than that prescribed by canon law for a Lenten fast.[48]

During the times of the hunt, worship took on the cultural stamp of the Indian more than at any other time. Since a priest was seldom present, native converts conducted the public worship on Sundays and on other specified days. Even those who settled at Sillery continued to hunt large game such as elk and moose when the snow was deep; for this was the only way to obtain meat in quantity. It was for their converts on the hunt or for nomadic tribes that the *calendar rosary* and *books of sticks* were devised. Ultimately in these books the days, months, and feasts came to be distinguished by various marks.[49] On the hunt a kind of brush shed was often erected as a place for a crucifix, before which devotions were held, devotions which, as Jérôme Lalemant wrote in 1659, ". . . penetrate Heaven just as well as from those great Temples where prayers are held with so much pomp."[50]

Among the nomadic Atikemegues, Sunday services began very early. With no priest present, the eldest Christian, or the captain, if he were a Christian, would cry out that the new day was to be honored in a special way: no smoking, eating or drinking was to be done until after Sunday prayers. A special cabin was then prepared and the floor carpeted with spruce branches. Non-Christians were welcomed to attend opening prayers, but then had to leave when the captain signified they were to do so. Various hymns dealing with the Mass and Christian beliefs were then intoned, after which the rosary was recited. According to Indian custom, the final *Ave Maria* of each decade was sung.[51] Prayers were conducted daily, but with special solemnity on Sundays, when the worshippers dressed in their best native attire:

> . . . they figure and paint their faces, after their fashion, with various colors; they take their great robes of Beavers, of Otters, of Lynxes, of black Squirrels, and of other animals, and their embellishments of porcupine quills, dyed in scarlet, are not wanting. The women put on their great bracelets, and the men their collars and crowns, or porcelain.[52]

Some of the Christians of Sillery, away on the hunt at Christmas, reported that they simply prayed all night long on this feast, which they had come to call "the night when we pray so long."[53]

When a priest was present on a Sunday or holy day, then, of course, Mass was celebrated; but the setting and the accompanying festivities were native to the culture. The missionaries not only adapted their life-style, their accustomed decorum at Mass, and the fasting rules of the church, but they also were willing to adapt the entire celebration of the church's chief festivals to the cultures they encountered. Father Henry Nouvel, living among some nomadic Algonquins, gave an Easter feast in a special kind of cabin put up for native festivals. The feast, following Mass, consisted of sagamité, moose, and tongues; dessert was a little tobacco. Some Easter songs were sung in Algonquian, after which a convert delivered a bit of native oratory, always a part of feasts, on the efficacy of prayer. The orator closed with the singing of two Christian songs, which, set to native music, were rendered in the native style. Many such songs followed, and the rosary closed the proceedings.[54]

Understandably, in some ways the spirit of adaptation was carried even farther in the work done among the tribes of the west. As was shown in chapter two, Allouez believed he had discovered a vestigial knowledge of the true God among the Illinois Indians in the 1660s. "Of all the spirits to whom they offer sacrifice, they honor with a very special worship one who is preeminent above all the others, as they maintain, because he is the maker of all things."[55] He went on to illustrate how he not only tolerated but apparently tended to favor the evolution of native forms in worship:

> I have proclaimed the name of Jesus Christ
> here to eighty people of this nation, and they have
> carried it and published it with approbation to the

whole country of the South . . . They honor our Lord among themselves in their own way, putting his Image, which I have given them, in the most honored place on the occasion of any important feast, while the Master of the banquet addresses it as follows: 'In thy honor, O Man-God, do we hold this feast; to thee do we offer these viands.'[56]

Where once the demons had customarily been invoked during the Indian ceremonial feasts, now Jesus Christ was similarly invoked and the accustomed food sacrifices were now offered to him. These Indians may not have been baptized Christians, but what is significant here is that the missionaries approvingly recorded all of this as a beginning, a foundation, for a native church. What has been allowed cannot altogether be undone, but built upon and allowed to evolve. Allouez does not object to another more spectacular custom, which he saw as a sign of a tribe's increasing inclination toward Christianity:

> The Savages of this country show sufficiently, by the honors that they pay to our holy Church, after their fashion, that, if they do not all pray as yet, they at least esteem Prayer. They are far from dreading it as a dangerous thing, as all the other Savages of this New France did when we began preaching the Gospel to them. Sometimes, even, in their councils they address their speeches to this house of God, and speak to it as to an animate being. When they pass by here they throw tobacco all around the church, which is a kind of devotion to their divinity; and, when they enter it, they think that they never can do enough to satisfy their inclination to honor the true God as the greatest divinity of whom they have ever heard. They also come

sometimes and offer presents, to beg God to have pity upon their deceased relatives. The Pouteouata-mus [Potawatomies] came here bringing theirs, to ask pardon from God.[57]

That there was more than just a willingness to be tolerant on the part of the Jesuits is apparent from the example of Father Louis André, who arrived among the Menomini in April, 1673, in the region to the west of Lake Michigan. He found them concerned over their failure to catch fish. They were engaged in beseeching the sun for aid in sending sturgeon into the river. One of them had painted an image of the sun on a piece of wood before which their prayers were offered. He described the scene and his response:

This picture was tied to the end of a pole which was also painted in the brightest colors; and on this pole, at the height of a man, was suspended a sheaf of small cedar sticks, cut so as to serve as floats for the nets that are used in catching sturgeon, like the pieces of cork that are fastened to all kinds of nets in France . . . They replied that it was a sacrifice . . . an 'exhortation'—which they had made to the sun, to entreat it to have pity upon them . . . they believed that the sun was the master of life and of fishing, the dispenser of all things . . . After disabusing them of the idea which they had of the sun, and explaining to them in a few words the principal points of our Faith, I asked them whether they would consent to my removing the picture of the sun, and replacing it by the image of Jesus crucified . . . they consented . . . I put my crucifix in the place of the picture of the sun. On the following morning, sturgeon entered the river, in . . . great abundance . . .[58]

The crucifix replaced the sun's image, but the context remained the same: the native rite was carried out; the native offering was placed before a new image, but was offered for the same purpose. The missionary might have lectured them on the error of their sacrifice, attempted to remove all of their symbols, and silenced their prayers with his own. Instead, he removed, with their permission, only one symbol and replaced it with another; all else was carried out as usual.

Aboriginal marriage customs presented the fathers with obstacles around which there could be little adaptation on their part if the church's moral teachings were to be kept intact. The missionaries found among the tribes of the St. Lawrence valley and Great Lakes regions varying degrees of marital stability. Polygamy was common, but not universal. Among the Iroquois, for instance, polygamy was occasionally found. Although some later writers deny its occurrence among the Hurons, the Jesuits have reported to the contrary. Among the Abenakis and Montagnais, it was common.[59] Whatever the case, there seems little disagreement that instability characterized most native marriages, even monogamous ones. Barthélemy Vimont wrote from Quebec in 1644:

> . . . of all the Christian laws which we propound to them, there is not one that seems so hard to them as that which forbids polygamy, and does not allow them to break the bonds of a lawful marriage.[60]

According to native custom, a boy of marriageable age was advised by his family as to which girl was most suitable for him to marry; the boy then asked the girl's parents for permission to marry her; this granted, he proceeded to visit her at night in her cabin. If she did not turn him away, the marriage could then be officially declared in effect. This seems to have been, with minor variations, generally the custom followed in the tribes of the region. The missionaries strongly condemned the custom of nocturnal visitation, not, they wrote, that it always led to sexual intercourse, but that such visits tended to end that way.[61] Even if sexual intercourse did result, the girl was not bound to marry her suitor. Only one thing did the missionaries admire in this procedure: if a suitor were refused, he did not wreak vengeance in any way upon the one who was accepted, but to the contrary, went and congratulated the groom-to-be. To do otherwise was, in the Indian view, to give evidence of weakness.[62]

Among the Hurons, when a boy had received the advice of his family, he asked the consent of the girl's parents; receiving this, he painted his face, dressed in his finest ornamental attire, went to the girl in the evening and offered her various presents. If she accepted the presents, her lover came and slept with her for three or four nights; but since she might only have allowed this out of respect to her father's or mother's wishes, the marriage was not a certainty until the marriage feast occurred, presided over by the girl's father or a tribal leader who then announced officially that the two were getting married.[63]

Marriages could be broken on a moment's notice, and this of course could lead to strife within the tribe. Le Jeune wrote of an Indian near Quebec who left home for a time, received word his wife had married another, and then proceeded himself to marry again. After a few months, he left his second wife, returned home, and demanded his first wife back again; this was refused by her new husband. However, her father declared that he would settle the matter by a contest, from which there would be no appeal: he placed a stick in the ground, some distance away, declaring that the one who could first retrieve it would be the husband of his daughter.[64] This whole approach to marriage was, of course, horrifying to the missionaries, and no matter how much they might respect aboriginal cultures, this particular aspect was not tolerated among their converts.

Some of the missionaries wished to postpone the baptism of single catechumens of marriageable age, until they had contracted what was shown to be a stable marriage. This was by no means a rule. The young men at Sillery, for example, leaving to fight the Iroquois, could put forth good arguments for their reception into the church. One fellow accused a priest of mentioning marriage every time baptism was brought up. He argued that a wife could not blot out his sins; besides, since the Jesuits had thus far refused him baptism, that then the missionary could answer for his soul, should he die in battle. The missionary, in response, could do nothing but baptize him and "hope" for a good marriage.[65]

In condemning nocturnal solicitations of a wife by their male converts, the Jesuits did not rule out the usual family or tribal participation in the selection of a mate. Among the converts of the Quebec region, the fathers urged the use of pictography to convey a suitor's wishes, instead of the night visit. A suitor painted on a piece of bark a figure of a young man and woman, hand in hand, the posture assumed by a couple during Christian marriage rites. With a friend serving as an intermediary, the painting was conveyed to the young woman. If the bark were kept, the proposal was deemed accepted; but if she claimed not to understand the message's meaning, the suitor knew he was refused.[66] This all occurred after the respective families had given the usual advice and consent. Where feasible, the Jesuits wanted their converts to marry fellow Christians, yet they respected and encouraged the influence of family figures, even the unconverted, so long as the choice fell upon a Christian girl. A Christian suitor was still to seek the consent of non-Christian parents of a Christian girl.[67]

Among the Christians at Sillery the tribal leaders had a voice in the selection of mates and continued to participate in the marriage feast and even in the nuptial Mass. For example, when the officiant asked the couple their consent to the vows, a prominent tribal leader stood, asked the priest to cease and allow him to speak, then went to the altar, and addressed the couple in the following manner:

> Take care; there is but one more step to be taken—if you go any further, you can never draw back. Your word is a bond that would unite you so closely that you will no longer be permitted to sever it. Keep your mouths closed, if you do not wish to be bound. If you speak, may your words be of iron, that they may never break. You are still free—no one compels you; but if you speak, we will force you to keep your word. Now then, speak, or be silent, as you please.[68]

After the speaker finished, he turned to the priest, telling him he could then continue the rite. In such an oration a tribal leader might speak specifically to one of the contracting parties, if he had doubts about the individual's suitability for marriage. Furthermore, if a married couple were having marital difficulty, a tribal leader might rise spontaneously at Mass to lecture them on their duty to each other.[69] This, of course, occurred at Sillery where although almost all of the Indians were Christians by the early 1640s, yet the tribal leadership had a place in the contracting of marriage. This authority seems not to have been opposed by the Jesuits. Although the record is not so explicit, it is reasonable to assume that similar customs, regarding family and tribe, prevailed in the Huron mission in those villages which became preponderantly Christian, prior to the defeat of the Hurons by the Iroquois in 1649.

In Europe, family participation in the choice of a mate was the custom of the time; but the missionaries seem to have accepted the concept of communal participation by the tribe, or at least by its elders, into other matters that in Europe would have been considered personal. In Europe, a murderer or thief was considered personally guilty; but among the Indians, some of the guilt, if not all, was borne by the tribe. Bressani wrote in 1653:

> It would be attempting the impossible, and ruining everything, rather than affording a remedy, to proceed with the Barbarians according to the judicial usage of nearly all nations, by condemning the murderer to death: it is the public that gives satisfaction for the crimes of the individual, whether the culprit be known or not. In fine, the crime alone is punished, and not the criminal; and this, which elsewhere would appear an injustice, is among them a most efficacious means for preventing the spread of similar disorders.[70]

As this whole concept of communal guilt could logically have some bearing on any penance imposed by the church upon commission of sin, the fathers made some interesting accommodations to native ways. The Christian Iroquois and Hurons dwelling at the mission village of Notre-Dame-de-Lorette in 1677, acting as tribal units, imposed upon themselves the requirement of making a present to be used for the poor among them whenever it was found that anyone of their nation had committed a notorious sin. This was viewed as a penance accepted by the tribe just as in the native system of justice retribution for crimes committed by an individual fell upon the entire village, clan, or tribe.[71]

Sometimes an individual Indian having committed a sin which could have been, in Catholic doctrine, settled in the privacy of the confessional, would feel so responsible to his tribe or village that he would perform acts not required by the missionaries but by his own sense of tribal responsibility. One young man at Tadoussac sought punishment at his fellow tribesmen's hands to atone for the stigma he had brought upon them through some sin committed while on the hunt in the woods. He knelt before the chapel doors, bare-shouldered, asking them to strike him for his offense which, in native understanding, had brought guilt upon the whole tribe.[72] Although, according to Catholic practice, none of this need have occurred, the missionary praised him for his zeal.

This same sense of communal guilt can be seen in the practice of mothers who brought children too young to make a confession to the confessional, and confessed for them and also carried out their penance. Offenses had been committed even though the perpetrators were too young to be in actual sin; yet sin, regardless of by whom it was committed, rested not upon the individual alone, but on his family, clan, and tribe. What these mothers were doing under the new religion was necessary to remove what was considered an offense in their culture's eyes.[73]

There was perhaps to the Indian, nothing more sacred than the rites surrounding the burial of the dead, the initial preparation of the body, the honors paid to it, and the ceremonies surrounding final disposition. The Catholic church—and the Jesuit missionaries, of course—had definite ideas on how and where the bodies of Christians were to be buried. But, as the years passed, the fathers came to have great respect for native burial customs, for they saw in them a consciousness of the survival of the soul in the afterlife. This, the Jesuits believed, was an element of truth that had survived among the Indians since the fall of man. It was a vestigial truth perceived through natural reason—the remaining natural good still present in unbaptized human beings. In 1653 Bressani wrote from Italy, where he then lived, that, although at the very start of the missions in the 1630s, the missionaries had condemned too much, they had later learned that much of what they had condemned was harmless and had discovered a "secret," which was that good resided in some of the very things which had been condemned. He warned that missionaries should not approach foreign cultures with preconceived notions, even those sanctioned "by the common approbation of centuries, believed to be beyond doubt." He went on to describe what he calls the Indians' "pious observance toward their dead, which was the most solemn ceremony that they had . . ."[74] Yet not even in this early work among the Hurons did the missionaries always demand that the bodies of converts be buried separately from unbelievers, and sometimes these bodies of Christians were even exhumed at the time of the "feast of the dead."[75]

In Huron tradition, the body of the deceased, having been prepared for burial, was covered with a beaver skin, placed on a mat, and borne to the burial place where a platform of bark had been erected, about eight or ten feet high. Gifts from the villagers were presented by the chief, most of which were to lighten the sorrow of the family. Some gifts, however, usually cakes of bread, a comb, a wampum collar, some tomahawks, and a gourd of oil, were sealed in the raised tomb for the use of the soul in the afterlife. The Iroquois were also buried in the same fashion. Occasionally the Indians in both tribes erected a kind of shrine-like cabin over the grave and enclosed it with a fence of stakes.[76] A *resuscitation* ceremony was held later by which the name, responsibilities, and position of the dead Indian were passed on.

The Huron feast of the dead was in some way related to the Iroquoian *condolence ceremony;* but, more elaborate, it involved the transferral of the bones of the dead from the village burial site to a central burial ground.[77] The Huron ceremony was done at intervals of eight, ten, or twelve years. Jesuits who attended a feast of the dead given in 1636 stated that the Indians usually referred to the feast as "the kettle" and, when indicating its occurrence, said that the fire would soon be stirred up under the kettle, there being a taboo against frequent reference to the dead. The bodies were removed from their graves, taken to the village where interment was to occur, and scraped clean of all remaining flesh. They were carefully washed, and wrapped in new animal skin robes. More necessities for the afterlife and great quantities of food were assembled. The participants dug a large pit or grave outside the village, lined it on the sides and bottom with beaver robes, and placed the gifts for the dead into it. They then erected a huge scaffold over the pit and from this emptied the bones into their new resting-place. More skins were placed over the bones, then wood and earth. Poles, driven into the ground, marked the site. Great feasting followed.[78]

While Brébeuf in this early period had litle good to say about the feast itself, it is significant that he allowed the bodies of fifteen or twenty Christians to be brought to the new burial site over which, at the ensuing feast, the fathers recited the *De profundis*—a Christian hymn for the dead. Brébeuf's only stipulation was that an adjacent pit be made for them so that the Catholic practice of burial in consecrated grounds might be maintained. While Brébeuf did not particularly care for the feast *per se*, he and the other missionaries did participate both by their presence and by allowing the bodies of Christians to be moved. He recorded further his hope that the ceremony would in the future either cease, or else, much revised, become a Christian feast for the souls of departed Indian converts. [79]

The Algonquins had a similar feast which seems to have evolved from their contact with the Hurons. [80] In September, 1641, Jérôme Lalemant joined Charles Raymbault and Claude Pijart, [81] who were living among some Algonquins encamped far to the north of the Huron villages, for what was their own annual feast of the dead. The Algonquins were joined by a few Hurons as well as by some of the Nipissiriniens. About two thousand people attended. When all were assembled according to nations, their choice possessions were exhibited: skins of otter, moose, wild cat, and caribou, along with beaver robes, glass beads, hatchets, and kettles. Those sponsoring the feast received gifts from the various chiefs as well as from the Jesuits who were there obviously as participants. Lalemant, as he offered their presents, did say that the gifts were not for the purpose of "drying their tears," but to signify their "wish to the living the same happiness that we hope to enjoy in Heaven when they shall have acknowledged the same God whom we serve . . ."[82]

Lalemant seemed to hold in awe much of what he beheld: it was not, he said, at all characterized by "sav-

155

agery," but seemed almost a "ballet," danced by about forty Indians with the voices and drums producing an agreeable musical sound to his European ears. The first "act" of the ballet, as he put it, was a battle scene, with the actors either giving or receiving death-blows. All movements, expressions, and gestures were done individually with intricate precision; yet the whole dance moved with incredible unity, as if to the beat of one directing intelligence. The second part consisted of a dance begun first by a group of eight, which then increased to twelve, then sixteen, and more, until it reached gigantic proportions, ever slowing or quickening as the singers chanted cadence. Then, suddenly, women appeared and danced the third act. After this rather solemn but beautiful event, proceedings centered around the scaling of a greased pole, and closed with a resuscitation ceremony, during which the names, responsibilities and honors of those recently deceased were conveyed to others.

The next day the women began decorating a house with an arched roof, about two hundred feet long, which was described by Jérôme Lalemant as *magnifique*. The women carried in the bones of the dead that had been encased in caskets of bark and covered with new beaver robes that were decorated with bead-studded scarves and collars. Then the women seated themselves, each near a casket, forming two lines facing each other. The chiefs entered, carrying food for the ensuing feast in which the women alone participated. This completed, men carefully selected for the quality and tone of their voices entered and joined with the women in a somber chant, which Lalemant called both sad and sweet. This continued through the night amidst a great display of reverence and devotion. By morning, when gifts were distributed by the singers, the chanting had turned to an invocation of the dead, which was intended to help send them on their way to the land of souls. As the morning progressed, a large group of men began to descend a hillside. As they did so, they moved into various configurations, but always toward the house containing the remains of the dead. When they reached the house, the women left it and yielded it to them, as if to a conquering army. Attention from then on gradually turned to the living. The conquerors became dancers and great feasting began with all the guests regaled with meal, beaver, and dog. The Jesuits were given places of honor.[83]

While the fathers opposed the spiritual entities who were invoked at such feasts, they nevertheless participated, and even allowed the remains of Christians to be transported to those feasts. Brébeuf seems to have considered that such feasts might at some point become a Christian Indian festival, and Bressani, years later, praised the pious treatment by the Indians of the remains of their dead. All things considered, there was on the missionaries' part a kind of affirmation of such a feast, not a condemnation. The fact that they participated even when the feast was obviously a non-Christian religious rite is most significant: vestigial good, which the Indian had preserved through the use of reason, was to be sought out and cultivated, wherever it might be found.

Some of the presents buried with the dead, both at the time of death and again at these feasts, were considered by native tradition to be for the soul's use in the spirit world, during the time a soul was believed to remain near its body after its first burial, and also after it left the body at the time of the feast of the dead. The fathers recorded that they, from time to time, advised their flocks that the soul had no need of such gifts, yet they did not forbid this practice since there was no absolute law against such a thing in Christian tradition. As they quoted one Indian, "since God forbids it not, I wish to honor the dead."[84] When some Algonquin converts in 1640 requested that their dead be buried in a Christian manner, the fathers refused, for, "the time for that has not yet come."[85]

The *time* for this probably never came for the nomadic tribes and never fully arrived even for those converts who dwelt in *Christian* villages. Among the Hurons, Indian mourning customs prevailed among converts at least as late as 1646. Ragueneau described such customs among convert women. Their practice, ". . . in this country . . . consists in not visiting anyone, in walking with the head and eyes lowered, in being ill-clad, ill-combed, and having a dirty face, and even sometimes all blackened with charcoal . . ."[86] Even in the Christian village of Lorette (located purposely away from white contact) after forty years exposure to the Jesuits' teachings, the funerary customs immediate upon death were little changed from those of former times. Certainly, requiem Mass was now said over the remains, but little else changed. The chief, by a sad, solemn cry, announced the individual's death; the body was dressed in its finest, covered with a red blanket, and borne to a bark-lined tomb in the ground, but the tomb was wide, capable of holding six bodies. At this point, a chief, as before, gave out the accustomed presents to the family and made an oration. Then, a present, usually a glass bead collar, was given to the church that prayers might continue to be said for the deceased's soul.

There was then, in the method of burial, a conflation of customs. The body was not placed on a raised platform nor directly into the ground, as previously had been the custom, but into a tomb reminiscent of that built for the feast of the dead. The tomb was carefully lined with bark, and had a top piece made of pieces of wood and a bark covering. It was a tomb designed to hold more than one body. The body did not come into direct contact with the earth, as was the case in the burial pit at the feast of the dead. Although the accustomed presents were given, there is no record that presents were buried with the dead. Some days later, however, there was a resuscitation ceremony, according to the old tradition. Dablon, in making his description, stated that the Jesuits had left much of Indian burial traditions untouched because these traditions served "to maintain the mutual union which exists between them [as a people] . . ."[87] Also, the annual celebration of All Souls' Day had great importance for the Hurons at Lorette. The celebration lasted for more than twenty-four hours, and prayers were continually offered for the dead by the Indians. The chiefs would cry out through the night that all should come to pray for the dead. The Indians saw this, said the missionaries, as a means of placing the souls "on the road to heaven . . ." just as the feast of the dead helped souls on their journey to the spirit-world.[88]

"Mutual union," or, rather, cultural identity, among the converts, was respected and fostered by the missionaries for the reason that, in the first instance, the Jesuits believed that vestigial good was to be found even in "savages." Since all men possessed reason and could apprehend natural revelation, the Jesuits sought to build on the truth, which could be found within the native cultures. In the second place, the Jesuits fostered native cultural integrity because they came to see that contact with the whites weakened the good they found within the native culture.

This chapter would not be complete without some discussion of how the Jesuits dealt with what was at times the major factor in an Indian's life, warfare. Of this and the horrible circumstances surrounding Indian disposal of prisoners, the fathers have much to say; yet they seem to have accepted established custom, mitigating it here and there when possible. There was, of course, little or no pacifism in seventeenth-century Christianity, and the Jesuits instilled none in their converts; they were proud of the valor of their Huron converts as they met the Iroquois in battle. Although the fathers personally abhorred the cruelties heaped upon prisoners taken in battle, they did not officially condemn the native custom of killing prisoners, but, when possible, they sought to save the prisoners or at least to lessen their torments. They admitted to the Indians that heretics and sorcerers were sometimes burned in Europe; but denied that such were customarily tortured to death. Where the Jesuits could affect change, then, they stopped protracted torture but saved captives only if the tribal leaders were likely to be favorable to the proposal. Prisoners were burned according to native custom even at Sillery.[89]

What the Jesuits did condemn outright was the kind of treatment of prisoners that was reported by several Huron women who escaped from the Iroquois. These women reported that they were forced to watch their men being killed, dismembered, boiled, and eaten before their eyes. The Iroquois "seized a thigh . . . a breast; some sucked the marrow from the bones; others broke open the skulls, to extract the brains."[90] In addition, each of these women had an infant child and saw it slowly roasted alive in their presence.

> They took our little children, and placed them on spits, held them to a fire, and roasted them before our eyes . . . They looked at us and cried with all their might . . . After they had put the poor little babes to death by fire, they drew them off the spit . . . threw them into their kettles, boiled them and ate them in our presence.[91]

Although the Iroquois were the perpetrators of the cruelties just cited, such acts were common among the other tribes as well.[92] The missionaries condemned the killing of children, torture, and cannibalism, all to little avail except as they were able to restrict the participation by their converts in these acts. The killing of captive warriors, however, was not condemned by the fathers, though they did not favor the custom. Even on this point, there was a reticence to interfere with what was a culturally accepted practice and where the only alternative was having the prisoner rejoin his tribe and become a threat once more on the field of battle.

In conclusion, it should be pointed out again that the Jesuits' mission, as they came to understand it, was not one of cultural destruction but rather of introducing into native cultures a form of Christianity which they believed could be assimilated, propagated, and practiced within the aboriginal cultural context. Since they believed that good resided within these native tribal cultures, they were willing to live their own lives within the contexts of these cultures, and they were willing to change themselves, not fearing innovation, if cultural compatibility could be served without sacrificing the essentials of their faith. Their pedagogical approach was based on the principle of cultural compatibility. The propagation of European civilization was neither complementary nor ancillary to their didactic approach. Where native custom required, not only the practice of piety but the liturgy itself was carried out in a context other than that created by European custom. The text of the liturgy as laid down by the Council of Trent could not be altered; nevertheless, through the introduction of native cultural elements into the rites, liturgical change did take place, but through the method of interpolation rather than by textual alterations.

In terms of burial rites, there was not only interpolation, but a conflation of Christian liturgy and the native rites of non-Christian origin. The missionaries, then, were willing to accommodate their own heritage, including the Catholic cultus itself, to native culture. Commensurate with this willingness to adapt their own customs and traditions was the adaptation of native social forms to a Christian purpose.

VII

Transformation of
Symbols and Ceremonies

The fathers were willing on the one hand to adapt their
didactic methods and much of Catholic observance to
Indian life and custom, and exhibited on the other hand a
pervading willingness to adapt, for their own purposes,
the institutions and customs found in native tradition.
The fathers, willingly and skillfully, adapted native oratory, dancing, gift-giving (the Indian means of transact-
ing social compacts), the Indian concept of the "feasts,"
and the ceremony of "resuscitation" into their and their
converts' experience of Christianity.

      No aspect of Indian social intercourse had more
prominence than oratory. Among the North American
tribes, oratory was such an important aspect of life that
proficiency therein raised a man to power and prominence within both village and tribe. Oratory was important in the presentation of a position before the tribal
council, in negotiations between villages or tribes, and,
not least of all, in the observance of native religious rites.
The gifted orator was considered to be a man endowed
with much wisdom and sagacity, and received the adula-
tion of his peers. Because the Indian view of the world was
full of symbolism, the various native languages contained
words that were many faceted in their meanings, and this

meant that in a relatively few words an orator could convey a highly embellished message.[1] "His vivid conceptions seemed often to thrill his frame, governing his attitude, the folds of his robe, his glance, and his gestures."[2]

In their work among the Hurons, the fathers, virtually from the start, enlisted when possible the aid of a *predicateur*, or preacher. This was an instructed layman who was commissioned to preach the faith and give instructions in the Christian religion. This was not a new custom. In the Middle Ages there had been many lay preachers. Usually, but not necessarily, they had been lay members of religious orders, who preached, possibly at the eucharist, but more often in less formal surroundings. What the Jesuits readily appreciated in the New World was the use of oratory at the core of Indian village life. But although they quickly learned native languages and dialects, the Jesuits realized they could not so quickly master the Indian style of oratory which one growing up in the culture might already possess. They, therefore, commissioned a native predicateur to fill this role, which few non-Indians could fill, at least not without the loss of much valuable time.

Among the Hurons, the most notable example of such a preacher was Chihwatenhwa, who was baptized at Ossossané on August 16, 1637, and given the baptismal name of Joseph. The missionaries came to consider him a shining light of the Huron church. Le Mercier said of him that he was "in no respect inferior to the most zealous Catholic of France."[3] His conversion took place after hearing Brébeuf speak to a gathering at the "feast of the dead" in 1636; his instruction began soon thereafter. Following his baptism, which occurred during an illness, he gave, with the father's approval, the "feast of rejoicing," prescribed by native tradition upon recovery of health, during which he delivered an oration to a large assembled crowd. He began with a recitation in his native language of the Christian hymn *Benedicite,* which is from the Catholic breviary and calls upon such elements of nature as frost, cold, sun, heat, and water, as well as upon all orders of creation, to praise and adore God. Chihwatenhwa continued his preaching to those in his cabin and at council meetings.[4] During the Christmas midnight Mass at Ossossané, in 1638, it was he who delivered an oration in the highly decorated, brightly-lit cabin that was the village church:

> Ah, my brothers . . . what do these lights shining and sparkling in the midst of the night mean, if not that he whose memory we are now honoring has through his birth dissipated the shadows and the ignorance of the world; having done this the first time so many centuries ago, he is about to grant us today, for the first time in these centuries, the same grace and mercy. There are purposes and reasons, which can only be adored, for which he has not done this sooner; but it is a grace and a favor toward us, which cannot be sufficiently estimated or acknowledged, that his providence has arranged this blessing for our country while we are still living.[5]

Judged from their writings, the Jesuits on the scene credited the flowering of the Huron church to the preaching of Chihwatenhwa, who preached not only at Ossossané but wherever opportunities arose at various mission stations maintained by the Jesuits in Huronia; whether they always took to heart his words or not, his countrymen never seemed to tire of his oratory.[6] In the Huron country in 1639, after the removal of the Jesuit residence from Ossossané to Ste. Marie, the chapel at Ossossané was often without a priest during weekdays.

Chihwatenhwa was placed in charge of it and led daily devotions, morning and evening, for the village congregation.[7] He was also believed to be gifted in ways other than oratory. Ragueneau reported in the *Relation* of 1640 that the preacher's niece had been stricken with strange nocturnal fears for several nights and that Chihwatenhwa was the instrument of her relief. Believing that evil forces were afflicting her, he took the cross in his rosary, held it before her eyes, told her to ardently believe the faith for which it stood, and to wear the cross about her neck. If she did this, he said, the fears would depart. According to Ragueneau, they did.[8] It is curious to note that this same Chihwatenhwa, who so ardently abjured and called upon his compatriots to abjure any consultation with the "demonic" spirits of the native religion, continued to participate in what was for the Indian a "religious" rite, the so-called *sweat*, or *sweat-bath*. The sweat-bath was nearly universal among the tribes north of Mexico and was done in a small, specially constructed building in which water was sprinkled over hot rocks to create steam. The participant in the sweat-bath often sang to his personal spirit or diety.[9] The fathers, who approved of his conduct, noted that Chihwatenhwa now sang to God during the sweat, promising to him greater valor in his hortative effort for the faith.[10] The murder of Chihwatenhwa by the Iroquois on August 2, 1640, already recounted in chapter four, was a great loss to the Huron church, but the fathers consoled themselves with the belief that the eloquent preacher was surely a saint who had entered the immediate presence of God where he prayed always for the Hurons. He would, therefore, have in death an even greater effect on the missionary effort than he had had in life.[11]

During the early 1640s another preacher of note among the Hurons was mentioned in the Jesuit reports.

This was Sondakwa, who had been given the name Thomas at his baptism. His preaching, said the missionaries, was characterized by a great gentleness toward his non-Christian detractors. He was credited with having a mitigating effect upon the severity that his fellow Indian co-religionists tended to exhibit in their relations with the unconverted. The Jesuits credit him with a gentleness and patience, which they believed was by far the best approach to their own work of conversion. With praise, they quoted him to this effect:

> . . . let us preach to the Infidels by our examples, and let us, above all, be careful not to embitter them. . . Let us win them over to God by love; let us bear with their weakness; let us have compassion on their faults; . . . [let us] make our lives so lovable by their innocence that the Infidels shall be constrained, in loving us, to love the Faith.[12]

In late 1640, a Montagnais named Meiachkawat was baptized at Quebec with Governor Charles Huault de Montmagny serving as his godfather. In honor of Montmagny he took the additional name of Charles. The Jesuits at Quebec, who praised his candor, fully accepted his account of the vision that led to his conversion. In 1638, while on a hunt, a figure, dressed as a Jesuit, appeared to him and exhorted him to forsake his native religion. This injunction he obeyed, and thereupon began to preach Christianity to the other Indians even before he had officially become a Christian himself. He so impressed his fellow tribesmen that they sent him to Quebec to obtain a missionary for them.[13] Much of his preaching was done at Sillery, where he lived for part of the year. He exhorted his hearers to either accept Christianity or become firmer adherents of it. Gambling occupied much of the time of some of the men at Sillery, and Meiachkawat spoke out against this pastime, which he called a "tyrant," a "passion."[14]

The Jesuits reported that Meiachkawat had a zeal to be a missionary himself, a zeal which he exercised at least on one occasion. In 1644 he set out to preach to the Abenaki in the area of present-day Maine. Before he had left, the missionaries wanted to hear a summary of what he would preach to the Abenaki. They described his discourse to them as ". . . a most judicious Sermon which included the principal mysteries of our Faith and the most important maxims of the Gospel."[15] Although his preaching was said by Vimont to have produced some good, no wholesale conversion occurred—a fact which Vimont attributed to the close proximity of the English.[16]

There were other outstanding orators who are mentioned in the *Jesuit Relations* of the 1640s: Jean Baptiste, a chief at Sillery who sought the conversion of the Atikemegues,[17] and a chief referred to as Noël, also at Sillery.[18] Almost any devout Christian, however, who in Indian eyes had an ability at oratory, could in a certain sense be termed a native preacher, and the Jesuits provided opportunities for them to address their fellow tribesmen, even at the Mass itself. Since oratorical ability was usually always accompanied by tribal respect and position, native leaders frequently preached at Mass in a spontaneous fashion, simply getting up during the rite, presumably at an appropriate time, or at the end of the liturgy, to announce their intention of speaking and that no one was to leave until they had finished. The phenomenon of the native preacher, whether at Sillery near Quebec or far away among the distant tribes, seems to have been a usual, and an ordinary, part of the Indian's ecclesiastical life under the guidance of the Jesuits.

The laity, both men and women, were used by

the missionaries as teachers or catechists. These people usually had the responsibility of leading public prayers and, in the absence of clergy, of visiting and praying for the sick.[19]

This kind of lay training and leadership paid off during the years when many converts were held in captivity among the Iroquois, for these very laymen kept Christianity alive among the captives in the absence of priests. Ragueneau wrote of one such Indian in 1650, a blind Algonquin woman, who served as a preacher to the women captives among the Iroquois. He wrote:

> She formed little gatherings; instructed, catechized, encouraged, and taught them, and induced her companions to pray. In a word, God enabled her to perform, in that land of horror and darkness, the office of . . . a preacher.[20]

The native preacher used the imagery familiar to him and his hearers. He preached at Mass, and often in the cabins as well. He spoke of God as a "father," just as the Jesuits said he was, but for the preachers and their hearers this was an Indian father, the kind of fathers who captivated the imaginations of small boys with tales of valor on the hunt or in battle. God was pictured by these preachers as a great leader and a warrior, who was victorious over evil spirits. Christ was proclaimed a great captain or chief, a victor in the struggle with evil. Easter and the Ascension were signs of his victorious combat.[21] Le Jeune wrote of the preachers' effectiveness, "Indeed, I have observed that one truly Christian Savage, who is zealous for the faith, accomplishes more among his people than do three Jesuits."[22]

Perhaps second in importance to oratory in tribal social life was the concept of the dance, which was used to express both joy and sorrow. The various dances of the American Indian were rife with symbolism and were often, but not always, related to an appeasement of the spirit-gods of the invisible world. They were performed on festive occasions as a means of rejoicing, or in anticipation of someone's death. There were also dances that the warrior would do before going off to battle. In order to insure their success and safe return, there was the custom in some tribes of the women continuing the dance after the warriors had departed.[23] Among the Iroquois tribes, the particular motion assumed by women during the dance gave rise to the word *wathonwisas,* one of their words signifying woman.[24] *Wathonwisas* means the one who sways or rocks, and it originated with the swaying, rocking motion of Indian women dancers—a motion that was distinct from the forceful, violent motion of the men dancers.

Among the Hurons, dancing was also a means of curing or preventing disease, and was sometimes done nude.[25] Because of the religious nature of many of the dances and the occasional nakedness of the dancers, some of the Jesuits, during the early years of their missionary work, frowned if their converts participated in the dances. Le Jeune recorded that the performance of the war dance at Sillery was not participated in by converts,[26] yet the next year he cited with approval the dancing of the girls at the Ursuline school in Quebec, "after the fashion of their country."[27] Whatever objections there may have been to the war dance at Sillery in 1639, it must have centered around the idea that a demon or diety was being thereby invoked, for it certainly had nothing to do with its connection with war and battle. It is possible that the war dance may have been among those things the Jesuits later believed had been too readily condemned in the mid-1630s, and which they approved later in the 1640s. Whatever the case, in 1640, Vimont recorded with approval that a Christian Indian at Montreal recently had led dancing around a band of warriors who bore the head of an enemy, and that the festivities ended with prayers in their chapel; the band with their grizzly prize was also led by a Christian chief.[28]

While the missionaries no doubt continued to frown on their converts participating in dances dedicated to deities of their former religion, there was no condemnation of dancing as such; dancing was accepted by the missionaries as an accompaniment to native ceremonies. The fathers themselves participated in dances at peace negotiations,[29] at festivals of welcome done expressly for the Jesuits,[30] and at the Christian festivals of Christmas, Easter, and the Ascension when they were a part of the native Christian rites.

If what the Jesuits considered evil could be eliminated from a practice, then there was no reason why the practice could not be used in the service of Christianity. In the region of Durango, Mexico, during Christmas of 1598, the Jesuit Juan Agustín was delighted that the Indian converts at the Santa Maria Mission danced the *mitote,* a dance once dedicated to Satan but now dedicated to Christ. In their native finery, with arrows in hand, the participants shouted praises to God in their native language as they once had shouted the praise of the devil.[31]

When Father Henry Nouvel was among some wandering Algonquins in 1664, he asked them not to dance during Holy Week, since Jesus Christ, their chief, had suffered that week, but to dance on Easter from the "noble" and "sacred" motive of celebrating the victory of Christ, their captain, over death.[32]

On Christmas Day, 1679, at Saint-Ignace, Mackinac, in the west, a statue was first processed through the village, then carried to a designated cabin where the women were to dance. First they formed two parallel lines on either side of the cabin. Each woman held a kind of rattle, or castanet, and danced to native tunes, keeping time to the rhythm of the rattles, all the while shouting cries of thanksgiving to the Christ child.[33]

Another aspect of Indian life that the missionaries came to appreciate and eventually adapt for use in the Catholic cultus was the custom of gift-giving. Among the Hurons, for instance, the giving of gifts was the means of: making and sealing social compacts; making peace between tribes and individuals; satisfying the needs of justice when crimes were committed; expressing grief; and healing the sick.[34] This seems to have been the practice of all the tribes north of Mexico. Vimont wrote of the tribes around Quebec that "Presents . . . despatch all the affairs of the country."[35] With them, anger was assuaged, he wrote; tears, stopped; and entrance obtained into the regions of alien tribes.

As one tribe might present gifts to another in order to pass through or dwell for a time in their territory, so the Jesuits presented gifts to a tribe when contacting it for the first time in order to secure permission to live in the Indian villages. When, in 1645, Isaac Jogues returned to the Iroquois, after having escaped from captivity, he took presents to them for this precise purpose.[36] Such gift-giving by the Jesuits to the Iroquois became routine over the next three decades, and was done in an effort to establish their work among the Iroquois—not always to much avail. Le Mercier wrote of this practice, ". . . one must needs adapt himself to the customs and methods of procedure of those whom he wishes to win, when these customs are not unreasonable . . ."[37] In 1655, when the Jesuits sought to strengthen the peace between the French and their Indian allies on the one hand, and with the Iroquois on the other, a grandoise gift-giving ceremony took place at Onondaga in Iroquois territory. The missionaries presented a gift to remove tears of grief for those lost in battle. Then, the priest:

> . . . to calm their minds, the seat of all these griefs, and, as the seat of the mind is in the head, he made them a crown of the proffered collar which he put on the head of each one successively. At first, they were surprised at this novelty; they were pleased, however, when they saw the Father holding a little kettle, full of an excellent beverage, of which he made them all drink, . . . in order to dispel their grief and apply the remedy to their very hearts and bowels.[38]

Other presents that were offered included a small tree whose upper branches were shorn to signify their prominent men who had been killed in battle. These branches were removed from the trees, ". . . but the tree had many other branches, strong and in full leaf, representing their children, through whom these departed heroes would be restored to life . . ."[39] The fathers reported that this symbolic tree attracted more attention than any of the other gifts.

It is an oversimplification to consider the giving of gifts as merely an attempt by the missionaries to *buy* their way into the Indians' favor, and the superficiality of such a conclusion is readily seen when one considers the symbolic nature of the gift-giving custom within the native cultures. Whether or not the Indians' reaction was as favorable to the presentation of the symbolic tree as the Jesuits related, the fact that such a gift was presented at all illustrates that the only possible value of some of the gifts exchanged was a symbolic one. Besides, the Jesuits themselves were willing recipients of such symbolic gifts. Furthermore, they allowed their use in devotional practice among the converts.

When one of the lay assistants, Jacques Douart, was murdered by Hurons in 1648, a general council of the Hurons met, according to custom, and decreed that presents of reparation must be made to the Jesuits. As the ceremony began, an eloquent oration delivered by an Indian asked the missionaries to state what would restore happiness to them. The missionaries, after being advised by some of the Indian converts on exactly how to respond on such an occasion, presented the Hurons with a bundle of sticks tied together, the number of which indicated how many presents it would take to provide satisfaction. A day was then set aside for the official ingathering of presents to mark the official rite of satisfaction. Such a rite usually lasted for more than a day, and this one was to be no exception. A great crowd gathered on the appointed day at the Jesuit residence of Ste. Marie. Several Huron chiefs, representing all their people, stepped to the door. They first offered a present to the fathers so that the Indians might be allowed in. Other gifts were given to the Jesuits so that all their tears might be removed; that their voices might have kind words; that their minds might be soothed; and that their hearts might be put at ease. These gifts consisted mainly of shells. Then several symbolic gifts were offered to erect a tomb for the deceased—each gift represented a particular part of the Indian-style scaffold-tomb. Another set of gifts was offered, each gift representing the bones of the arms, the thighs, and the feet of the deceased. After these formalities, custom dictated that those wronged make an oratorical response full of righteous anger. In accordance with this custom then,

Ragueneau presented a gift of three thousand glass beads, which he told them:

> . . . was to make their land level, so that it might receive them more gently when they should be overthrown by the violence of the reproaches that I was to address to them for having committed so foul a murder.[40]

The next day, a scaffold was erected, upon which fifty presents were hung, these comprising the substance of the principal act of reparation. Included were symbolic clothing for the dead, a gift symbolizing the fatal hatchet blows, in order that the wound might be closed. The Jesuits performed the last act of the rite by presenting gifts symbolic of their satisfaction that justice was now done, and their hope that any animosity to Christianity would fade. By this, they officially acknowledged that reparations had been done for the wrong they had suffered.[41] The gifts had symbolically expressed sorrow and the restoration of joy.

When an Indian, suspected of thievery, was wounded by a Frenchman at Quebec in 1657, Father Le Moyne applied a plaster to the wound in the shape of a glass bead collar which apparently settled the situation. Tribesmen responded by presenting presents to pay for a Frenchman's cow that they had eaten. The exchange of these presents was symbolic; the Jesuits accepted this and apparently persuaded a few of the French to do likewise.[42]

With obvious important symbolic significance behind the offering of presents, it was an easy matter for this to enter the Indians' perception of, and consequent adaptation of, the Catholic cultus. The Christian teachings concerning sin, repentence, and thanksgiving provided the logical places for this to appear. The fathers taught that although Jesus Christ, the *Agnus dei,* had been sacrificed for the sins of mankind, and consequently had provided the means for the faithful believer to find forgiveness for his sins, the penitent, for his part, had to be truly sorry for his sins and be determined to foresake them. Acts of reparation as signs of sorrow, as signs of thanksgiving, and as signs of gratitude for Christ's sacrifice, were declared to be a necessary part of the faithful Christian's piety. Since rites of reparation were public acts among the Indians, when the convert brought the concept of reparation into a Christian context, the public nature of such an offering was often maintained. A chief at Sillery who had helped a friend get drunk expressed his sorrow by going to Mass where, before both Indians and French, he stopped the priest just as the rite was about to begin and prayed aloud for forgiveness. He then threw a bead collar on the altar step as an act of atonement. This was reported with approval by the Jesuits.[43] Similar presents were made to seek God's favor or the Virgin's prayers in times of sickness, need, and thanksgiving.[44]

In 1675 at the Huron village of Lorette, the Indians adopted the custom of making special offerings on Good Friday, a practice the Indians had witnessed in French Quebec. The Indians, however, echoing overtones from their own tradition of funerary gift-giving, said that they offered presents on that day to the Virgin, to "wipe away the tears that she sheds for the death of her first-born . . ."[45]

In the west, around the Great Lakes, the giving of gifts to God and the Blessed Virgin as a form of reparation had an equally prominent place. In 1679 when a cross was damaged at Saint-Ignace Mission at Mackinac, the Indians placed a glass bead collar on the arms of a crucifix to express their regret.[46] That same year, it was reported that the Indians customarily offered glass beads to Jesus Christ in order to unite their own offering with his offering for sin in the sacrifice of the Mass.[47] By the final years of the century, Jesuit chapels in the St. Lawrence Valley, as well as in the west, were laden with this type of offering. Beaded belts, collars, and small colored glass tubes covered the walls, beams, and the altars themselves.[48]

Among all tribes north of Mexico, the concept of the feast played an important role. A feast might be a part of an occasion as serious as a religious commemoration or as lighthearted as a simple event staged by a child for his playmates. Some feasts were meant to insure the success of the planting; others, to celebrate the season when the corn matured or when it was eaten for the first time.

The Iroquois held feasts from time to time just to insure that the spiritual power resident in their shamanism did not die out. Other feasts were given for the benefit of the dead. However, most frequently feasts occurred to commemorate an event such as the completion of a house, the curing of a sick person, the naming of a child, or some other joyous event.[49] Feasts might, as among the Hurons, be given to announce any joyous or sorrowful event.[50] They were held when individuals approached death. The feasts, whether given to announce joy or sorrow, consisted of ladling out to all present whatever was cooking in the kettle. The meal was accompanied by much oratory and usually some singing and dancing. Various invocations of deities or spirits were common during the proceedings. When Le Jeune first arrived among the Indians of Quebec, he compared their feasts to those of the ancient Greeks who, he said, feasted amidst simplicity, without the pretense of later times.[51]

177

Other than the dedication of feasts to the spirit-gods, and nakedness or orgiastic behavior, only one aspect of the Indian feast did the Jesuits condemn.[52] This was the so-called *eat all* method of feasting, in which the participants had to eat until all food was consumed, even though regurgitation might have to be induced in order to accomplish this feat. To the missionaries, this was the sin of gluttony and was to be avoided by their converts just as were murder, adultery, thievery, and lying. Although the missionaries condemned this aspect of native feasting, they soon began to adopt the feast itself as a part of Christian observance. For example, a feast in native fashion was given in the Huron country at the time of the baptism of the first adult not baptized in illness.[53] During the winter of 1637-38 at Ossossané, Brébeuf began to use the feast as a means of presenting his views to the village leaders. An impressive native-style feast was held at Ossossané on the solemnity of the Immaculate Conception on December 8, the patronal day of their village chapel. The village leaders agreed to sponsor other feasts themselves, at which the Jesuits' teachings could be presented. On January 9, 1638, the head chief sponsored a feast for various prominent men at which he further extolled Christianity and announced plans for other feasts in its honor. At the next feast, Brébeuf delivered a lengthy discourse. Soon after this, several families gave feasts in order to officially announce their intention of embracing Christianity.[54]

The missionaries themselves gave the *atsataion,* or "farewell feast," when the outbreak of disease among the Hurons, blamed on the missionaries by the Indians, brought the fathers threats of death. This feast was customarily given by the Indians as death approached. The fathers assured the villagers of Ossossané that they were prepared to die rather than flee these threats, and to vividly illustrate this readiness, Brébeuf gave the atsat-aion. The whole village was invited and the residence overflowed with guests, who maintained a mournful silence. The missionaries used the occasion to speak on the Christian doctrine of the future life. In the face of their determination not to run away, the threats dissipated for the time being.[55]

It follows, of course, if the missionaries themselves gave such a feast, that their converts continued to do so as well. In 1649 Ragueneau wrote of a Christian Huron mother who gave such a feast for her son, also a Christian, as he approached death. The missionaries approved of such feasts as occasions when the convert's belief might be declared before his fellow villagers.[56]

At baptismal feasts, which were frequently given, the local customs were followed. De Quen, at Sillery, records giving such a solemn feast. In accordance with a Montagnais custom, he solemnly presented to the guests, for their approval, each ingredient with which he intended to season the sagamité; and just before adding it, he would wait for their approval, an approval which they signified by shouts of "ho!"[57] At Sillery, the Christians continued to give the condolence feast when death occurred in the village or among a nomadic tribe encamped near them. Vimont recorded in 1642 that a feast was given by the Sillery Christians to console some Algonquins who had lost several warriors to the Iroquois. The feast followed all the native customs, but with the inclusion of Christian prayers and orations that were centered around the Jesuits' teachings. Presents were distributed to aid in drying the Algonquins' tears, to "resuscitate" or restore life to the nephew of a leading Algonquin and to express the host's desire that more among them might embrace Christianity.[58]

Feasts were often given before going into battle,

and the converts continued to give such feasts and participate in them. They might use the occasion for urging the acceptance of the missionaries' teachings or else to declare the determination and valor of Christian warriors.[59]

The fathers did not disapprove of their converts' continuing to give traditional feasts following recovery from illness; and these, of course, provided additional occasions when Christian doctrine could be declared to a large group, or when the mercies and power of God could be proclaimed—particularly if the cure had in any way seemed miraculous.[60]

In addition to the regular occasions in an Indian's life when a feast was customary, converts began to give them on occasions that were important to their new religion. Since most of the converts took a saint's name at their baptism in addition to their original name, that saint's day in the Catholic liturgical calendar provided an obvious occasion for a feast in native style. Vimont, writing of such feasts, had nothing to say but praise:

> [these] . . . feasts . . . served not a little to confirm the fervor of our Christians. In fine, these generally consist of . . . a great kettle or two of Indian corn, or of peas, with a quarter moose or of beaver, according to the number of those invited, and they make them in order to comfort one another in their poverty, and to bestow charity upon one another—insomuch that to make a feast is at the present the same here as to feed those who are in necessity, and to exercise an act of mercy.[61]

The feast, then, served a didactic purpose and also was an obvious means of feeding people, a work of mercy in times of famine.

A convert might also give a feast to announce

his joy upon going to confession and receiving absolution, especially if his conscience had been particularly troubled by any matter.[62] A feast might also be given to declare a rededication to one's faith in the midst of opposition by family or village.[63]

The missionaries themselves continued throughout the period to use the feast for various didactic purposes. Father Pierre Millet, among the Iroquois at Onondaga during the late 1660s, gave a feast on Sundays to point out the special significance of that day and to expound his teachings in a context that was both familiar and attractive to the villagers. The Iroquois sang as they prepared a feast, so Millet did likewise, singing, he said, of "the mercies of God, the coming of the Savior into the world, and the victory that he gained over the demons."[64] Among the displaced Hurons near Quebec in the 1670s, it became the custom to hold a great Easter feast in native style. The Jesuits were eager to amalgamate tribal traditions with Christian observances. A woman is quoted thusly in the *Relations* of 1672:

> My Father, I beg your approval of my plan to give a feast today [Easter] to the principal people of the village, in testimony of our joy at the glorious Resurrection of our Lord. You know our custom: when one of our allies has escaped from the enemies' clutches, we give him, after making the whole village ring with shouts of joy at his arrival, a feast of the best things we have, to show him our delight at his happy deliverance. Should we do less for our Lord Jesus Christ, who today comes to us in the glory of his Resurrection, after freeing himself from his enemies' hands? It seems to me, my Father, that it would be . . . an intolerable instance of ingratitude on our part to neglect this duty.[65]

The words no doubt reflect the views of the missionaries as much as those of the Indian quoted. The amalgamation of rites took place with the Huron victor's feast now set amidst singing and Christian prayers.

In the distant regions of the west, Jacques Gravier, at the Immaculate Conception Mission near present-day Peoria, Illinois, used the feast as a means of preaching in complete frankness to a large number of people. He was among the Peorias, one of the principal tribes of the Illinois confederation of Indians of Algonquian derivation.[66] Since among this tribe it was customary that the giver of a feast was free to say whatever he wished without fear of giving offense, Gravier used the feast to severely upbraid by name some of his neophytes for their lack of zeal in keeping the tenets of the faith. He saw such an occasion as being ideal for presenting his teachings with great boldness and declared to his lax neophytes the mortal danger of turning away or rejecting the faith.[67]

By the 1640s, the Jesuits in the Huron country and those at the missions along the St. Lawrence also began to take a more lenient view toward feasts with a pagan motif. If converts' attendance at feasts dedicated to "demons" was likely to engender in the unconverted a favorable attitude toward Christianity, then attendance was advised. Even attendance at the "eat-all" feast was not always opposed. This more lenient attitude evident in the 1640s has already been cited.[68] The "eat-all" feast could be attended so long as the Indians avoided gluttony; however, converts could not host such feasts since, presumably, the unconverted would commit gluttony, and the convert would have provided the occasion for sin. Le Jeune also recorded that the Indians around Quebec were exhorted to use the "eat-all' feasts, which were often given to bring health to someone stricken with serious illness, as a means of feeding the destitute or sick among them. Le Jeune freely admitted that, in that region at least, they could ". . . do away gradually with this superstition . . ." and that the best course to take was to at least introduce some virtue into it by making it a means of charity.[69]

The *resuscitation* rite was common to the Hurons, Iroquois, Montagnais and Algonguins. When a man died, his resposibilities, name, and honors were bestowed upon someone deemed worthy of them, and the one receiving these gifts was thenceforth referred to as if he were that person. The chosen successor gave his previous name to a relative and was never called by it again. This rite was carried on in the midst of great feasting and giving of presents to the "resuscitated" Indian. This individual often believed it incumbent upon him to perform some notable exploit, if the one resuscitated in him was particularly valorous, so as to prove that he had inherited more than just the name of the deceased.[70] Following this ceremony, all mourning for the deceased stopped. Since this ceremony conceivably might imply some concept of reincarnation, it is, at first glance, surprising that almost from the start the missionaries had no difficulty with this native rite, and, in fact, praised it highly. To their satisfaction, the custom in no way signified a belief in reincarnation, but was seen as a means of perpetuating the name and memory of the deceased and for providing for the care of widows and orphans; this could only be praiseworthy, Le Jeune wrote in 1639.[71] Both the missionaries and their converts participated in these rites, and a Christianized version resulted.[72] The fathers also used such occasions to advance the faith before the unconverted. When an unconverted chief was resuscitated in his convert brother in the Huron country in 1642, the missionaries took an active part in the native ceremonies.

As the gifts were presented, each one said what he hoped the gift would do for the resuscitated warrior. The priests presented several gifts, and with the presentation of the most valuable, one of them uttered the following:

> The gift is intended to restore the Voice of the deceased, but a Voice that will no longer be the Demon's to proclaim and command forbidden Ceremonies—I say, a Voice worthy of a Christian, who loves and encourages every one to defend his Country, to overthrow Impiety, and to promulgate the Holy Gospel.[73]

The fathers sought to instill in the converts a symbolic relationship between the resuscitation rite and the Church's doctrine of the resurrection of Jesus Christ and of the faithful Christians. This was particularly appropriate if the deceased had been a convert; then the resuscitation rite became an "image" of the resurrection, a time when tears should truly be put away. Much oratory to this effect by convert tribal leaders accompanied their "Christianized" rite. At one such rite, at Sillery, following the orations, one convert chief began to sing various Indian chant melodies to which he set new words: "He who is to bring me back to life is he who consoles me." Le Jeune said of it all, "God grant that they may of themselves change their ancient customs into actions replete weith devotion and piety."[74]

When the Huron preacher, Joseph Chihwatenhwa, was killed by the Iroquois in 1640, his brother soon sought baptism and was given the name Joseph, the baptismal name his brother had borne. The missionaries obviously sought to build upon the ideas surrounding the rite of resuscitation, for Lalemant wrote that the name was given ". . . in the hope we had that the virtue of his late brother, as well as his name, might be made to live again in his person."[75]

The converts were also encouraged to draw a parallel between the passing on of certain characteristics at the rite of resuscitation, and the taking of a saint's name at baptism; the convert was to imitate the saint as the native had been taught to imitate the deceased whose name he bore.

Father Thierry Beschefer,[76] as he worked among the Hurons then near Quebec in 1666, was the means by which Isaac Jogues was "resuscitated" among his former neophytes. The Hurons had named Jogues during his lifetime, "Ondesonk," and this name was duly passed to Beschefer in the resuscitation rite. The new Ondesonk wrote:

> I have changed my language and my name, and at present I am called Ondessonk [*sic*] which means "a bird of prey." Such is the name that the Hurons have given me, and which was born by Father Isaac Jogues . . . Pray God that he may make me inherit his virtues, as I have his name. My baptism took place on the feast of St. Francis Xavier, after I had myself baptized 2 savages . . . it was necessary, before getting . . . [my name] to have a great feast . . . They sang, they danced; in a word, they observed all the ceremonies of the savages.[77]

This was in a "Christian" village, thirty years after the arrival of the permanent Jesuit mission among the Hurons.

It was not destruction of the Indian cultures which the Jesuits set out to accomplish, but a change "in their ancient customs" which would communicate and celebrate the new teachings in forms that the tribal cultures had produced. Native oratorical customs were respected and utilized, and the new religion was skillfully communicated through the dance, gift-giving customs, and festal observances, which tribal traditions dictated. While the Puritan effort in North America during the same period had grave theological difficulty with any concept of a festival connected with religious observance,[78] without this philosophical barrier the Jesuits entered into the social life of the tribes and were able to put the forms of social intercourse to the use of their own didactic purpose.

VIII

Style and Substance

In the foregoing chapters, it has been shown how the Jesuit fathers respected, participated in, and adapted to the cultural environment around them as they worked among the Indian tribes in the seventeenth century. During the early part of this period, they experimented in fostering cultural contact between the Indians and the French. By mid-century they had rejected such contact on almost all levels, and had become an opposing force to those who favored *civilizing* the Indians in the European manner. As will be shown, they exerted this opposition at the risk of jeopardizing their order's standing with the civil authorities, both in Quebec and in Paris.

During their early period of contact with the Indians, the missionaries believed that their purposes could best be accomplished if the nomadic tribes were encouraged to become sedentary. Prior to their contact with Europeans, the Hurons were sedentary, but the Montagnais and Algonquins were nomadic. It appeared to the missionaries that the ordered life of a village was a better context for the advancement of the faith—they found it much more difficult to instruct nomadic tribes, who were almost constantly on the move.

The idea of French colonists coming to the New World and settling among the Indians was popular with the Jesuit leadership during the 1630s. The presence of the French, it was felt, would aid in the acculturation process; moreover, it would afford added protection for the Indians against the onslaught of the Iroquois. From the writings of Le Jeune it is possible to get an insight into what the Jesuits at this time hoped for: some colonists, not in large numbers, who would live among or near the Indians and help them in the cultivation of the soil:

> . . . men to clear and cultivate the land, who . . . would work for the Savages, on condition that they would settle down and themselves put their hands to the work, living in houses that would be built for their use; by this means becoming located, and seeing this miracle of charity in their behalf, they could be more easily instructed and won.[1]

Also, the presence of French colonists among tribes that were threatened by hostile Iroquois might cause the Paris government to send enough soldiers to the New World to permanently remove a threat which the fathers early saw as potentially destructive to all of their hopes. In the mid-1630s there was a positive response to this desire for colonists,[2] and by the 1640s a few dozen soldiers were stationed at Ste. Marie in the Huron territory. But a few dozen soldiers was hardly an effective force against the Iroquois; and the influx of colonists proved to be a disappointment. Le Jeune wrote, "It is to be feared that in the multiplication of our French, in these countries, peace, happiness, and good feeling may not increase in the same ratio as do the inhabitants of New France."[3] Still, he believed the possible good to be achieved by this colonization outweighed the problems.

Most of the French who moved out into the Indian country, however, were fur traders, not settlers.

They were hardly less nomadic than the Indians them-selves. The establishment of the Indian village of Sillery near Quebec was to provide a gathering point for Indians who wished, at least part of the year, to forsake their nomadic life-style. Yet, even here, the Indians were free to come and go at will and appear to have forsaken their nomadic ways only when it suited them to do so.[4] Their style of dress for the most part remained Indian—the neophytes went to Mass each morning wrapped in blan-kets, which served both as bedcover and garment.[5] French-style cottages were built for some Indians by 1643, but most of the natives continued to live in their traditional bark houses.[6]

French civil officials in Quebec encouraged the Indians to elect chiefs to govern them while they were in residence at Sillery, and the Jesuits helped the Indians organize the first election for village leaders in 1640. Since most of the Sillery Indians were converts by that time, the positions all went to Christians, although the chiefs did appoint one non-Christian to the relatively important position of overseer of the young men; but even he shared this duty with a convert.[7]

A similar attempt to establish a French-style village was begun for the Algonquins at Three Rivers in 1640, but it met with little success and ultimately fell victim to the Iroquois onslaught.[8]

In 1637 missionaries began to operate a school for Huron youths at Quebec. Since they believed at this time that Christianity might be easier to instill in the young Indian if he were taken out of the pagan context and brought into close contact with the Christian French, the young Hurons were housed in the French manner, clothed as young Frenchmen, and assigned beds that were covered with linen. The French colonists were pleased to see these youths aping French ways, and for a

189

time the young Indians seemed to enjoy it as well. To a certain extent, no doubt, this school was an agency of French culture, but the fathers remained pragmatic in their approach to teaching their charges, whose cultural differences they appreciated.

The Huron seminary was not a carbon copy of European pedagogical enterprises typical of the time. The missionaries often wrote that restraints imposed from without were foreign to the American aborigines; therefore, their seminary, in order to function at all, had to allow for what Europeans might consider great laxity. If a boy really wanted to leave the school, he could. Furthermore, he was allowed to retain what had been given him in the way of clothing and personal items.

The native propensity to overindulge in food, when it was available, repelled the Jesuits at first, but it was tolerated, and the youths were gently cared for when this overindulgence led to sickness. Hunting in the nearby woods was permitted each afternoon. If hunting did not suit them, they could make bows and arrows; fish; work at cultivating a crop; or do "anything else that is agreeable to them."[9] Absence without permission at other times was even tolerated.

By 1639, the missionaries had also established a school for Algonquin and Montagnais youths where they, too, could be shielded from the temptation of their former religion and could be housed in a European fashion.[10] But education of youths in the ways of Christianity, not Europeanization *per se*, was the real motive behind these schools.

After only a few years, however, the missionaries became convinced that almost any contact with the French was damaging to the moral and religious well-being of the Indians. Even as Le Jeune wrote of his hopes regarding colonization and the possibility of making nomadic tribes sedentary, he expressed his fears of evil European influence. This influence, he felt, could be far more debilitating to Jesuit missionary efforts than the nomadism of the tribes. But, he wrote, the Jesuits would never forsake the nomadic Indians.[11]

Although the Jesuits never opposed intermarriage between the Indians and the French (provided both were good Catholics) they seem only to have encouraged such marriages as a kind of policy of missionary strategy in the 1630s and early 1640s, and only when they had hoped that contact with the French might create a stable atmosphere for their work. Thereafter, such marriages were put on the same basis as any marriage which had the prospects of being stable according to the teachings of the Catholic church.

Ultimately, the Jesuits viewed Indian contact with the French as something to be avoided. In the 1670s and 1680s they pursued this policy of non-contact in direct opposition to the Paris authorities and the local governor, Count Frontenac. Forces from some quarters within the Catholic church opposed the Jesuits on this matter as well. The Recollect missionary, Father Hennepin, and the English Puritans of New England would have been in full accord on the necessity of Europeanizing the Indians as a precondition to conversion.[12] Hennepin wrote:

> These tribes must absolutely first be civilized to make them embrace Christianity, for so long as Christians are not absolutely their masters we shall see little success, without a most special grace of God, without a miracle which he does not work in regard to all nations.[13]

Frontenac and Jean Baptiste Colbert both favored the Recollect Order and its Indian work in North America over the Jesuits and their missionary efforts.[14] Hennepin's words leave little reason to question why.

The Jesuits, after only a few years, decided that instead of passing on to the Indians practices that were compatible with, and supportive of, Catholicism, the French settlers tended to pass on practices that were considered to be destructive elements from European civilization. Even the integrity of Catholic doctrine was not secure around some of the French. Le Jeune, in 1639, decried the fact that some of the French had beliefs, such as wearing amulets about the neck for the curing of disease, that were as foreign to Christianity as were many of the native customs.[15] Most of the Jesuits' opposition to contact with the French, however, rested upon French immorality and the sale of intoxicants to the Indians.

From the beginning of their work in French North America, the Jesuits pressed the colonial authorities to forbid the sale of brandy and wine or any other alcoholic beverage to the Indians. In 1639 Le Jeune wrote approvingly of colonial policy against such trade, saying that without such opposition, the ruination of the Indians would surely result.[16] While the civil authorities suppressed this traffic at Quebec during the 1630s and 1640s, the sale of alcohol tended to go on unmolested in the hinterland, although the Jesuits continually castigated the brandy merchants and traders as enemies of the faith. Any Frenchman involved in this illicit trade, declared the *Relation* for 1642, could receive no "great blessing from Heaven, since they raise an obstacle against the Blood of Jesus Christ, by preventing it from sanctifying these poor Souls."[17] In the late 1650s, the Jesuits were ardent supporters of Bishop Laval in Quebec who sought to impose the penalty of excommunication upon all involved in supplying intoxicants to the Indians.[18] During this period a few Frenchmen were flogged or executed for dealing in this traffic.[19]

Separation from the French, rather than close contact or assimilation, became the Jesuit ideal for their converts. All European contact in their view became suspect: the English, they believed, considered the Indians beasts; and the Dutch, who traded with them and supplied them with rifles, drove them from their churches, or so the missionaries thought.[20] And their own fellow Frenchmen were just as destructive in different ways. For this reason the Jesuit Louys Nicolas[21] took his flock of Algonquins into the interior in 1667, in an attempt to protect them from the influence of French settlers along the St. Lawrence, an influence that seemed only to produce among the natives drunkenness and immorality.[22]

This movement on the part of the Jesuits came at the very time Louis XIV and Colbert were intent on "civilizing" the Amerind according to European standards. The bishop of Quebec, in cooperation with this desire, established at Quebec in the late 1660s a school where Indian children were to be taught French ways. He sought to enhance the process of acculturation by having French children attend the same school. But the Jesuits soon came under fire from authorities in Paris for their unrelenting opposition to the brandy traffic and for their failure to spread civilization in their schools as well as in their mission enterprises.[23] As discussed in chapter one, the clash of aims between the Paris government and the Jesuits was a major source of Governor Frontenac's opposition to their work, a work, he charged, that had failed to convey to the Indians even the rudiments of French civilization. He complained that even after almost forty years of being exposed to the French-Jesuit influence, the converts at Sillery, so close to Quebec, hardly had any knowledge of the French language and that they had retained the habits, food, and dress of their native past. The priests at Sillery, he said, were content to teach Catholicism in that uncivilized context.[24]

When Jean de Lamberville[25] presented his draft *Relation* for the years 1672 and 1673 to the superior, Father Dablon, Dablon first edited out of it all that could be construed by anyone as anything favoring Colbert's policy, before sending it on to the Jesuit authorities in France and Rome. Furthermore, he added an account to this document, which he penned himself, of how French influence threatened the very existence of the Jesuit missions. He marvelled that the mission at La Prairie, so close to the French along the St. Lawrence, had not already been destroyed by the sale of brandy to the Indians and by other acts of the colonists. Sale of intoxicants "has ruined the Algonquin missions; and it still prevents many Savages from being converted." He went on to say that the ". . . insatiable avarice of the French" led some colonists to go hundreds of miles to cheat an Indian out of his furs by getting him drunk.[26]

By 1682 conditions were such that the priests at Sillery exhorted the villagers to have nothing to do with the French at nearby Quebec, in order to avoid alcoholic contamination and other misconduct.[27] The same year, from upriver near Montreal, at St. Francis Xavier Mission, Claude Chauchetiere[28] wrote that the French were giving him and his flock "much trouble," and that whereas the converts once thought the French were good Christians, they now saw them as the opposite.[29] He wrote his brother some years later in 1694 that the Jesuits and their flocks would be far better off if they could divorce themselves in everyway from the corrupting influence of "civilized nations." "We all desire," he wrote, "as did St. Francis Xavier, to see ourselves so far away from the French with our beloved savages that we may no longer have such stumbling blocks.''[30] What was good and fine in the Indian was soon corrupted by the European, he concluded.

The Jesuit outcry against French influence continued on into the eighteenth century. Military garrisons, of which there had been so few during the struggle with the Iroquois, had become more plentiful by the turn of the century. Now, however, this was only to the dismay of the missionaries. Far from being a help, these French enclaves became centers of all the evil influences European civilization could heap upon their neophytes. In 1702 Father Étienne de Carheil[31] wrote the governor in Quebec from Saint-Ignace mission at Mackinac that the missionaries might as well abandon their missions, since they could not compete with the brandy traffic the government allowed to emanate from the military garrisons. He wrote that the garrisons should be withdrawn, for they had become a combination of taverns, headquarters for brandy traders and peddlers, brothels that employed native women, and gambling houses where brawls frequently occurred. This, he said, had gone on for years and had made the work of nearby missions difficult, if not impossible. The moral impact on the Indians was extremely destructive.[32]

Because the Jesuits hoped to transform nomadic tribes into sedentary village dwellers, to educate young Indians, and to provide defense against the Iroquois, they did wish for a time to bring the aborigines into contact with Europeans. This attitude existed in the 1630s and to some extent in the 1640s. The Jesuits, however, soon realized that such contact was detrimental to the practice of Christianity among the neophytes, and began to oppose extensive European contact with the Indians.

Ultimately, the Jesuits refused to see either

themselves or their work as agents of Europeanization, and they opposed the exploitation of the aborigines by their fellow Europeans. They were willing to take such a stand in spite of the opposition from civil authorities in Paris and Quebec, who sought to use the Jesuits and their work to foster cultural assimilation.

As Cotton Mather put it, God had called his reformers, the Puritans, to the isolated New World—a place free of Old World corruptions—in order that they might set up a church to be a light to the churches of the Old World.[33] Ironically, the French Jesuits came to have a similar hope that they might set up churches among the various tribes, which, if kept isolated from European moral corruption, might outshine European Christianity in morality, piety, and devotion, and point the way for "spiritual reformation."

IX

Conclusion

In North America the French Jesuits of the seventeenth century contradicted two major trends of the European world from which they came. First, on the material level, they showed themselves willing and able in almost every way to become savages among savages, a thing particularly difficult for the French of the *grand* century to do.[1] Second, the Jesuits both championed and conveyed to their Indian converts a faith based on the premise that the natural world and the invisible, eternal order were inexorably bound together. They did this at a time when many Christians were losing the conceptual understanding of this unity. The intellectual life of western Europe was being caught up in an emerging Deism, which tended to divorce the activity and intervention of God from the daily life of man and the mechanical universe in which man was seen to exist. According to this concept of God, the Creator in a limited sense might be said to re-create the world and to conserve it, but not to interfere with it, or to change the workings of nature.[2] This concept was antithetical to the Jesuits' teachings.

The Jesuits' willingness to accept and participate in the life-style of the savages was influenced by their concept and understanding of the nature of man. While Calvinists believed that original sin had so corrupted every faculty of body and soul to the extent that man without the intervention of divine grace was incapable of any good,[3] the Jesuits held to the common pre-Reformation view that, in spite of the 'fall,' man still possessed some residual good. Through the use of reason men and women could apprehend and choose right actions. They might even, through reason, have an inchoate understanding of God. Brébeuf said that although certain pagan Indians were ignorant, they, nevertheless, honored the true God.[4] If the pagan or savage possessed some generic or natural good, it was incumbent upon the missionary not to deny its existence but rather to seek it out and build upon it. The existence of this good provided a ready foundation, endemic to the native culture, upon which a native Christianity could be built. The assumed existence of this good made the lice, filth, cold, starvation, and threat of an excrutiatingly painful death easier for the Jesuits to bear, and it helped produce an example of self-sacrifice which even some of the Jesuits' detractors have admired.[5] Since this good was present in the Indians by virtue of their creation by God, their ignorance of the accouterments of modern civilization—European customs, dress, and lifestyle in general—was not a consequential factor. Indeed, it has been shown that in seventeenth-century French America, the Jesuits finally came to oppose all efforts aimed at the frenchification of the Indians.

From the start of their missionary labors among the Indians, even when their shock of cultural change was at its height, these educated French Jesuits expressed the conviction that the Creator had left his mark upon the pagan, primitive Amerind.

To the Jesuits, the languages of the Indians were signs of divine activity among them and their ancestors. In 1646 Jérôme Lalemant wrote in his report that he found grammatical construction of the Indian languages both intricate and admirable. This was further evidence, he wrote, of the existence of God. No human wisdom, in his estimation, could have caused so many people to develop the intricate order around which the native languages centered, an order entirely unlike that of any European language. Only God could have supplied such order and guided its development in a people.[6] The presence of the Creator's activity among the Indians since the beginning of time had insured a richness in their languages, a richness Le Jeune first described in the early 1630s.[7] Any language which had developed under divine guidance could, without doubt, convey the truths of Christianity. Christianity was not bound by either French or Latin. Any language, including Indian dialects, through which an appeal could be made to reason, would suffice. Indeed, wrote Lalemant in 1648, the Indians' minds were so endowed with the divinely inspired quality of reason that they "relished" the arguments that the missionaries presented to them.[8]

Although the Indians possessed reason and might even have a shadowy idea of the existence of the true God, the native religions, of course, were corrupt and the Indians' salvation could be assured only if they converted to the religion preached by the Jesuits. Yet, here again, the missionaries came to develop a degree of respect for the corrupt religions of the natives, for they came to see in them more than just the naive imaginings of primitive people. The native religions were demonic in the missionaries' view, and they came to believe that Satan communicated directly with at least some of the tribal shamans. Such demonic intervention in the lives of the Indians could not be ignored, but called for confrontation on the Jesuits' part. If the Indians' understanding of existence were based on the premise that supernatural forces intervened in the daily events of human life, then the Jesuits, to a significant extent, were prepared to agree. In so doing, of course, they had much more in common with the Indian and his world than with the emerging seventeenth-century European deist.

Although the Jesuits believed that, in general, whatever provided the power within native shamanistic rites was evil or Satanic in origin, and although, of course, they were certain that the operative forces within their own cultus were of God, His saints, and the angelic host, the point is that they also believed a spiritual force existed within the native rites, and it was this that they sought to supplant. As this evil force sometimes manifested its presence in the physical world, so, they believed, the divine power at the heart of Christianity revealed its power in the physical order through the sacraments of the Catholic church; and, at times, in miracles, signs, and visions. When Father Le Jeune wrote lightheartedly of confronting the devil in an Indian village in 1634, it was not because he did not take the incident seriously, but because as a priest Le Jeune accepted it as a rather simple and commonplace event. There was no fear on Le Jeune's part because, as he told the Indians, the devil was powerless before those who believed in God. While he was not certain at this time as to the extent to which Satan revealed himself to the Indians, he had no doubt that Satan did reveal himself in their physical world. He was just as certain that Satan feared Catholics and was powerless in the presence of the faithful.[9] Jérôme Lalemant concluded in 1647 that the missionaries' work among the Indians had verified the words of St. Paul that are found in the sixth chapter of Ephesians and are concerned with the warfare true Christians are bound to carry on against the evil forces of the spiritual world.[10]

In combating these spiritual opponents, the Jesuits were convinced that divine supernatural intervention came to their aid, not only by giving the missionaries strength of will but by giving definite signs which Jérôme Lalemant called extraordinary favors.[11] These "favors" took the form of various kinds of miracles; for instance, the ability to temporarily speak or understand a native language beyond one's ordinary ability to do so; or to experience a miraculous healing following the use or application of holy water, the crucifix, or a sacred relic of a saint or a person for whom canonization was deemed a real possibility.[12]

The *combat* waged by the Jesuits against native religious beliefs was, therefore, fought within a world in which spiritual forces made themselves known to men and sometimes altered the ordinary course of physical existence.

Since the missionaries believed that good existed within the native culture and that, therefore, the foundation for a native Christianity existed among the Indians, they did not hesitate to adopt native social forms such as the dance, or the ceremony of exchanging gifts, or any native religious ceremonies if these could be separated from pagan imagery. The ritual use of tobacco at solemn gatherings of dignitaries was accepted by the missionaries and certain forms of this ceremony were possibly spread by them to tribes living farther to the west.[13]

As the Jesuits did in other areas of the world, so did the Jesuits in French America seek to make the natives themselves vehicles for the new faith by encouraging them to become preachers, teachers, or lay administrators in the missions.[14] In addition, wherever they could conscientiously do so, the fathers adapted the Catholic cultus itself to the native life-style.

The belief that residual good existed among the Indian tribes not only strengthened the missionaries' willingness to adopt a primitive life-style themselves but led them to reject almost all contact between the French and the Indian converts whenever it was possible to do so. In the Jesuits' view it was all too likely that the French would introduce the Indians to the corruptions that plagued European society. If any proof is needed of the veracity of their published reports from the North American missions during the years from 1632 to 1672, it can be found in the fact that these reports show a resolve to respect Indian culture and adapt to it when at all possible, even though the Paris government opposed this approach and called more and more for a policy of "Europeanizing" the Indians. In their reports published in Paris during these years, the missionaries gave detailed descriptions of the costumes, mores, and beliefs of the Indians at least twenty-one times.[15] The missionaries made no attempt in these reports to cloud the fact that the government's approach to the Indians was not their own.

The Jesuits' emphasis on the principle of seeking good and building upon it gave a vitality to their missionary efforts never equaled by the Puritans of New England. In the seventeenth-century writings of the Jesuit missionaries there is evidence of an acute consciousness of sin and evil by both the missionary authors themselves and the Indians around them. Yet this concern does not reach the levels of morbidity found in the writings of the Puritan divines who, perhaps because of their conviction of their own natural total depravity, seem locked in a dismal self-searching introspection. Perhaps the perpetual concern over salvation, set in a context where salvation was always in doubt, so drained the Puritans' spiritual energy and zeal that there was little of either left for any large scale efforts at converting the Indians. (This is certainly exemplified in their revivalistic concern in the eighteenth century.)[16] The Jesuits, while at times extremely conscious of sin, seem to have been, to a far greater degree, impelled beyond themselves. Without the concept of natural man's total depravity, they seem to achieve great joy in describing what they believed were praiseworthy reflections of the divine image in a pagan people who were also, by European standards, both primitive and savage.

During the seventeenth century, when the Jesuits labored in French North America, a fellow Jesuit, Matthew Ricci, worked in China—against what proved to be insurmountable odds—to establish Christianity in a Chinese framework. What was written of him by a modern Jesuit historian could also have been written of Le Jeune, Jogues, Brébeuf, Marquette, and numerous other French missionaries in North America:

> He realized that grace does not operate in a vacuum. It makes use of human instrumentalities; it moves in a thousand mysterious ways "its wonders to perform." It is the duty of those instrumentalities to put no obstacles in the way of the operation of grace, and to scorn no means, provided in itself good, which might serve, by whatever winding ways, to carry grace and inspiration to human souls.[17]

Appendix A

Biographical Data of French Jesuit Missionaries Cited in this Work[1]

Claude Allouez. Born at St. Didier-en-Forest, France, in 1622, Allouez entered the Society of Jesus at Toulouse in 1639 and went to French North America in 1658.[2] He died at his mission among the Miamis near present-day Niles, Michigan in 1689.

Louis André. Born on May 28, 1631, at Saint-Remy, Bouches-du-Rhône, André entered the Society of Jesus on September 12, 1650, at Lyon and went to French North America in 1669. He worked among the Ottawas in the 1670s and 1680s. He died on September 19, 1715 at Quebec.[3]

Jacques Bertric. Bertric joined the Society of Jesus in 1580 and in 1626 was closely associated with the Jesuit provincial of France, Pierre Coton. He was later rector of the Jesuit colleges at Bourges and Rouen. He died in 1639.[4]

Thierry Beschefer. Born at Châlons-sur-Marne, France, in 1630, Beschefer entered the Society of Jesus at Nancy in 1647. He arrived at Quebec in 1665 and returned to France in 1690. He died at Rheims in 1711.

Pierre Biard. Born at Grenoble, circa 1567, Biard entered the Society of Jesus in 1583 and arrived in Acadia in 1611. After his capture by the English in 1613, he returned to France and died at Avígnon in 1622.

Vincent Bigot. Born at Bourges on May 15, 1649, Bigot entered the Society of Jesus at Paris on September 2, 1664. He worked in Canada from 1680 to 1713, when he returned to France. He died at Paris on September 7, 1720.

Étienne Binet. Binet was the Jesuit provincial of France from 1636 to 1638.[5]

Jean de Brébeuf. Born in France in 1593, Brébeuf entered the Society of Jesus in 1617 and first arrived at Quebec in 1625. After years of missionary activity among the Hurons, he was killed in 1649 by the Iroquois at St. Ignace village, located in what is now Simcoe County, Ontario. He was canonized by Pope Pius XI in 1930.

Frances Joseph Bressani. Born at Rome in 1612, Bressani entered the Society of Jesus there in 1626. He went to French North America in 1642 and returned to France in 1650. He died at Florence in 1672.

Jacques Buteux. Born at Abbeville in 1600, Buteux entered the Society of Jesus at Rouen in 1620. In 1634, he went to French North America and was killed by the Iroquois in 1652.

Étienne de Carheil. Born at the Château de la Guichardaye in Carentoir, France, in 1633, Carheil entered the Society of Jesus in 1652 and went to French North America in 1666. He died at Quebec in 1726.

Noël Chabanel. Chabanel was born in France in the diocese of Mende on February 2, 1613, and joined the Jesuit Order at Toulouse on February 9, 1630. He went to French North America in 1643. While laboring among the Hurons he was killed on December 8, 1649. He was canonized by Pope Pius XI in 1930.

Pierre Chastelain. He was born in France in 1604. After entering the Society of Jesus, he went to French North America in 1636; he died in Quebec in 1684.

Claude Chauchetiere. Born at Saint-Porchaire-de-Poitiers in 1645, Chauchetiere entered the Society of Jesus at Bordeaux in 1663 and went to French North America in 1677. He died at Quebec in 1709.

Pierre-Joseph-Marie Chaumonot. Born at Châtillon-sur-Seine, France, in 1611, Chaumonot entered the Society of Jesus at Rome in 1632. He arrived in Quebec in 1639 and died there in 1693.

Pierre Coton. Born in 1564 at Neronde, France, Coton entered the Society of Jesus and became in turn confessor to both Henry IV and Louis XIII. He became the Jesuit provincial of France in 1624 and died at Paris in 1626.[6]

François de Crepieul. Born in Arras, France, in 1638, he entered the Society of Jesus in 1658 at Tournay. He went to French North America in 1670 and died at Quebec in 1702.

Claude Dablon. Born at Dieppe in 1619, Dablon entered the Society of Jesus in 1639 in Paris. He went to French North America in 1655 and died at Quebec in 1691.

Antoine Daniel. Born at Dieppe in 1601, he entered the Society of Jesus at Rouen in 1621. He arrived at Quebec in 1633. He was killed by the Iroquois in 1648 at the Huron village of Teanaustaiyé, located in what is now Simcoe County, Ontario. In 1930 he was canonized by Pope Paul XI.

Ambrose Davost. After arriving at Quebec from France in 1633, he worked for ten years in French North America. He died aboard ship while returning to France in 1643.

Gabriel Druillettes. Born near Limoges in 1610, Druillettes entered the Society of Jesus at Toulouse in 1629 and went to French North America in 1643. He died at Quebec in 1681.

Charles Garnier. Born in Paris in 1605, Garnier entered the Society of Jesus there in 1624. He arrived in Quebec in 1636 and was killed by the Iroquois in 1649 at the Huron village of St. Jean, or Etharita, in what is now Grey County, Ontario. He was canonized in 1930 by Pope Pius XI.

Jacques Gravier. Born at Moulins, France, in 1651, Gravier entered the Society of Jesus in 1670 at Paris. He went to French North America in 1685 and died in Louisiana in 1708, shortly after his return from a sojourn in France.

Isaac Jogues. Born at Orleans in 1607, he entered the Society of Jesus at Paris in 1624 and first arrived in America in 1636. He was killed by the Iroquois near what is now Auriesville, New York, in 1646. He was canonized by Pope Pius XI in 1930.

Charles Lalemant. Born in Paris in 1587, Lalemant entered the Society of Jesus in 1607 and first arrived in French North America in 1625. In 1638, he left North America for the last time and died in Paris in 1674.

Gabriel Lalemant. Born in Paris on October 10, 1610, Lalemant entered the Society of Jesus there on March 24, 1630. He was the nephew of Charles and Jérôme. Arriving at Quebec in 1646, he went to the Huron country where he was brutally killed by the Iroquois on March 17, 1649. He was canonized by Pope Pius XI in 1930.

Jérôme Lalemant. The brother of Charles, he was born at Paris in 1593, entered the Society of Jesus there in 1610, and arrived at Quebec in 1638. He died there in 1673.

Jean de Lamberville. Born at Rouen in 1633, Lamberville entered the Society of Jesus at Paris in 1656 and went to French North America in 1669. He returned some years later to France and died at Paris in 1714.

Paul Le Jeune. Born in Châlons-sur-Marne, France, in 1591, he entered the Society of Jesus at Rouen in 1613. He came to French North America in 1632 and returned to France in 1649. He died in Paris in 1664.

François Le Mercier. Born at Paris in 1604, Le Mercier entered the Society of Jesus there in 1620 and went to French North America in 1635. Le Mercier was superior of the whole Jesuit mission in New France from 1653-56 and 1665-71. In 1673, he returned to France and went later to the Island of Martinique, where he died in 1690.

Simon Le Moyne. Born in 1604, Le Moyne entered the Society of Jesus at Paris in 1623 and went to French North America in 1638. He died at Three Rivers in 1665.

Jacques Marquette. Born at Laon on June 1, 1637, Marquette entered the Society of Jesus at Nancy in October, 1654. He arrived in America in 1666. He labored in the west from 1668 until his death near present-day Ludington, Michigan on May 18, 1675.[8]

Ennemond Massé. Born at Lyons in 1574, Massé entered the Society of Jesus at Avignon in 1595. He arrived in Acadia in 1611. After being forced by the English to return to France, he came back to French North America and died at Sillery in 1646.

René Ménard. Born at Paris circa 1605, Ménard entered the Society of Jesus in 1642 at Quebec, where he had arrived in 1640. He died in northeastern Wisconsin in 1661.

Pierre Millet. Born in Bourges on November 19, 1635, Millet entered the Jesuit Order on October 3, 1655. He worked in French North America from 1667 until his death at Quebec in 1709.

Louÿs Nicolas. Born at Aubenas, France, in 1634, Nicolas entered the Society of Jesus at Toulouse in 1654. By 1667, he was in French North America with the Algonquins in the St. Lawrence valley. He returned to France in 1675 and left the Society in 1678.

Anne de Nouë. Born in the region of Rheims in 1587, Nouë entered the Society of Jesus at Paris in 1612 and first went to French North America in 1626. While crossing on the ice from Three Rivers to the settlement of Sorel in February, 1646, he was frozen to death.

Henri Nouvel. Born at Pézanas, France, in 1624, he entered the Society of Jesus in 1648. Nouvel went to French North America in 1662 where he labored at Tadoussac and in the Ottawa missions. He returned to France in 1695 and died at Aix-la-Chapelle in 1696[9] near present-day Green Bay, Wisconsin in 1702.

François du Peron. Born at Lyon in 1610, du Peron entered the Society of Jesus at Avignon in 1627 and went to French North America in 1638. He died there at the village of Chambly in 1665.

Jean Pierron. Born at Dun-sur-Meuse, France, in 1631, Pierron entered the Society of Jesus in 1650 at Nancy. He was in

French North America from 1667 to 1678. He returned to France, where he died in 1700.

Claude Pijart. Born in 1600 in Paris, Pijart entered the Society of Jesus in 1621 and labored in the French American missions from 1637 until his death. The date of his death is not certain. According to Thwaites he died in Quebec probably in 1680 or 1683.

Pierre Pijart. Born on May 17, 1608, in Paris, Pijart entered the Society of Jesus in 1629 and arrived in French North America in 1635. In 1650, he returned to France and died at Dieppe in 1676.

Jean de Quen. Born in Amien in 1603, de Quen entered the Society of Jesus in 1620. He went to French North America in 1635 and died at Quebec in 1659.

Jacques Quentin. Born in Abbeville in 1572, Quentin entered the Society of Jesus in 1604. He arrived at Canada in 1613 but was forced by the English to go back to France the following year. He never returned to North America and died in 1647.

Paul Ragueneau. Born in Paris in 1608, he entered the Society of Jesus there in 1626. Ragueneau went to French North America in 1636 and returned to France in 1662; he died in Paris in 1680.

Sébastian Rasle. Born in Pontarlier, France, in 1657, Rasle entered the Society of Jesus at Dôle in 1675 and went to French North America in 1689. He was killed by New England troops at his mission in Norridgewock, Maine, in 1724.

Charles Raymbault. Born in France at Le Bois, Ile-de-Ré, in 1602, Raymbault entered the Society of Jesus at Rouen in 1621 and went to French North America in 1637. He died in Quebec in 1642.

Anthoine Sylvy. Born in Provence in 1638, Sylvy entered the Society of Jesus in 1658 and went to French North America in 1673. He died in Quebec in 1711.

Gilbert du Thet. A member of the Society of Jesus, not in priests's orders, du Thet arrived in Canada in 1612. He was killed in the English attack on St. Sauveur, the Jesuit settlement on the Maine coast, in 1613.

Barthélemy Vimont. Born at Lisieux in January, 1594, Vimont entered the Society of Jesus in 1613 in Rouen. He worked in the North American missions from 1629 until his return to France in 1659. He died there in 1667.

Appendix B

Selected List of Indian Tribes*

Abenaki A tribe of the Algonquian linguistic group who lived in western Maine along the Kennebec, Androscoggin, and Saco Rivers near and along the coast.

Algonquin. This tribe, whose name has been applied to a far reaching linguistic family, lived, at the time of their first contact with the Jesuits, on the northern tributaries of the Ottawa River. They suffered much in the wars with the Iroquois.

Arendaronon (or *Arendahronon*). Meaning "rock people," this was the name of one of the four chief clans of the Hurons. At the time of the Iroquois triumph over the Hurons, some of the Arendaronon surrendered to the Seneca and were adopted by them.

Atikemegue (or *Attikamegue*). A group of the Montagnais who, when first encountered by the Jesuits, lived north of the St. Maurice basin in what is now Quebec province. They ascended the St. Lawrence to trade at Quebec. They virtually became extinct in 1670 because of smallpox. They were of the Algonquian linguistic family.

Attiwandaronk. The name given by the Hurons to a tribal confederation known to the French as the "Neutrals" because they were neutral in the conflicts between the Huron and Iroquois.

The Neutrals were related to the Iroquois and lived north of Lake Erie. The Huron appellation "Attiwandaronk" means "those whose language is awry" They were of the Iroquoian linguistic group.

Bayagoula. A small tribe living in 1700 in what is now Iberville Parish, Louisiana. Their language was of the Southern Muskhogean division.

Cayuga. One of the five Iroquois tribes. The Cayuga were centered around the shores of Lake Cayuga, New York.

Cherokee. A large well-known tribe, speaking a language of the Iroquoian linguistic family. In the seventeenth-century they lived in the highlands of the southern Appalachians.

Erie. Related to the Iroquois and the Iroquoian linguistic group, this tribe in the seventeenth century inhabited a region comprised of the southern shore of Lake Erie and the neighboring area to the south. In the *Jesuit Relations* they are sometimes referred to as the "Cat Nation," cat being the original meaning of Erie. The tribe was devastated by the Iroquois in the 1650s, and several hundred survivors were adopted by the victors.

Huron. This confederation of four clans lived south and east of the Georgian Bay in what is now Ontario. They were of the Iroquoian linguistic group. They called themselves the "Wendat;" the name Huron was given them by the French about 1600, probably used as a term of derogation since it referred to an uncivilized or unkempt person. The Hurons were closely related to the Iroquois by whom they were devastated in the late 1640s. A portion of the tribe took refuge near the French at Quebec while others fled to the west.

Illinois. Belonging to the first Algonquian linguistic family, the Illinois, when first contacted by the Jesuits, lived mainly along the Illinois and Mississippi Rivers, although one division ranged as far south as northeastern Arkansas.

Iroquois. Of the Iroquoian linguistic group, the Iroquoian, at the time of Jesuit contact, lived in the upper and central part of the Mohawk Valley and around the lakes of central New York. They were then composed of five powerful nations known as the Cayuga, the Mohawk, the Oneida, the Onondaga, and the Seneca.

Island Nation. A term used to designate a group of Algonquins living on Allumette Island in the Ottawa River in Quebec province.

Khionontateronon. The Huron name for the Tionontati or what the French called the "Tobacco Nation." They were of the Iroquoian linguistic group and at the time of Jesuit contact lived in what is now Grey and Simcoe Counties, Ontario. After the Iroquois onslaught, they were absorbed by those Hurons who moved west.

Menomini (or *Menominee*). Of the Algonquian linguistic family, they originally lived on and near the Menominee River in present-day Wisconsin. Their name means "wild rice people" since the wild rice of their region supplied much of their food.

Miami. Of the Algonquian linguistic group, they were living near Green Bay, Wisconsin, in the early 1600s. Shortly after 1670 they began to form new settlements on the Kalamazoo River in Michigan and at the southern end of Lake Michigan, beginning a general involvement to the southeast which continued for several decades.

Micmac. Called by the French "Souriquois," this Algonquian tribe lived in what is now northern New Brunswick, Nova

Scotia, and Prince Edward and Cape Breton Islands. The Jesuits first encountered them in 1611.

Mohawk. One of the five nations of the Iroquois.

Montagnais. A tribe of the Algonquian linguistic group and called "Montagnais" ("Mountaineers") by the French because of the nature of their homeland, a region ranging all the way from the St. Lawrence below Quebec to James Bay.

Nadouessi (or *Nadouessioux*). This is the French version of the Chippewa name for the Dakotas and the origin of the name Sioux. They are of the Siouan linguistic family. When the Jesuit's were working along the western Great Lakes, this tribe were living on and near the Mississippi in northeastern Iowa, southern Minnesota, and northwestern Wisconsin.

Natchez (or *Natches*). The largest tribe on the lower Mississippi River at the time a missionary arrived among them in 1699. The Natchez were located in present-day southwestern Mississippi. Their main village was located near the modern city that bears their name. They spoke a language related to the Muskhogean linguistic family. They were noted for their monarchic form of government and social structure.

Nipissirien. An Algonquin clan whose name means "little water people." Their traditional home is Lake Nipissing which means "little lake or water." They are also known simply as Nipissing.

Ojibway or *Chippewa*. Of the Algonquian linguistic group, and dwelling originally farther to the east, the Ojibway had located themselves along both shores of Lake Superior by the seventeenth century. Later they spread into what is now northern Minnesota and southern Manitoba.

Oneida. One of the five nations of the Iroquois.

Onondaga. One of the five nations of the Iroquois.

Ottawa. Originally living on the northern shore of Georgian Bay and nearby Manitoulin Island, the Ottawas were allies of the Hurons and fled westward when the Iroquois turned on them after the Huron defeat. After briefly returning to Manitoulin Island, they migrated into what is now eastern Michigan around 1700. They are of the Algonquian linguistic group.

Outagami (or *Kickapoo*). Of the Algonquian linguistic group, and closely related to the Foxes, this tribe had migrated from the lower Michigan Peninsula to what is now Columbia County, Wisconsin where the Jesuits contacted them.

Peoria. A division of the Illinois tribe.

Potawatomie. Closely related to the Ottawa and Ojibway, the Potawatomie were a part of the Algonquian linguistic family and lived in the lower Michigan peninsula before moving westward to the region of Green Bay. At the time of Jesuit contact they were in the process of slowly migrating from there to southeastern Wisconsin and northeastern Illinois.

Seneca. One of the five Iroquois nations.

Sioux. See Nadouessi.

Wenrohronon. Belonging to the Iroquoian linguistic group, the Wenrohronon probably lived originally near the oil spring at Cuba, New York. Their name probably means "those who are of the place of floating scum." Fear of the Iroquois caused them in 1639 to take refuge with the Hurons and the Neutrals.

Yaqui. A division of the Cahita tribe, they dwell along the Yaqui River in the western Mexican state of Sinaloa.

Appendix C

Alphabetical List of Major Jesuit Missions[1]

Assumption, Kennebec River, Maine. Father Gabriel Druillettes founded this mission among the Abenaki in 1646. After Druillettes' departure in 1657, intermittent work followed until the 1680s when Fathers Vincent Bigot and Sébastian Rasle took up the Abenaki mission.

Conception, Ossossané. A Huron mission founded in 1636 by Father Brébeuf and his companions.

Conception, Three Rivers. Founded in 1633 by Jacques Buteux, the site of this mission was for several tribes an important gathering place for trade. From here, Buteux set out on numerous mission journeys to tribes in the interior.

Immaculate Conception, Kaskaskia. Founded in 1674 by Father Jacques Marquette at the Indian town of Kaskaskia in present-day Illinois, this mission served not only the Kaskaskia Indians but the various other subdivisions of the Illinois tribe as well.

Iroquois Missions. Father Isaac Jogues, as a prisoner of the Mohawks in 1642, was the first Jesuit to enter the lands of the Iroquois. After being taken to France through the aid of the Dutch, Jogues returned twice to the Iroquois country where he finally suffered martyrdom. Other members of the order contacted the Iroquois in the years following. In 1655 under the leadership of Fathers Claude Dablon and Pierre-Joseph-Marie Chaumonot, more intense missionary work began which, by the end of 1656, had touched all of the five Iroquois nations. The missionaries were driven out, however, in 1658 when the Iroquois once more went to war against the French and their Indian allies. In 1667 Jesuits were once again among the Iroquois; and, by late 1668, a mission was functioning among each of the five nations. It was in these years that the now canonized St. Catherine Tegakouita became one of the fathers' converts. The missionaries were driven out once more in 1687. While attempts would be made to reopen the work in the remaining years of the century, the Jesuits concentrated their efforts on the St. Francis Xavier mission near Montreal which they had established for Iroquois Christian refugees.

Mission to the Bayagoulas. Located in what is now Iberville Parish, Louisiana, northwest of New Orleans, this work among the Bayagoulas was begun by Father Paul du Ru in 1699–1700.

Mission to the Natches. Begun in the same period as the above by Father Paul du Ru among the Natches near present-day Natchez, Mississippi, this mission as well as that among the Bayagoulas would be served after the departure of du Ru by Fathers Joseph de Limoges and Pierre Dongé.

St. Anne, Cape Breton. Founded in 1634 by Father Julian Perrault, St. Anne's was a mission to the Micmacs of Cape Breton Island.

St. Charles, Miscou. Established in the late 1630s by Father Charles Turgis, St. Charles served as a mission to the Micmacs in what is now northeastern New Brunswick.

St. Croix, Tadoussac. Founded in 1640 by Father Jean du Quen, this mission served the Montagnais and other tribes of the lower St. Lawrence who periodically gathered at the trading center of Tadoussac below Quebec.

St. Esprit, Chequamegon Bay. Founded in 1665 by Father Claude Allouez at the western end of Lake Superior, originally among refugee Hurons and Ottawas, this mission is often referred to as "La Pointe" from its location on what the fathers named "La Pointe du St. Esprit."

St. Francis Xavier, Caughnawaga. Founded in 1669 by Christian Iroquois immigrants opposite Montreal, this mission and village were later moved upriver to Sault St. Louis where the village was given the name Caughnawaga after an Iroquois town located on the Mohawk River.

St. Francis Xavier, Green Bay. Established by Father Claude Allouez in 1669 on Green Bay in what is now Wisconsin, this mission was primarily to the Fox tribe.

Saint-Ignace, Mackinac. Father Jacques Marquette in 1670 founded this mission among the refugee Hurons and Ottawas who, having taken refuge around Chequamegon Bay in the west, were then driven east by the Sioux.

Saint-Ignace, Taenhatentaron. Founded in the 1630s, this, like most other Huron missions, was abandoned in 1649 after the Iroquois attack. It was here that Fathers Brébeuf and Lalemant were brought after their capture at the St. Louis Mission.

St. Joseph, Ihonatiria. Founded in 1634 by Fathers Jean de Brébeuf, Antoine Daniel, and Ambrose Davost, this was the first mission established when work was reopened in the Huron country around Georgian Bay.

St. Joseph's, Lake Michigan. Located at the southern end of Lake Michigan in what is now Indiana, St. Joseph's was founded in 1690 among the Miami by Father Claude Aveneau.

St. Joseph, Sillery. Established in 1637, a few miles south of Quebec, this mission was the focal point of a new village named "Sillery" in honor of the French donor whose funds made the venture possible, Noël Brulart de Sillery. At its founding, it was hoped that this walled village would attract certain of the Montagnais to a sedentary life-style.

St. Louis, Huronia. Located about four miles from the residence of Ste. Marie, this Huron mission was founded in the 1630s. It was here that Fathers Brébeuf and Lalemant were captured by the Iroquois in March, 1649.

Ste. Marie among the Hurons.[2] Founded in 1639 on the Wye River in the Huron country, this Jesuit residence was the headquarters of the Huron missions until its abandonment in 1649 during the Iroquois onslaught. Constructed of logs, native stone, and locally-made mortar, Ste. Marie served as a retreat center for priest and convert alike and as a fortress against the Iroquois. Some French soldiers, inadequate in number, and a few hired workers, who were French colonists from the St. Lawrence Valley, lived there for a time in the 1640s.

Ste. Marie, Sault Ste. Marie. Founded by Fathers Isaac Jogues and Charles Raymbault in 1640 among the Ojibway, or Chippawa, through the years this mission was able to reach other tribes as well, since it was located in what was an Indian gathering place.

St. Mark among the Outagami. Located inland and to the west of the mission on Green Bay in what is now Wisconsin, Father Claude Allouez founded this mission among the Outagami in 1671.

FRENCH NORTH AMERICA

N
W   E
S

0   100   200
Miles

Lac Superieur

CHIPPEWA
Sault Ste. Marie
✝ **Ste. Marie**

Lake Nip

OTTAWA
(Refugee)

OTTAWA
St. Ignace ✝ Mackinac

**Huron
Missio**

**Mission
du St. Esprit** ✝

SIOUX

HURONS
(Refugee)

MENOMINI

POTAWATOMIE

✝ St
✝ M

**TOBACCO
NATION**

✝ ✝

St. Mark ✝

SAUK
✝ St. Francis
Xavier

Lac Huron

HURONS

WINNEBAGO

**OUTAGAMI
FOX**

MIAMI

NEUTRALS

*Lac Des Illinois
(Michigan)*

MIAMI

✝ St. Joseph

Lac Erie

Mississippi River

**ERIE
(CAT)
NATION**

ILLINOIS ✝

Immaculate
Conception

PEORIAS

Missouri River

La Belle Riviere

(Ohio)

A P P A L A C H I A N

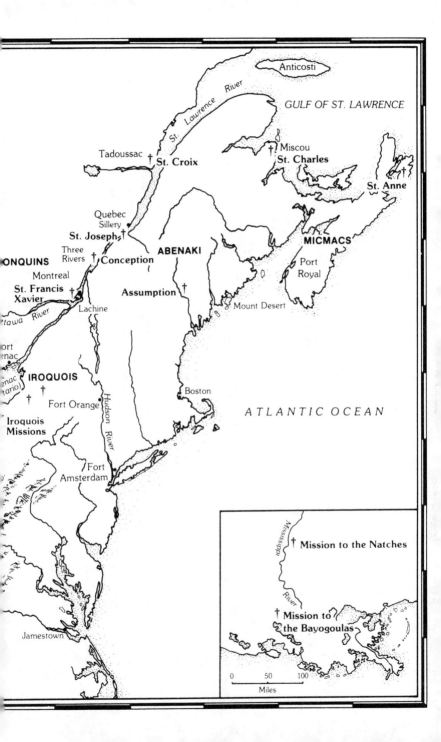

Notes

Chapter I
French Jesuits among the Amerind

1. *See* Appendix A for biographical data.
2. *Ibid.*
3. Reuben Gold Thwaites, ed., *The Jesuit Relations and Allied Documents*, 73 vols. (New York, 1959), 1:73–83.
4. *Ibid.*, pp. 127–37, 313, n. 33.
5. Peter Masten Dunne, *Pioneer Black Robes on the West Coast* (Berkeley, 1940), pp. 22, 128.
6. Clifford Merle Lewis and Albert J. Loomie, *The Spanish Jesuit Mission in Virginia* (Chapel Hill, 1953), pp. 28–62.
7. Thwaites, *Jesuit Relations*, 1:139–83.
8. *Ibid.*, p. 211.
9. *Ibid.*, pp. 213–15.
10. *See* Appendix A.
11. *Ibid.*
12. Thwaites, *Jesuit Relations*, 1:227, 313, n. 33.
13. *Ibid.*, pp. 227–31; Ethelred L. Taunton, *The History of the Jesuits in England, 1580–1773* (London, 1901), pp. 13 and 116; Lewis Owen, *The State of the English Colledges in Forraine Parts* (New York, 1968), pp. A2–A3, 4; Thomas Bell, *The Anatomie of Popish Tyrannie* (Norwood, New Jersey, 1975), pp. 1–15, 18–24, 31–33, 35–45, 69–77; T. S. Healy, *John Donne, Ignatius, His Conclave* (Oxford, 1969), pp. xvii–xlii; Samuel Eliot Morison, *Samuel de Champlain: Father of New France* (Boston, 1972), p. 98.

14. Christopher Hollis, *The Jesuits, A History* (New York, 1968), pp. 106–17; Thomas Joseph Campbell, *The Jesuits, 1534–1921* (Boston, 1971), pp. 134–65; Thomas Graves Law, ed., *The Archpriest Controversy*, 2 vols. (London, 1896–98), 1:ix–xxvii.

15. Thwaites, *Jesuit Relations*, 1:231–35; 2:249–75; 3:275–83; 4:9–75.

16. Auguste Carayon, *Bibliographie Historique de la Compagnie de Jésus* (Genève, 1970), pp. 178–79.

17. Ludwig von Pastor, *The History of the Popes from the Close of the Middle Ages*, 40 vols. (London, 1938), 27:220–22.

18. *Ibid.*, 28:391–95.

19. *See* Appendix A.

20. *Ibid.*

21. Frederick Webb Hodge, ed., *Handbook of American Indians*, Bureau of American Ethnology Bulletin 30, (Washington, 1907), 1:933.

22. *Ibid.*, pp. 584–90.

23. *See* Appendix A.

24. Thwaites, *Jesuit Relations*, 4:171–227.

25. *Ibid.*, pp. 255–56, n. 20.

26. *See* Appendix A.

27. Thwaites, *Jesuit Relations*, 5:25.

28. Thomas A. Hughes, *Loyola and the Education System of the Jesuits* (New York, 1912), p. 86.

29. Thwaites, *Jesuit Relations*, 5:33.

30. *Ibid.*, pp. 11–73.

31. *Ibid.*, 4:255–56, n. 20; Francis X. Talbot, *Saint Among the Hurons: the Life of Jean de Brébeuf* (New York, 1949), pp. 91, 94–95.

32. *See* Appendix A.

33. *Ibid.*

34. Thwaites, *Jesuit Relations*, 6:49.

35. *Ibid.*, p. 103.

36. *Ibid.*, 15:159.

37. *See* Appendix A.
38. Thwaites, *Jesuit Relations*, 21:293–307, 318–19, n. 23; 28:181.
39. *See* Appendix A.
40. *Ibid.*
41. *Ibid.*
42. Thwaites, *Jesuit Relations*, 13:95–143.
43. *See* Appendix A.
44. Thwaites, *Jesuit Relations*, 14:57, 73.
45. *Ibid.*, pp. 286–87, n. 12.
46. Hodge, *Handbook of American Indians*, Bureau of American Ethnology Bulletin 30, 1:38–39.
47. Thwaites, *Jesuit Relations*, 11:221–23.
48. *Ibid.*, 16:179.
49. As quoted, *Ibid.*, 16:181.
50. *Ibid.*, pp. 21–23.
51. As quoted, *Ibid.*, 19:15.
52. *Ibid.*, pp. 21–23.
53. *Ibid.*, 23:291–301; 11:276–77, n. 4.
54. *See* Appendix A.
55. *Ibid.*
56. Thwaites, *Jesuit Relations*, 23:303–11.
57. Frederick Webb Hodge, ed., *Handbook of Indians of Canada* (New York, 1969), pp. 224–26.
58. Lewis H. Morgan, *League of the Ho-De-No-Sau-Nee or Iroquois*, 2 vols. (New York, 1966), 1:25.
59. J. N. B. Hewitt, *Iroquoian Cosmology* (New York, 1974), p. 460.
60. Bruce G. Trigger, *The Children of Aataentsic*, 2 vols. (Montreal, 1976), 2:849–50.
61. Conrad Heidenreich, *Huronia* (Ottawa, 1971), pp. 280, 295–96.
62. Thwaites, *Jesuit Relations*, 17:31–39.
63. *Ibid.*, p. 39.
64. *See* Appendix A.
65. Thwaites, *Jesuit Relations*, 21:229–35.

66. *Ibid.,* p. 241.
67. *See* Appendix A.
68. *Ibid.*
69. Thwaites, *Jesuit Relations,* 23:225–33.
70. *Ibid.,* 24:145–47, 153–55, 310, n. 11.
71. *Ibid.,* pp. 191, 195–99.
72. Isaac Jogues, *The Jogues Papers,* tr. John Gilmary Shea, *New York Historical Society Collections,* Second Series, (1857), 3:182.
73. *Ibid.,* p. 180.
74. John Gilmary Shea, tr. and ed., *Perils of the Ocean and Wilderness* (New York, 1976), pp. 16–85; John Anthony O'Brien, *The American Martyrs* (New York, 1953), p. 104.
75. *See* Appendix A.
76. Shea, *Perils of the Ocean and Wilderness,* pp. 104–21.
77. Thwaites, *Jesuit Relations,* 24:273.
78. *Ibid.,* 33:259–65; Talbot, *Saint Among the Hurons,* pp. 283–85; O'Brien, *The American Martyrs,* pp. 236–37.
79. Thwaites, *Jesuit Relations,* 34:25–35.
80. *See* Appendix A.
81. Thwaites, *Jesuit Relations,* 35:79–81.
82. As quoted, *Ibid.,* 35:111.
83. *Ibid.,* pp. 113–15.
84. *Ibid.,* pp. 147–51.
85. William J. O'Malley, *The Fifth Week* (Chicago, 1976), p. 52.
86. Thwaites, *Jesuit Relations,* 34:213–21.
87. *Ibid.,* 36:50–51.
88. *Ibid.,* 35:205.
89. *See* Appendix A.
90. Increase Mather, *A Relation of the Troubles Which Have Happened in New England, by Reason of the Indians There* (New York, 1972), pp. 62, 70, 74.
91. Bartlett Burleigh James and J. Franklin Jameson, eds., *Journal of Jasper Danckaerts* (New York, 1913), pp. 137, 249, 269.

92. Gabrielle Druillettes, "Journal of an Embassy," *New York Historical Society Collections,* Second Series, (1857), 3:303–28; John Eliot, *The Christian Commonwealth* (New York, 1972), p. A4; Jonathan Mayhew, *Seven Sermons* (New York, 1969), pp. 38–40.

93. Daniel Gookin, *Historical Collections of the Indians in New England* (New York, 1972), pp. 16–28.

94. Francis Parkman, *The Jesuits in North America in the Seventeenth Centuy: France and England in North America,* Boston, 1906), pp. 541, 542; J. H. Kennedy, *Jesuit and Savage in New France* (New Haven, 1950), p. 43.

95. *See* Appendix A.

96. Thwaites, *Jesuit Relations,* 41:95–129; 42:42–97.

97. *See* Appendix A.

98. Thwaites, *Jesuit Relations,* 42:61–83.

99. *See* Appendix A.

100. Kennedy, *Jesuit and Savage in New France,* p. 45.

101. Thwaites, *Jesuit Relations,* 44:322, n. 10.

102. *Ibid.,* 1:221–23; 65:187.

103. Reuben Gold Thwaites, *Father Marquette* (New York, 1902), pp. vii–x.

104. Thwaites, *Jesuit Relations,* 1:317, n. 52; Kennedy, *Jesuit and Savage in New France,* p. 45.

105. Thwaites, *Jesuit Relations,* 63:147–51.

106. Druillettes, "Journal of an Embassy," *New York Historical Society Collections,* Second Series, pp. 309–10, fn.; Kennedy, *Jesuit and Savage in New France,* pp. 46–47.

107. *See* Appendix A.

108. Thwaites, *Jesuit Relations,* 71:157; James Joseph Walsh, *American Jesuits* (Freeport, New York, 1968), pp. 196–216.

109. William John Eccles, *Frontenac, the Courtier Governor* (Toronto, 1959), pp. 52–54; Francis Parkman, *Count Frontenac and New France* (Boston, 1966), pp. 23–24; Francis Parkman, *The Old Regime in Canada* (Boston, 1906), pp. 388–92; Alfred G. Bailey, *The Conflict of European and Eastern Al-*

gonkian Cultures, 1504–1700: A Study in Canadian Civilization (Toronto, 1969), pp. 107–8.

110. Blaise Pascal, *Pensées* (New York, 1965), pp. 411–13, 465, 469, 473; Pablo José de Arriaga, *The Extirpation of Idolatry in Peru*, tr. and ed. L. Clark Keating (Lexington, Kentucky, 1965), pp. 90–144; Malcolm Vivian Hay, *The Prejudices of Pascal* (London, 1962), pp. 15–26, 52–54; James Broderick, *The Economic Morals of the Jesuits* (New York, 1972), pp. 50–52.

111. Heinrich Boehmer, *The Jesuits: An Historical Study*, tr. Paul Z. Strodach (Philadelphia, 1928), p. 182; Wenceslaus Linck, *Wenceslaus Linck's Diary of His Expeditions to Northern Baja California*, tr. Ernest J. Burrus (Los Angeles, 1966), pp. 43–95; Wenceslaus Linck, *Reports and Letters, 1762–1778*, tr. and ed. Ernest J. Burrus (Los Angeles, 1967), pp. 25–42; Ignacio María Nápoli, *The Cora Indians of Baja California*, tr. and ed. James Robert Moriarty III and Benjamin F. Smith (Los Angeles, 1970), p. 31.

112. Felix Alfred Plattner, *Jesuits Go East* (Westminster, Md., 1952), pp. 118–214.

113. "Pope Clement X, in an effort to ease the acrimony of the debate on the Chinese rites . . . forbade the publication of any literature on the missions without the approval of the Congregation of Propaganda . . . Although the permission of Propaganda could have opened the way to the renewal of publication, the French Jesuits were not able to employ this device, because France, ever conscious of her Gallican liberties, refused to recognize within her boundaries the jurisdiction of the Roman Congregation." William Bangert, *A History of the Society of Jesus* (St. Louis, 1972), p. 265; Joseph P. Donnelly, *Thwaites' Jesuit Relations: Errata and Addenda* (Chicago, 1967), pp. 35–37.

114. John Winthrop Platner, *The Religious History of New England* (Cambridge, Mass., 1917), pp. 17–18; Cotton Mather,

Bonifacius: An Essay Upon the Good, ed. David Levin (Cambridge, Mass., 1966), pp. 153–54, 157.

115. Peter Wraxall, *An Abridgement of the Indian Affairs Contained in Four Folio Volumes, Transacted in the Colony of New York, 1678–1751,* ed. Charles Howard McIlwain (Cambridge, Mass., 1915), pp. 33–35.

116. Paul du Ru, *Journal of Paul du Ru, February 1 to May 8, 1700,* ed. Ruth Lapham Butler (Chicago, 1934), pp. vii, 1–71; William Bennet Munro, *Crusaders of New France* (New Haven, 1921), p. 123; Gilbert J. Garraghan, *The Jesuits of the Middle United States,* 3 vols. (New York, 1938), 2:175.

117. Parkman, *The Jesuits in North America in the Seventeenth Century,* pp. 551–52.

Chapter II
"Maker of the Earth"

1. Thwaites, *Jesuit Relations,* 26:213.
2. David Brainerd, *Memoirs of the Reverend David Brainerd* (St. Clair Shores, Michigan, 1970), pp. 149–320.
3. Joseph P. Donnelly, *Jean de Brébeuf* (Chicago, 1975), p. xii; Pierre F. X. de Charlevoix, *Journal of a Voyage to North America,* 2 vols. (Ann Arbor, 1966), 1:117; Pierre F. X. de Charlevoix, *History and General Description of New France,* 6 vols. (New York, 1870), 1:266–67; 2:65; Charles E. O'Neill, ed., *Charlevoix's Louisiana: Selections from the History and the Journal of Pierre F. X. de Charlevoix* (Baton Rouge, 1977), p. 243; François du Creux, *The History of Canada or New France* (Toronto, 1951), p. 99; Ward Barrett, tr., *Mission in the Marianas: An Account of Father Diego Luis de Sanvítores and His Companions, 1669–1670* (Minneapolis, 1975), pp. 22–23.
4. Johan Jakob Baegert, *Observations in Lower California,* tr. M. M. Brandenburg and Carl L. Baumann (Berkeley,

1952), p. 20; Peter Masten Dunne, *Black Robes in Lower California* (Berkeley, 1952), pp. 18–19.

5. Marc Lescarbot, *The History of New France,* tr. W. L. Grant, 3 vols. (Toronto, 1907–14), 1:65, 283.

6. John Lederer, *The Discoveries of John Lederer, With Unpublished Letters by and about Lederer to Gov. J. Winthrop, Jr.,* edited by William P. Cumming (Charlottesville, 1958), p. 14.

7. Thwaites, *Jesuit Relations,* 15:157.

8. *Ibid.,* 6:229–31.

9. *Ibid.,* 8:117, 121.

10. *Ibid.,* 14:135–37.

11. *Ibid.,* pp. 191–93.

12. *Ibid.,* 18:145–47, as quoted.

13. *Ibid.,* 23:25–29.

14. *Ibid.,* 33:225–27.

15. *Ibid.,* 39:13.

16. *Ibid.,* 51:29–31.

17. *Ibid.,* p. 49.

18. The "cultus" of a religion is the central system of rites and acts of devotion upon which that religious system is based.

19. Lescarbot, *History of New France,* 1:283.

20. Jean de Brébeuf, *Les Relations de ce que s'est passé au Pays des Hurons (1635–1648)* (Genève, 1957), p. 107.

21. Thwaites, *Jesuit Relations,* 26:125–27.

22. *Ibid.,* 29:225–27.

23. Donnelly, *Jean de Brébeuf,* p. xii.

24. Thwaites, *Jesuit Relations,* 3:89–111; Lescarbot, *History of New France,* 1:65.

25. Thwaites, *Jesuit Relations,* 3:185.

26. *Ibid.,* p. 73.

27. *Ibid.,* 5:33–35.

28. *Ibid.,* p. 123.

29. *Ibid.,* p. 241.

30. *Ibid.*, 6:243.
31. *Ibid.*, p. 247.
32. *Ibid.*, pp. 247–55.
33. *Ibid.*, 5:105.
34. *Ibid.*, 6:233.
35. *Ibid.*, pp. 229, 235–37.
36. *Ibid.*, p. 239.
37. *Ibid.*, p. 241.
38. *Ibid.*, 9:139.
39. Donnelly, *Jean de Brébeuf,* pp. 151–52.
40. Thwaites, *Jesuit Relations,* 8:131.
41. *Ibid.*, p. 87.
42. Donnelly, *Jean de Brébeuf,* p. 151.
43. Thwaites, *Jesuit Relations,* 17:145.
44. *Ibid.*, 28:63.
45. *Ibid.*, 32:283.

Chapter III
"Holding out One's Hands"

1. Thwaites, *Jesuit Relations,* 4:195–97.
2. *Ibid.*, 5:169.
3. *Ibid.*, pp. 169–71; 89–91.
4. *Ibid.*, 9:277.
5. *Ibid.*, 10:91.
6. *Ibid.*, p. 101.
7. *Ibid.*, 15:163.
8. *See* Appendix A.
9. Thwaites, *Jesuit Relations,* 29:47–49.
10. *Ibid.*, 35:149.
11. *Ibid.*, 7:81, 89–93; 105–9.
12. *Ibid.*, 17:15.
13. *Ibid.*, 9:279.
14. *Ibid.*, 16:239.

15. *Ibid.*, 6:135–41; 29:175–77.
16. *Ibid.*, 13:113.
17. *Ibid.*, 13:113–17; 54:79–81.
18. *Ibid.*, 15:27–29.
19. Louis Thomas Jones, *Aboriginal American Oratory* (Los Angeles, 1965), p. 24; George A. West, *Tobacco, Pipes, and Smoking Customs of the American Indians*, Part I (Westport, Connecticut, 1970), p. 66; Lewis Spence, *The Myths of the North American Indians* (New York, 1972), pp. 115–16.
20. Thwaites, *Jesuit Relations*, 17:87–93.
21. As quoted, *Ibid.*, 21:97.
22. *Ibid.*, pp. 121–25.
23. *See* Appendix A.
24. Thwaites, *Jesuit Relations*, 51:259.
25. *Ibid.*, 48:263–65.
26. *See* Appendix A.
27. Thwaites, *Jesuit Relations*, 65:43–49.
28. Robert Ignatius Burns, *The Jesuits and the Indian Wars of the Northwest* (New Haven, 1966), p. 38.
29. Edna Kenton, ed., *Letters From Missions* (New York, 1954), pp. 118–21.
30. Denis Meadows, *A Popular History of the Jesuits* (New York, 1958), pp. 75–76.

Chapter IV
Native Religions

1. Thwaites, *Jesuit Relations*, 3:33–35; 119–23; 131–35; Convers Francis, *Life of John Eliot* (Boston, 1836), pp. 34–35.
2. Thwaites, *Jesuit Relations*, 6:157–63.
3. Elisabeth Tooker, *The Iroquois Ceremonial of Midwinter* (Syracuse, 1970), pp. 84–103; Thwaites, *Jesuit Relations*, 1:127–39.
4. Brébeuf, *Les Relations . . . au Pays des Hurons*, p. 107.

5. Claude Mélançon, *Indian Legends of Canada* (Toronto, 1974), pp. 27–29.
6. W. Vernon Kinietz, *The Indians of the Western Great Lakes, 1615–1760* (Ann Arbor, 1965), pp. 284–85.
7. Thwaites, *Jesuit Relations*, 50:289–91; 51:49.
8. *Ibid.*, 7:273.
9. *Ibid.*, 6:163–71.
10. *Ibid.*, 8:123–25.
11. *Ibid.*, 16:149.
12. *Ibid.*, 6:187.
13. *Ibid.*, 10:125–39.
14. *Ibid.*, 12:7.
15. *Ibid.*, 8:123.
16. *Ibid.*, 6:193–201.
17. *Ibid.*, 12:17–21.
18. *Ibid.*, pp. 59–63.
19. *Ibid.*, 14:63.
20. *Ibid.*, 20:263.
21. *Ibid.*, 19:83–87.
22. *Ibid.*, pp. 179–80.
23. *Ibid.*, 14:37–39.
24. *Ibid.*, 12:237–39.
25. *Ibid.*, 21:133–35.
26. *Ibid.*, 17:207–11.
27. Deward E. Walker, ed., *Systems of North American Witchcraft and Sorcery* (Moscow, Idaho, 1970), pp. 210, 252–54.
28. Thwaites, *Jesuit Relations*, 19:191–93; 24:249–53.
29. *Ibid.*, 4:217–19.
30. *Ibid.*, 5:213.
31. *Ibid.*, 15:177–83.
32. *Ibid.*, p. 99.
33. *Ibid.*, 21:161–63.
34. *Ibid.*, 54:65–73.
35. Walker, *Systems of North American Witchcraft and Sorcery*, pp. 194–95.

36. *See* Appendix A.
37. Thwaites, *Jesuit Relations,* 61:149.
38. *Ibid.*, 58:51.
39. *Ibid.*, 23:155–59.
40. *Ibid.*, p. 159.
41. *Ibid.*, pp. 153–55.
42. *Ibid.*, p. 153.
43. Jogues, *The Jogues Papers,* pp. 202–3; William M. Beauchamp, *A History of the New York Iroquois* (New York, 1976), pp. 131–32.
44. The phenomenon of human sacrifice was not uncommon to the tribes north of Mexico, especially in wartime. Among tribes such as the Natches and Pawnee it was codified and carried out at a stated time. *See* Thwaites, *Jesuit Relations,* 65:137–45; Charles C. Jones, Jr., *Antiquities of the Southern Indians* (New York, 1973), p. 23; and Robert Redfield, *The Primitive World and Its Transformations* (Ithaca, 1953), pp. 130–31.
45. Richard Erdoes, "My Travels with Medicine Man John Lame Deer," *Smithsonian* vol. 4 (May, 1973), p. 34.

Chapter V
Angels, Demons, and Visions

1. Parkman, *The Jesuits in North America,* p. 418.
2. Mason Wade, ed., *The Journals of Francis Parkman,* 2 vols, (New York, 1947), 1:180.
3. William of Occam, 1300–1349, a principal advocate of *nominalism* in the fourteenth century, stated that God and things pertaining to Him can be known only through faith, not reason. Occam laid the foundation for the Reformation.
4. *Nominalism* is the denial of the possibility of objective knowledge of universal truths. Only knowledge of indi-

vidual objects can really be perceived by means of the intellect and reason. In this view, neither reason nor intellect can demonstrate the existence of God. On another level, nominalism tended to question the reality of the objective presence of divine grace in the sacraments of the Church.

5. Luther, as quoted, Increase Mather, *Remarkable Providences Illustrative of the Earlier Days of American Colonization* (London, 1890), p. 155; Hartmann Grisar, *Martin Luther, His Life and Work* (New York, 1971), pp. 382–84.

6. Mather, *Remarkable Providences,* pp. 96–175.

7. Cotton Mather, *Diary of Cotton Mather,* 2 vols. (New York, n.d.), 1:150–75, 178.

8. Thwaites, *Jesuit Relations,* 7:183.

9. *Ibid.,* 31:87.

10. *Ibid.,* 20:41.

11. *Ibid.,* 23:147.

12. *Ibid.,* pp. 141–49.

13. *Ibid.,* 18:209–11.

14. *Ibid.,* 30:103–5.

15. *Ibid.,* 34:119, 131.

16. *Ibid.,* 19:195–97.

17. *Ibid.,* 14:201–3.

18. *Ibid.,* 22:57.

19. *Ibid.,* 21:291.

20. *Ibid.,* 34:161, 171–73, 175–77, 185, 191.

21. *Ibid.,* p. 187.

22. *Ibid.,* pp. 171, 193.

23. *See* Appendix A.

24. *Ibid.*

25. *Ibid.*

26. Thwaites, *Jesuit Relations,* 31:75–77.

27. *Ibid.,* 34:97; Talbot, *Saint Among the Hurons,* p. 287.

28. Thwaites, *Jesuit Relations,* 34:117–19.

29. *Ibid.,* 23:79.

30. *Ibid.,* p. 81.

31. *Ibid.*, 18:25–29.
32. *Ibid.*, 24:21–23.
33. *Ibid.*, 56:75.
34. *Ibid.*, 10:73; 50:87–89.
35. *Ibid.*, 29:199.
36. *See* Appendix A.
37. Thwaites, *Jesuit Relations*, 56:103–5.
38. *See* Appendix A.
39. Thwaites, *Jesuit Relations*, 65:109.
40. *Ibid.*, 19:143.
41. *Ibid.*, 32:213.
42. *Ibid.*, 24:135.
43. *Ibid.*, 20:275.
44. *Ibid.*, 22:75.
45. *Ibid.*, 31:227–29.
46. *Ibid.*, 20:27; 19:129–31.
47. *Ibid.*, 19:203–7.
48. Alban Butler, *Lives of the Saints*, 4 vols. (New York, 1962), 1:631.
49. Thwaites, *Jesuit Relations*, 15:73.
50. Charles M. Segal and David C. Stineback, *Puritans, Indians, and Manifest Destiny* (New York, 1977), pp. 146–47; Norman Earl Tanis, "Education in John Eliot's Indian Utopias, 1646–1675," *History of Education Quarterly* (1970), 10:308–23.

Chapter VI
Old Customs – New Ways

1. Thwaites, *Jesuit Relations*, 5:245.
2. Jerome V. Jacobsen, *Educational Foundations of the Jesuits in Sixteenth-Century New Spain* (Berkeley, 1938), pp. 237–39.
3. Anonymous, "The Historical Account of John Eliot," *Massachusetts Historical Society Collections*, First Series (1968),

8:15–17; "Communications from the Town Clerk of Dorchester," *Ibid.*, 2:9.

4. *The Ledger for the Years 1650–1660 and The Record Book of Meetings Between 1656 and 1686 of the Corporation for the Propagation of the Gospel in New England* (New York, 1967), pp. xlv, xlviii–xlix; 52–53; 70–71; Ola Elizabeth Winslow, *John Eliot, Apostle to the Indians* (Boston, 1968), pp. 180–83.

5. Thwaites, *Jesuit Relations*, 10:15–21.

6. *Ibid.*, 13:9–11.

7. *Ibid.*, 24:125–27, 137; Spence, *The Myths of the North American Indians*, pp. 115–16; Jones, *Aboriginal American Oratory*, p. 24.

8. Thwaites, *Jesuit Relations*, 20:155–59.

9. *Ibid.*, p. 147.

10. *Ibid.*, p. 291.

11. Barry Fell, *America B. C.* (New York, 1976), pp. 63–155.

12. Thwaites, *Jesuit Relations*, 24:83, 95–97.

13. *See* Appendix A.

14. Thwaites, *Jesuit Relations*, 24:83, 95–97; 52:117–21.

15. *Ibid.*, 56:125, 129, 135.

16. *Ibid.*, 18:151.

17. *Ibid.*, 29:45–46.

18. *Ibid.*, p. 103.

19. J. W. Powell, "On Limitations to the Use of Some Anthropologic Data," *First Annual Report of the Bureau of Ethnology* (1881), p. 75.

20. For a possible explanation of the origins of Indian pictography, *see* Fell, *America B. C.*, pp. 63–155.

21. Thwaites, *Jesuit Relations*, 67:227.

22. *Ibid.*, 24:83.

23. J. W. Powell, "Introduction," *Ninth Annual Report of the Bureau of Ethnology* (1892), pp. xxxii–xxxv.

24. Garrick Mallery, "Sign Language Among North American Indians," *First Annual Report of the Bureau of Ethnology* (1881), pp. 368–70.

25. Thwaites, *Jesuit Relations,* 24:93.
26. *Ibid.,* 23:243.
27. *Ibid.,* 26:287; 37:63.
28. *Ibid.,* 40:235.
29. The "porcelaine beads" were glass beads, prized by the Indians, introduced in quantity by Europeans as trade items.
30. Thwaites, *Jesuit Relations,* 13:169–73.
31. *Ibid.,* 17:113, 115.
32. *Ibid.,* 64:217.
33. *Ibid.,* 33:279–81.
34. *Ibid.,* 25:173; 15:93.
35. *Ibid.,* 17:141.
36. *Ibid.,* 22:171.
37. *Ibid.,* 18:151.
38. *Ibid.*
39. *Ibid.,* p. 153.
40. *See* Appendix A.
41. Thwaites, *Jesuit Relations,* 60:209.
42. *Ibid.,* 24:171–73.
43. *Ibid.,* 21:159–61; 24:29–31.
44. *Ibid.,* 16:145.
45. *Ibid.,* 30:79–81.
46. *Ibid.,* 57:209.
47. *Ibid.,* 15:193.
48. *Ibid.,* 19:201; 22:141; 23:63–65.
49. *Ibid.,* 18:167.
50. *Ibid.,* 45:49.
51. *Ibid.,* 31:217.
52. *Ibid.,* p. 221.
53. *Ibid.,* 25:169.
54. *Ibid.,* 49:31–35.
55. *Ibid.,* 51:49.
56. *Ibid.,* pp. 49–51.
57. *Ibid.,* 58:267.

58. *Ibid.*, pp. 273–75.
59. Elisabeth Tooker, "An Ethnography of the Huron Indians, 1615–1649," *Bureau of American Ethnology Bulletin 190* (1964), p. 125; 125, fn. 32; Thwaites, *Jesuit Relations*, 3:99–101; 27:39; Hodge, *Handbook of Indians of Canada*, p. 276.
60. Thwaites, *Jesuit Relations*, 25:247.
61. *Ibid.*, 16:63; Emma H. Blair, ed. and tr., *The Indian Tribes of the Upper Mississippi Valley and Region of the Great Lakes*, 2 vols. (Cleveland, 1911–12), 1:67.
62. Thwaites, *Jesuit Relations*, 22:71.
63. Tooker, "An Ethnography of the Huron Indians, 1615–1649," *Bureau of American Ethnology Bulletin 190*, pp. 126–27.
64. Thwaites, *Jesuit Relations*, 14:261–63.
65. *Ibid.*, 20:211–13; Jesuit missionaries whether in French North America or elsewhere seem never to have rushed conversion and baptism regarding those who were of the age of discretion; to be unbaptized was a preferable condition to apostacy. *See also*, Francesco Maria Picolo, *Informe on the New Province of California, 1702* (Los Angeles, 1967), pp. 56–57.
66. Thwaites, *Jesuit Relations*, 22:71.
67. *Ibid.*, 20:171.
68. *Ibid.*, 25:139–41.
69. *Ibid.*, 29:77; René Fülöp-Miller, *The Power and Secret of the Jesuits* (New York, 1956), p. 274.
70. Thwaites, *Jesuit Relations*, 38:275–77.
71. *Ibid.*, 60:307–9.
72. *Ibid.*, 41:191.
73. *Ibid.*, 32:305.
74. *Ibid.*, 39:27–29.
75. *Ibid.*, 15:91.
76. Tooker, "An Ethnography of the Huron Indians, 1615–1649," *Bureau of American Ethnology Bulletin 190*, pp. 130–31; 131, fn. 50.

77. *Ibid.*, pp. 134–40; 134–35, fn. 58.
78. Thwaites, *Jesuit Relations,* 10:279–305.
79. *Ibid.*, pp. 301, 305–7; Talbot, *Saint Among the Hurons,* pp. 137–38.
80. Tooker, "An Ethnography of the Huron Indians, 1615–1649," *Bureau of American Ethnology Bulletin 190,* pp. 134–35, fn. 58.
81. *See* Appendix A.
82. Thwaites, *Jesuit Relations,* 23:211.
83. *Ibid.*, pp. 209–23.
84. *Ibid.*, 24:173.
85. *Ibid.*, 20:41.
86. *Ibid.*, 29:285.
87. *Ibid.*, 60:33.
88. *Ibid.*, pp. 33–41.
89. *Ibid.*, 37:111.
90. *Ibid.*, 22:255.
91. *Ibid.*, p. 257.
92. *Ibid.*, 13:39–83.

Chapter VII
Transformation of Symbols and Ceremonies

1. Hodge, "Handbook of American Indians," *Bureau of American Ethnology Bulletin 30* Part 2 (Washington, 1910), p. 144.
2. *Ibid.*
3. Thwaites, *Jesuit Relations,* 15:77.
4. *Ibid.*, pp. 77–91.
5. *Ibid.*, 17:39–41.
6. *Ibid.*, p. 47.
7. *Ibid.*, 19:257.
8. *Ibid.*, pp. 255–57.

9. Hodge, "Handbook of American Indians," *Bureau of American Ethnology Bulletin 30* Part 2, pp. 660–62.

10. Thwaits, *Jesuit Relations*, 19:259.

11. *Ibid.*, 20:77–85.

12. *Ibid.*, 26:269.

13. *Ibid.*, 20:185–91.

14. *Ibid.*, 22:97.

15. *Ibid.*, 25:177.

16. *Ibid.*, pp. 175–79.

17. *Ibid.*, 24:67–71, 75.

18. *Ibid.*, 25:149–51.

19. *Ibid.*, 35:275–77.

20. *Ibid.*, p. 249.

21. *Ibid.*, 20:251.

22. *Ibid.*, p. 231.

23. Hodge, "Handbook of American Indians," *Bureau of American Ethnology Bulletin 30* Part 1, pp. 381–82.

24. *Ibid.*, p. 381.

25. Tooker, "An Ethnography of the Huron Indians, 1615–1649," *Bureau of American Ethnology Bulletin 190*, p. 76.

26. Thwaites, *Jesuit Relations*, 16:65.

27. *Ibid.*, 19:43.

28. *Ibid.*, 24:259–61; 20:281–87.

29. *Ibid.*, 27:267, 289.

30. *Ibid.*, 37:39.

31. Peter Masten Dunne, *Pioneer Jesuits in Northern Mexico* (Berkeley, 1944), pp. 28–29.

32. Thwaites, *Jesuit Relations*, 49:29–31.

33. *Ibid.*, 61:113–21.

34. Tooker, "An Ethnography of the Huron Indians, 1615–1649," *Bureau of American Ethnology Bulletin 190*, pp. 45, 46, 52, 53, 110, 130–31.

35. Thwaites, *Jesuit Relations*, 22:291.

36. *Ibid.*, 29:45–49.

37. *Ibid.*, 40:167.

38. *Ibid.*, 42:101–3.
39. *Ibid.*, p. 103.
40. *Ibid.*, 33:243.
41. *Ibid.*, pp. 229–49.
42. *Ibid.*, 43:39–41.
43. *Ibid.*, 27:145–47.
44. *Ibid.*, 56:23–25; 52:235–37.
45. *Ibid.*, 60:41.
46. *Ibid.*, 61:139–45.
47. *Ibid.*, p. 107.
48. *Ibid.*, 63:27–31, 243.
49. Hodge, ''Handbook of American Indians,'' *Bureau of American Ethnology Bulletin 30* Part 1, p. 454.
50. Tooker, ''An Ethnography of the Huron Indians, 1615–1649,'' *Bureau of American Ethnology Bulletin 190*, p. 72.
51. Thwaites, *Jesuit Relations*, 6:279.
52. *Ibid.*, 9:111.
53. *Ibid.*, 14:91, 95–97.
54. *Ibid.*, 15:111–23.
55. *Ibid.*, p. 61; the *atsataion* cited here was given on October 28, the day of St. Simon and St. Jude; in Catholic hagiography St. Jude is considered the patron of hopeless or gravely threatened causes. While the record does not say so, it is possible the fathers chose this day for their farewell feast since they were in grave danger.
56. *Ibid.*, 34:113.
57. *Ibid.*, 25:137.
58. *Ibid.*, 22:51–53.
59. *Ibid.*, 23:161–63.
60. *Ibid.*, 29:169–71.
61. *Ibid.*, 24:51.
62. *Ibid.*, 30:77–79.
63. *Ibid.*, pp. 108, 119–23.
64. *Ibid.*, 53:269.
65. *Ibid.*, 55:271–73.

66. Hodge, "Handbook of American Indians," *Bureau of American Ethnology Bulletin 30* Part 1, pp. 597–99; Part 2, p. 228.
67. Thwaites, *Jesuit Relations,* 64:165–67.
68. *Ibid.,* 33:145–47.
69. *Ibid.,* 20:269–71; 24:87–89; 16:49; 25:183.
70. Tooker, "An Ethnography of the Huron Indians, 1615–1649," *Bureau of American Ethnology Bulletin 190*, pp. 44–45.
71. Thwaites, *Jesuit Relations,* 16:201–3.
72. *Ibid.,* 26:155–61; 27:293; 32:109–211; 50:171.
73. *Ibid.,* 23:169.
74. *Ibid.,* 32:211.
75. *Ibid.,* 21:149–55.
76. *See* Appendix A.
77. Thwaites, *Jesuit Relations,* 50:171.
78. Increase Mather, *Testimony Against Prophane Customs* (Charlottesville, 1953), pp. 18–41.

Chapter VIII
Style and Substance

1. Thwaites, *Jesuit Relations,* 6:145–47.
2. *Ibid.,* 7:309–10, n. 8.
3. *Ibid.,* 8:9.
4. *Ibid.,* 18:111.
5. *Ibid.,* p. 123.
6. *Ibid.,* 23:305–7.
7. *Ibid.,* 18:95.
8. *Ibid.,* pp. 243–45.
9. *Ibid.,* 12:45–59, 65.
10. *Ibid.,* 16:179–83.
11. *Ibid.,* 14:181.

12. Winslow, *John Eliot, Apostle to the Indians,* pp. 180–83; Tanis, "Education in John Eliot's Indian Utopias, 1646–1675," *History of Education Quarterly,* X (1970), pp. 308–23; Anonymous, "The Historical Account of John Eliot," *Massachusetts Historical Society Collections, First Series,* (1968), 8:15–17; David McClure, *Memoirs of Rev. Eleazar Wheelock, D.D.* (New York, 1972), pp. 259–63; Jonathan Edwards, *The Nature of True Virtue,* (Ann Arbor, 1960), pp. 60–61.

13. Louis Hennepin, *A Description of Louisiana,* tr. John G. Shea (Ann Arbor, 1966), p. 338.

14. Parkman, *Count Frontenac and New France,* p. 435.

15. Thwaites, *Jesuit Relations,* 16:195–97.

16. *Ibid.,* 9:201–7.

17. *Ibid.,* 22:243.

18. *Ibid.,* 46:105.

19. *Ibid.,* p. 187.

20. *Ibid.,* 62:209; 53:185.

21. *See* Appendix A.

22. Thwaites, *Jesuit Relations,* 50:207.

23. W. J. Eccles, *The Canadian Frontier, 1534–1760* (New York, 1969), p. 57; Bailey, *The Conflict of European and Eastern Algonkian Cultures, 1504–1700,* pp. 107–8; Alain Grandbois, *Born in Quebec* (Montreal, 1964), pp. 162–63; F. X. Garneau, *History of Canada* (Montreal, 1860), pp. 246–48.

24. Parkman, *Count Frontenac and New France,* pp. 23–24.

25. *See* Appendix A.

26. Thwaites, *Jesuit Relations,* 58:83.

27. *Ibid.,* 62:125.

28. *See* Appendix A.

29. Thwaites, *Jesuit Relations,* 62:183.

30. *Ibid.,* 64:131.

31. *See* Appendix A.

32. Thwaites, *Jesuit Relations,* 65:190–99.

33. Cotton Mather, *Selections from Cotton Mather* (New York, 1926), pp. 7–8.

Chapter IX
Conclusion

1. Leon Pouliot, *Étude sur les Relations des Jésuites de la Nouvelle-France 1632–1672* (Paris, 1940), p. 155.

2. Franklin L. Baumer, *Modern European Thought* (New York, 1977), pp. 75–76.

3. Jonathan Edwards, *The Philosophy of Jonathan Edwards from His Private Notebooks*, ed. Harvey G. Townsend (Eugene, Oregon, 1955), pp. 154–56; Jonathan Edwards, *Representative Selections* (New York, 1962), pp. lxiv, 261–339; David E. Stannard, *The Puritan Way of Death* (New York, 1977), p. 83.

4. François Roustang, *Jésuites de la Nouvelle-France* (Paris, 1960), p. 19; Thwaites, *Jesuit Relations,* 10:158–60.

5. Mary Purissima Reilly, O.P., ''Francis Parkman and the Spiritual Factors at Work in New France,'' (Ph.D. dissertation, St. Louis University, 1942), p. 285.

6. Thwaites, *Jesuit Relations,* 29:225–27.

7. *Ibid.*, 7:21–29.

8. *Ibid.*, 33:25–27.

9. *Ibid.*, 7:85–87, 183, 201–3.

10. *Ibid.*, 31:243.

11. *Ibid.*, 19:129–31.

12. *Ibid.*, 65:31–33.

13. Reginald and Gladys Laubin, *Indian Dances of North America* (Norman, 1976), p. 230.

14. Eusebio Francisco Kino, *Kino's Plan for the Development of Pimería Alta, Arizona, and Upper California,* tr. Ernest J. Burrus (Tucson, 1961), p. 30; Sigismundo Taraval, *The Indian Uprising in Lower California, 1734–1737,* tr. Marguerite Eyer Wilbur (Los Angeles, 1931), pp. 6–8.

15. Roustang, *Jésuites de la Nouvelle-France,* p. 20.

16. Jonathan Edwards, *Jonathan Edwards on Evangelism* (Grand Rapids, 1958), pp. 17–34.

17. George Harold Dunne, *Generation of Giants: The Story of the Jesuits in China in the Last Decades of the Ming Dynasty* (London, 1962), p. 87.

Appendix A
French Jesuit Missionaries Cited

1. Except where cited otherwise, information regarding those listed is taken from Thwaites, *Jesuit Relations*, 71:137–81.
2. Joseph P. Donnelly, *Jacques Marquette, S.J.* (Chicago, 1968), p. 91, n. 46.
3. *Ibid.*, p. 157, n. 82.
4. Thwaites, *Jesuit Relations*, 31:289, n. 4.
5. *Ibid.*
6. *Ibid.*, 2:306, n. 68.
7. Donnelly, *Jacques Marquette, S.J.*, p. 69, n. 8.
8. *Ibid.*, pp. 9; 41–42; 253–66.
9. *Ibid.*, p. 95, n. 9.

Appendix B
Selected List of Indian Tribes

* Information on the tribes cited is taken from the appropriate listings in Hodge, *Handbook of Indians of Canada* and John R. Swanton, *The Indian Tribes of North America* (Washington, D.C., 1952).

Appendix C
Alphabetical List of Major Jesuit Missions

1. Thwaites, *Jesuit Relations*, 1:1–37.
2. For a thorough examination of the ruins of Ste. Marie, *see* Kenneth E. Kidd, *The Excavation of Ste. Marie I* (Toronto, 1949).

Bibliography

Primary Sources
Books:

Arriaga, Pablo José de. *The Extirpation of Idolatry in Peru.* Translated and Edited by Clark Keating. Lexington: University of Kentucky Press, 1968.

Baegert, Johan Jakob. *Observations in Lower California.* Translated by M. M. Brandenburg and Carl L. Baumann. Berkeley: University of California Press, 1952.

Barrett, Ward, tr. *Mission in the Marianas: An Account of Father Diego Luis de Sanvítores and His Companions, 1669–1670.* Minneapolis: University of Minnesota Press, 1975.

Bell, Thomas. *The Anatomie of Popish Tyrannie.* Norwood, New Jersey: W. J. Johnson, 1975.

Blair, Emma Helen, ed. and tr. *The Indian Tribes of the Upper Mississippi Valley and Region of the Great Lakes, as Described by Nicolas Perrot, French Commandant in the Northwest; Bacqueville de la Potherie, French Royal Commission to Canada; Morrell Marston, American Army Officer; and Thomas Forsyth, United States Agent at Ft. Armstrong.* Two volumes. Cleveland: A. H. Blair Co., 1911–1912.

Brainerd, David. *Memoirs of the Rev. David Brainerd.* Edited by Jonathan Edwards. St. Clair Shores, Michigan: Scholarly Press, 1970.

Brébeuf, Jean de. *Les relations de ce que s'est passé au Pays des Hurons (1635–1648).* Genève: Theodore Besterman, 1957.

Charlevoix, Pierre François Xavier de. *History and General*

Description of New France. Translated by John Gilmary Shea. Volumes I and II. New York: John Gilmary Shea, 1870.

Charlevoix, Pierre François Xavier de. *Journal of a Voyage to North America.* Volume I. Ann Arbor: University Microfilms, 1966.

Donnelly, Joseph P. *Thwaites' Jesuit Relations: Errata and Addenda.* Chicago: Loyola University Press, 1967.

du Ru, Paul. *Journal of Paul du Ru, February 1 to May 8, 1700.* Translated by Ruth Lapham Butler. Chicago: Printed for Caxton Club, 1934.

Edwards, Jonathan. *Jonathan Edwards on Evangelism.* Edited by Carl J. C. Wolf. Grand Rapids: Eerdmans, 1958.

Edwards, Jonathan. *The Nature of True Virtue.* Ann Arbor: University of Michigan Press, 1960.

Edwards, Jonathan. *The Philosophy of Jonathan Edwards From His Private Notebooks.* Edited by Harvey G. Townsend. Eugene: University of Oregon Press, 1955.

Edwards, Jonathan. *Representative Selections.* Edited by Clarence H. Faust and Thomas H. Johnson. New York: Hill and Wang, 1962.

Eliot, John. *The Christian Commonwealth.* Research Library of Colonial Americana Series. New York: Arno Press, 1972.

Gookin, Daniel. *Historical Collections of the Indians in New England.* New York: Arno Press, 1972.

Hennepin, Louis. *A Description of Louisiana.* Translated by John G. Shea. Ann Arbor: University Microfilms, 1966.

James, Bartlett Burleigh and J. Franklin Jameson, eds. *Journal of Jasper Danckaerts.* New York: Charles Scribner's Sons, 1913.

Kenton, Edna, ed. *Letters from Missions.* New York: Vanguard Press, 1954.

Kidd, Kenneth E. *The Excavation of Ste. Marie I.* Toronto: University of Toronto Press, 1949.

Kino, Eusebio Francisco. *Kino's Plan For the Development of Pimería Alta, Arizona and Upper California.* Translated by

Ernest J. Burrus. Tucson: Arizona Pioneers Historical Society, 1961.

Law, Thomas Graves, ed. *The Archpriest Controversy*. (Edited from Petyt Manuscript of the Inner Temple). Two volumes. London: Camden Society, 1896–98.

Lederer, John. *The Discoveries of John Lederer, With Unpublished Letters by and about Lederer to Governor John Winthrop, Jr.* Edited by William P. Cumming. Charlottesville: University of Virginia Press, 1958.

The Ledger for the Years 1650–1660 and The Record Book of Meetings between 1656 and 1686 of the Corporation for the Propagation of the Gospel in New England. New York: Burt Franklin, 1967.

Lescarbot, Marc. *The History of New France*. Translated by W. L. Grant. Three volumes. Toronto: The Champlain Society, 1907–1914.

Linck, Wenceslaus. *Reports and Letters, 1762–1778*. Translated by Ernest J. Burrus. Los Angeles: Dawson's Book Shop, 1967.

Linck, Wenceslaus. *Wenceslaus Linck's Diary of His 1766 Expedition to Northern Baja California*. Translated and edited by Ernest J. Burrus. Los Angeles: Dawson's Book Shop, 1966.

Mather, Cotton. *Bonifacius: An Essay Upon the Good*. Edited by David Levin. Cambridge: Harvard University Press, 1966.

Mather, Cotton. *Diary of Cotton Mather*. Two volumes. New York: Frederick Ungar, n.d.

Mather, Cotton. *Selections From Cotton Mather*. Edited by Kenneth B. Murdock. New York: Harcourt, Brace and Company, 1926.

Mather, Increase. *A Relation of the Troubles Which Have Happened in New England, by Reason of the Indians There, From the Year 1614 to the Year 1675*. New York: Arno Press, 1972.

Mather, Increase. *Remarkable Providences Illustrative of the Earlier Days of American Colonization*. London: Reeves and Turner, 1890.

Mather, Increase. *Testimony Against Prophane Customs*. Charlottesville: University of Virginia Press, 1953.

Mayhew, Jonathan. *Seven Sermons*. New York: Arno Press, 1969.

McClure, David. *Memoirs of Rev. Eleazar Wheelock, D.D.* New York: Arno Press, 1972.

Mélançon, Claude. *Indian Legends of Canada*. Toronto: Gage Publishing, Ltd., 1974.

Nápoli, Ignacio María. *The Cora Indians of Baja California*. Translated and edited by James Robert Moriarty III and Benjamin F. Smith. Los Angeles: Dawson's Book Shop, 1970.

O'Neill, Charles E., ed. *Charlevoix's Louisiana: Selections from the History and the Journal of Pierre F. X. de Charlevoix*. Baton Rouge: Louisiana State University Press, 1977.

Owen, Lewis. *The State of the English Colledges in Forraine Parts*. New York: Da Capo Press, 1968.

Pascal, Blaise. *Pensées*. New York: Pantheon Books, 1965.

Picolo, Francesco Maria. *Informe on the New Province of California, 1702*. Translated and edited by George P. Hammond. Los Angeles: Dawson's Book Shop, 1967.

Shea, John Dawson Gilmary, tr. and ed. *Perils of the Ocean and Wilderness. The Garland Library of Narratives of North American Indian Captivities*. Volume 73. New York: Garland, 1976.

Taraval, Sigismundo. *The Indian Uprising in Lower California, 1734–1737*. Translated by Marguerite Eyer Wilbur. Los Angeles: Quivira Society, 1931.

Thwaites, Reuben Gold, ed. *The Jesuit Relations and Allied Documents, Travels and Explorations of the Jesuit Missionaries in New France, 1610–1791*. Volumes 1–46; 48–58; 60–65; 67; 71. New York: Pageant Book Company, 1959.

Wade, Mason, ed. *The Journals of Francis Parkman*. Volume 1. New York: Harper and Brothers, 1947.

Walker, Deward E., Jr., ed. *Systems of North American Witchcraft and Sorcery*. Moscow, Idaho: University of Idaho, 1970.

Wraxall, Peter. *An Abridgement of the Indian Affairs Contained in Four Folio Volumes, Transacted in the Colony of New York, 1678–1751*. Edited by Charles Howard McIlwain. Cambridge: Harvard University Press, 1915.

Articles:

"Communications from the Town Clerk of Dorchester," *Massachusetts Historical Society Collections*. First Series II (1968) p. 9.

Druillettes, Gabrielle. "Journal of an Embassy," *New York Historical Society Collections*. Second Series III (1857), pp. 303–28.

Erdoes, Richard. "My Travels with Medicine Man John Lame Deer," *Smithsonian* IV (1973), pp. 30–36.

Jogues, Isaac. "The Jogues Papers." Translated and edited by John G. Shea. *New York Historical Society Collections*. Second Series III (1857), pp. 161–229.

Secondary Sources
Books:

Bailey, Alfred Goldsworthy. *The Conflict of European and Eastern Algonkian Cultures, 1504–1700: A Study in Canadian Civilization*. Toronto: University of Toronto Press, 1969.

Bangert, William V. *A History of the Society of Jesus*. St. Louis: Institute of Jesuit Sources, 1972.

Baumer, Franklin L. *Modern European Thought*. New York: Macmillan Publishing Company, 1977.

Beauchamp, William M. *A History of the New York Iroquois*. New York: AMS Press, 1976.

Boehmer, Heinrich. *The Jesuits: An Historical Study*. Translated by Paul Z. Strodach. Philadelphia: Castel Press, 1928.

Broderick, James. *The Economic Morals of the Jesuits*. New York: Arno Press, 1972.

Burns, Robert Ignatius. *The Jesuits and the Indian Wars of the Northwest*. New Haven: Yale University Press, 1966.

Butler, Alban. *Lives of the Saints*. Volume I. New York: P.J. Kenedy & Sons, 1962.

Campbell, Thomas Joseph. *The Jesuits, 1534–1921*. Boston: Milford House, 1971.

Carayon, Auguste. *Bibliographie Historique de la Compagnie de Jésus*. Genève: Slatkine Reprints, 1970.

Donnelly, S.J., Joseph P. *Jean de Brébeuf*. Chicago: Loyola University Press, 1975.

Donnelly, S.J., Joseph P. *Jacques Marquette*. Chicago: Loyola University Press, 1968.

Du Creux, François. *The History of Canada or New France*. Translated by Percy J. Robinson. Edited by James B. Conacher. New York: Greenwood Press, 1969.

Dunne, George Harold. *Generation of Giants: The Story of the Jesuits in China in the Last Decades of the Ming Dynasty*. London: Burns and Oates, 1962.

Dunne, Peter Masten. *Black Robes in Lower California*. Berkeley: University of California Press, 1952.

Dunne, Peter Masten. *Pioneer Black Robes on the West Coast*. Berkeley: University of California Press, 1940.

Dunne, Peter Masten. *Pioneer Jesuits in Northern Mexico*. Berkeley: University of California Press, 1944.

Eccles, William John. *Frontenac, The Courtier Governor*. Toronto: McClelland and Stewart, 1959.

Eccles, William John. *The Canadian Frontier, 1534–1760*. New York: Holt, Rinehart and Winston, 1969.

Fell, Barry. *America B. C.* New York: The New York Times Book Company, 1976.

Francis, Convers. *Life of John Eliot*. Boston: Hilliard, Gray, and Company, 1836.

Fülöp-Miller, René. *The Power and Secret of the Jesuits*. Trans-

lated by F. S. Flint and D. F. Tait. New York: G. Braz-
iller, 1956.

Garneau, F. X. *History of Canada*. Montreal: J. Lovell, 1860.

Garraghan, Gilbert Joseph. *The Jesuits of the Middle United States*. New York: American Press, 1938.

Grandbois, Alain. *Born in Quebec*. Montreal: Palm, 1964.

Grisar, Hartmann. *Martin Luther, His Life and Work*. New York: AMS Press, 1971.

Hay, Malcolm Vivian. *The Prejudices of Pascal*. London: N. Spearman, 1962.

Healy, T. S. *John Donne, Ignatius, His Conclave*. Oxford: Clarendon Press, 1969.

Heidenreich, Conrad. *Huronia*. Ottawa: McClelland and Stewart, 1971.

Hewitt, J. N. B. *Iroquoian Cosmology*. New York: AMS Press, 1974.

Hodge, F. W., ed. "Handbook of American Indians," *Bureau of American Ethnology Bulletin 30*. Parts I and II (1907).

Hodge, F. W., ed. *Handbook of Indians of Canada*. New York: Kraus Reprint Co., 1969.

Hollis, Christopher. *The Jesuits, A History*. New York: Macmillan, 1968.

Hughes, Thomas A. *Loyola and the Educational System of the Jesuits*. New York: C. Scribner's Sons, 1912.

Jacobsen, Jerome Vincent. *Educational Foundations of the Jesuits in Sixteenth-Century New Spain*. Berkeley: University Press, 1938.

Jones, Charles C., Jr. *Antiquities of the Southern Indians*. New York: AMS Press, 1973.

Jones, Louis Thomas. *Aboriginal American Oratory*. Los Angeles: Southwest Museum, 1965.

Kennedy, John Hopkins. *Jesuit and Savage in New France*. New Haven: Yale University Press, 1950.

Kinietz, W. Vernon. *The Indians of the Western Great Lakes, 1615–1670*. Ann Arbor: University of Michigan Press, 1965.

Laubin, Reginald and Gladys. *Indian Dances of North America.* Norman: University of Oklahoma Press, 1976.

Lewis, Clifford Merle, and Albert J. Loomie. *The Spanish Jesuit Mission in Virginia.* Chapel Hill: University of North Carolina Press, 1953.

Mallery, Garrick. "Sign Language Among North American Indians," *First Annual Report of the Bureau of Ethnology.* (1881), pp. 269–552.

Meadows, Denis. *A Popular History of the Jesuits.* New York: Macmillan, 1958.

Morgan, Lewis H. *League of the Ho-De-No-Sau-Nee or Iroquois.* Vol. I. New York: Burt Franklin, 1966.

Morison, Samuel Eliot. *Samuel de Champlain: Father of New France.* Boston: Little, Brown and Company, 1972.

Munro, William Bennet. *Crusaders of New France.* New Haven: Yale University Press, 1921.

O'Brien, John Anthony. *The American Martyrs; the Story of the Eight Jesuit Martyrs of North America.* New York: Appleton-Century-Crofts, 1953.

O'Malley, William J. *The Fifth Week.* Chicago: Loyola University Press, 1976.

Parkman, Francis. *Count Frontenac and New France.* Boston: Beacon Press, 1966.

Parkman, Francis. *The Jesuits in North America in the Seventeenth Century: France and England in North America, Part Second.* Boston: Little, Brown and Company, 1906.

Parkman, Francis. *The Old Regime in Canada.* Boston: Little, Brown and Company, 1906.

Pastor, Ludwig von. *The History of the Popes from the Close of the Middle Ages.* Vol. 27. London: Kegan and Co., 1938.

Platner, John Winthrop, and others. *The Religious History of New England.* Cambridge: Harvard University Press, 1917.

Plattner, Felix Alfred. *Jesuits Go East.* Translated by Lord Sudley and Oscar Blobel. Westminster, Maryland: Newman Press, 1952.

Pouliot, Léon. *Étude sur les Relations des Jésuits de la Nouvelle-France, 1632–1672.* Paris: Desclée de Brouwer, 1940.

Powell, J. W. "Introduction," *Ninth Annual Report of the Bureau of Ethnology.* (1892), pp. xxiii–xlvi.

Powell, J. W. "On Limitations to the Use of Some Anthropologic Data," *First Annual Report of the Bureau of Ethnology.* (1881), pp. 73–86.

Redfield, Robert. *The Primitive World and Its Transformations.* Ithaca: Cornell University Press, 1953.

Roustang, François. *Jesuites de la Nouvelle-France.* Paris: Desclée de Brouwer, 1961.

Segal, Charles M., and David C. Stineback. *Puritans, Indians, and Manifest Destiny.* New York: G. P. Putnam's Sons, 1977.

Spence, Lewis. *The Myths of the North American Indians.* New York: Kraus Reprint Co., 1972.

Stannard, David E. *The Puritan Way of Death.* New York: Oxford University Press, 1977.

Swanton, John R. *The Indian Tribes of North America.* Washington: Smithsonian Institution Press, 1952.

Talbot, Francis Xavier. *Saint Among the Hurons: the Life of Jean de Brébeuf.* New York: Harper, 1949.

Taunton, Ethelred Luke. *The History of the Jesuits in England, 1580–1773.* London: Methuen and Co., 1901.

Thwaites, Reuben Gold. *Father Marquette.* New York: D. Appleton & Company, 1902.

Tooker, Elisabeth. "An Ethnography of the Huron Indians, 1615–1649," *Bureau of American Ethnology Bulletin 190.* (1964), pp. 1–183.

Tooker, Elisabeth. *The Iroquois Ceremonial of Midwinter.* Syracuse: Syracuse University Press, 1970.

Trigger, Bruce G. *The Children of Aataentsic. Vol. 2.* Montreal: Queen's University Press, 1976.

Walsh, James Joseph. *American Jesuits.* Freeport, New York: Books for Libraries Press, 1968.

West, George A. *Tobacco, Pipes, and Smoking Customs of the American Indians.* Part I. Westport, Connecticut: Greenwood Press, 1970.

Winslow, Ola Elizabeth. *John Eliot, Apostle to the Indians.* Boston: Houghton Mifflin Company, 1968.

Articles:

Duignan, Peter. "Early Jesuit Missionaries: A Suggestion for Further Study," *American Anthropologist* (1958) 60:725–32.

"The Historical Account of John Eliot," *Massachusetts Historical Society Collections.* First Series (1968) 8:5–35.

Tanis, Norman Earl. "Education in John Eliot's Indian Utopias, 1646–1675," *History of Education Quarterly* (1970) 10:308–23.

Unpublished Material:

Reilly, Mary Purissima. "Francis Parkman and the Spiritual Factors at Work in New France," Ph.D. dissertation, St. Louis University, 1942.

Index

261

DATE DUE	
MAR 1 2 2006	

GAYLORD   PRINTED IN U.S.A.